# GROWING LITERACY

**The Eighteenth Yearbook
A Peer Reviewed Publication of
The College Reading Association
1996**

## *Editors*

**Elizabeth G. Sturtevant**
George Mason University

**Wayne M. Linek**
Texas A&M University-Commerce

## *Editorial Assistants*

**Vicki Parsons Duling**     **Debby Deal**
George Mason University

**Syamsundar Uppuluri**     **Leslie Nation**
Texas A&M University-Commerce

## Photocopy/Reprint Permission Statement

ISBN 1-883604-02-8

Printed at Texas A&M University-Commerce

Cover Design: Lee Sturtevant, age 11, Springfield, Virginia
Vivian Freeman, Texas A&M University-Commerce

# COLLEGE READING ASSOCIATION BOARD MEMBERS 1996-1997

# CRA Editorial Advisory Board 1995-1996

# TABLE OF CONTENTS

# INTRODUCTION

What is literacy and how does it grow? Simple-sounding questions, with far from simple answers. Around the globe, educators, parents, authors newspaper columnists—even politicians—argue issues related to literacy definitions and literacy growth. These are "hot topics" in the 1990s. Everyone, it seems, favors "literacy;" few, however, can agree on what "literacy" is, much less how to help it develop.

From our perspective, exploration of these important questions is what the College Reading Association has always been about, now and in the past. While the CRA membership is diverse in goals, background, and location, we share a dynamic interest in literacy development at all levels. As an organization and as individuals, our diversity is a strength that compels us to work together in the search for answers to vital questions. Various aspects of CRA, such as the four divisions, the annual conference, the publication, the committees, and most recently, the CRA Listserve, all contribute to the growing knowledge and literacy of the membership. Individual members then contribute to the literate growth of others through continued discussion in their own educational communities, regions, and nations.

The articles in this 18th Yearbook reflect the theme, growing literacy. Once again, the papers submitted illustrate both the broad professional interests of the CRA membership and current discussion in the field as a whole. School-based and university researchers explore literacy growth in young children, teens, college students, and adults. Teacher educators discuss ways to expand understanding of literacy teaching and learning. And "early leaders"—long term members of our profession—expand our vision of growth in the field through the decades, while their former students provide connections through personal stories of growth under the guidance of these mentors. Last, but certainly not least, the final section illustrates our continuing foray into new ways of teaching, collaborating, and researching. As you read, expect your horizons to expand: You won't be disappointed.

Not surprisingly, it took many hands to create this publication. First thanks go to the authors—all authors who submitted papers. As in other years, there were more papers than could be accepted, and all authors, both published and unpublished, are commended for their efforts to support CRA through a strong Yearbook.

Second, thanks go to the reviewers. Every editor of every peer-reviewed publication knows that good reviewers are worth their weight in gold. Yet, no one sees the reviewer's anonymous work except for authors and editors. CRA reviewers this year gave tremendous care in preparing their reviews. Reviews were thoughtful, thorough, and extremely helpful to both authors and the editors. Support in the reviewer-selection process and in other editorial matters was provided by the CRA Publications Committee, chaired by Bill Henk of Penn State, Harrisburg.

Third, thanks go to our hard-working, behind-the-scenes editorial assistants. At George Mason University, Debby Deal assisted with the creation of the review board last fall, while Vicki Duling sorted and sent all manuscripts for review, tracked the review process, and communicated with authors. At Texas A&M University-Commerce, Syamsundar Uppuluri assisted with tracking manuscripts and sending out galley proofs, while Leslie Nation assisted extensively with reading and copy-editing so that authors received relatively clean galley proofs.

We also greatly appreciate the support our universities have provided for this project throughout the years of our editorship. At George Mason University, President Alan Merten, Provost David Potter, Dean Gustavo Mellander, Associate Dean Martin Ford, and the Faculty of the Graduate School of Education provide financial and moral support, while Firzana Ahmad provides secretarial assistance. At Texas A&M University-Commerce, President Jerry Morris, Academic Vice President Donna Arlton, Dean Donald Coker, Assistant Dean Jerry Hutton, and Department Head Michael Sampson provide financial assistance, time, and moral support. Vivian Freeman and Lyndal Burnett provide technical expertise in the production of the book, Frances Norman, Jan Hazelip, and Regina Strickland provide secretarial assistance, while Michelle England, Angela McGill, and Kenneth Edwards provide assistance with mailing.

Finally, Growing Literacy is dedicated to our family members: Dave, Dan, Paul, and Lee; Dana, Jennifer, and Laura. Through the years their caring support has inspired confidence, new journeys, and growth. In their individual ways, each also reminds us that ". . . all work is empty save when there is love" (Gibran, 1923/1968, p. 26).

EGS & WML, 1996
CRA Yearbook Editors

# Reference

Gibran, K. (1923/1968). *The prophet*. New York: Knopf.

# Awards in
# Literary Research

# KINDERGARTEN CHILDREN'S USES OF ORAL LANGUAGE AND SOCIAL INTERACTION IN LITERACY ACTIVITIES DURING UNSTRUCTURED PLAY

## Jan K. Bryan

Southwest Missouri State University

## Abstract

*The purpose of this qualitative study is to document literacy activities that occur during unstructured play and describe relationships among young children's uses of oral language, social interaction, and literacy activities that occur naturally during unstructured play. The findings suggest that relationships between children's use of oral language and social interaction in literacy activities are built from understandings they develop about ways adults purposefully use oral and written discourse and the communicative nature of literacy.*

## Introduction

Conceptual changes in the way that reading is perceived have led to dramatic shifts in reading research and the terminology used to describe reading and reading research. Historically, reading has been defined as it relates to society's ideas about children, teachers, what should be taught, and how reading ability should be assessed (Morrow & Smith, 1990). In contrast, literacy is now being described by many experts as a cognitive and social process in which people use language to construct meaning and communicate that meaning as they interact with others (Clay, 1986; Goodman, 1984; Hall, 1987; Heath, 1991; Teale & Sulzby, 1986; Vygotsky, 1967). To illustrate, Pearson (1992, 1993) writes that during the 1980s, reading was "recontextualized as a process that is intimately related to its sibling linguistic processes—writing, listening, and speaking—and to the basic process of thinking underlying all these linguistic processes" (p. 1075).

Young children are naturally predisposed to engage in speaking, listening, reading, and writing as they make sense of their world and communicate to others what they have come to understand (Pearson, 1993; Vygotsky, 1967). The emergent literacy perspective (Clay, 1966) focuses on young children's earliest attempts to make sense of their world through speaking, listening, reading, and writing and to the cognitive development that supports the emergence and refinement of these linguistic processes. Often, young children attempt to make sense of their world through repeated opportunities to participate in unstructured play, or play without adult direction or interference. In some school settings, young children are provided a time, physical space, and appropriate props for play. Adults typically structure the logistical aspects of play, such as when children are allowed time to play, access to play areas, and the types of props available in each play area. However, children's play remains unstructured because the children decide where to play, what to play, and with whom to play. In addition, play is considered unstructured because children also decide how play areas and props will be used. For example, children use imaginative language to create new meanings for props to facilitate their play (Vygotsky, 1967).

Traditionally, the emergent literacy literature describes literacy activities as those actions associated with constructing meaning through reading and writing. However, more recent explanations of emergent literacy legitimize young children's participation in play activities that include speaking and listening, as well as reading and writing, as literacy activities and indicators of literacy development (Guthrie & Greaney, 1991; Roskos, 1991). While literacy activities that include reading and writing are intricately associated with children's uses of oral language and social interaction, oral language and social interaction are not typically described as literacy activities in the same way as reading and writing. Strickland and Morrow (1988) state, "Oral language development begins before literacy and then parallels it. It supports literacy, but it need not be fully developed for reading and writing to begin" (p. 240). On the other hand, Sulzby and Teale (1991) state that "reading, writing, and oral language develop concurrently and interrelatedly in literate environments" (p. 728). What appears to be lacking in the emergent literacy literature is a consensus concerning the relationships among oral language, social interaction, and literacy activities.

This study is grounded in Vygotskian theory and the larger theoretical perspective: social constructivism. The Vygotskian perspective capitalizes on children's natural propensity toward interaction with others. The social constructivist perspective emphasizes interactions among learners within the environment. From the social constructivist perspective, literacy is described as a social phenomenon developed through interactions within a community of learners who are participating in shared literacy activities (Harste, 1985).

There is abundant research about children's uses of oral language and social interaction during both unstructured and structured play (i.e., play settings and activities that are designed and directed by adults). Structured play settings, where children have been removed from their natural setting to be observed in a contrived environment, have been used to examine specific functions of language, such as vocabulary acquisition, word usage, and use of narrative language (Andersen, 1984; Pellegrini, 1985; Pellegrini, Galda, Dresden, & Cox, 1991; Pellegrini, Galda, & Rubin, 1984; Schober-Peterson & Johnson, 1989; Schober-Peterson & Johnson, 1991; Vygotsky, 1967). For example, Pellegrini, Galda, and Rubin (1984) found that structure in writing, specifically the syntactic structure, may be influenced by children's uses of oral language and social interaction as they engage in literacy activities during structured play. Likewise, Rowe (1989) and Thomas, Rinehart, and Wampler (1992) describe such a strong link between children's participation in literacy activities that involve writing during structured play that when opportunities for oral language and social interaction were diminished, children's writing was likewise diminished.

Studies of young children's use of oral language and social interaction in literacy activities in unstructured play settings (Grugeon, 1988; Jacob, 1984; Neuman & Roskos, 1990, 1992) illustrate some of the connections among young children's use of oral language and social interaction and literacy development. For example, in a study that examined young girls' participation in playground chants and songs during unstructured play, Grugeon (1988) found that young children rehearse a syntactic competence during unstructured play that is seen in adult oral and written communication. Similarly, Jacob (1984), Isenberg and Jacob (1985), Dyson (1993), and Neuman and Roskos (1990, 1991) found that young children rehearse literacy with others during unstructured play as they establish scenarios and communicate to themselves and others through pretend shopping lists, purchasing goods, and obtaining prescriptions from imagined doctors.

Although there is abundant research that examines young children's use of oral language in literacy activities during structured and unstructured play, there is a lack of naturalistic studies that observe children's uses of oral language and social interaction in literacy activities as a regular part of their school day. More importantly, there is a lack of naturalistic studies that observe children without disruption to their normal classroom activities or regular classroom setting.

The purposes of this study are to document literacy activities that occur during unstructured play and to describe relationships among young children's uses of oral language, social interaction, and the literacy activities that occur naturally during unstructured play. The guiding question for this research is as follows: What understandings about emergent literacy can be clarified through an examination of young children's uses of oral language and social interaction in literacy activities that occur spontaneously during unstructured play? This research question is delineated as four related questions:

- In what ways are kindergarten children's uses of oral language displayed in literacy activities that occur spontaneously during unstructured play?
- In what ways are kindergarten children's uses of social interaction displayed in literacy activities that occur spontaneously during unstructured play?
- What relationship exists between kindergarten children's use of oral language and literacy activities that occur spontaneously during unstructured play?
- What relationship exists between kindergarten children's use of social interaction and literacy activities that occur spontaneously during unstructured play?

## Methods

I observed kindergarten children during their regular 45 minute unstructured play period three days each week for a total of 20 weeks during the Fall, 1993 and Spring, 1994 semesters. Participant observation data were collected and unstructured play sessions were audio and video taped. Interview data and children's artifacts also were collected. Research questions were addressed by analyzing audio taped and video taped unstructured play sessions, interviews, children's artifacts, and participant observation data.

### Participants

One self-contained kindergarten classroom in a rural public school district was purposefully selected (Lincoln & Guba, 1985) as the site for this study. This site was chosen because a period of unstructured play was a naturally occurring, everyday event at this site, and I would have the opportunity to observe children's spontaneous interactions without interruption to their regular school day.

One teacher and nineteen children participated in this study. Eleven of the nineteen children were boys and eight were girls. Fourteen of these children were Mexican American and five were European American (Nieto, 1992).

### Data Source

Data were collected through participant observation (Bogdan & Biklen, 1992), video taping, and audio taping. Wireless microphones with FM receivers were used to collect audio data throughout the study. Two additional sources of data were a collection of children's artifacts (Bogdan & Biklen, 1992) and informal interviews (Hatch, 1988).

I took descriptive field notes (Bogdan & Biklen, 1992) each day of observation and wrote them up each day as soon as possible after leaving the field. Field notes were used to provide a written account of the activities observed in the kindergarten classroom each day of participant observation. In addition, these field notes served to support video and audio taped data (Bogdan & Biklen, 1992).

Children were video and audio taped each day of observation as they interacted during unstructured play. Audio taped data were used to generate accurate transcriptions of the children's conversations. Video taped data were used to support field notes and audio taped data. Video tapes were also used to record the physical context of the interactions observed (Green & Wallet, 1988). In addition, video tapes were viewed repeatedly so that I could reexamine events (Erickson, 1986). In some instances, the video taped data were used to clarify transcriptions of audio taped data.

Throughout the study, I conducted informal interviews (i.e., casual conversations) with the participants. I sought the participants' perspectives concerning what they played, with whom they played, and how they decided those things. During the interviews, I also sought information about the 33 artifacts children produced as naturally occurring literacy activities during unstructured play. These artifacts were collected, photocopied, and returned immediately to the children.

In addition to interviews with the children, I engaged in interviews with Ms. Casey (a pseudonym used to identify the kindergarten teacher). I sought to understand Ms. Casey's perspective about what she had observed during the children's play, specifically if she recognized children's attempts to communicate via oral and written language during unstructured play as indicators of children's participation in authentic literacy activities.

### *Data Analysis*

Data were analyzed using inductive data analysis as described by Lincoln and Guba (1985). Initial data analysis began while I was in the field. I read the field notes each day after participant observation, recording my thoughts, observations, and notes in the margins of the field notes. In addition, I revisited the scene each day after participant observation as I transcribed the audio taped data and viewed the video taped data, once again recording my thoughts, observations, and notes. Initial codes emerged from these notes. For example, *copying names and making lists* and *reading as a part of unstructured play* were notes that I used as codes. I read and reread the data and my notes to see if I was meeting the purposes of my study. I wanted my data collection to remain focused (Erickson, 1986). Therefore, it was important that I examine my data to see if I was indeed documenting children's participation in literacy activities during unstructured play.

Initial data analysis yielded 51 codes. Using Bogdan and Biklen's (1992) guidelines for coding, I re-read the data to discover if a single code could be used to describe patterns or similar properties of behavior or events. I began to merge codes, or as Bogdan and Biklen (1992) write, "play with different coding possibilities" (pp. 176-177). As I worked with the data and began to write up the findings, I discovered that many of my codes were too narrowly defined. For example, the *literacy activities* code initially had seven separate codes. As I reread the data and wrote the code descriptions for these codes, I observed that *literacy activities* could be coded as a "major code" (Bogdan & Biklen, 1992, p. 177) with descriptors used to identify "subcodes" (Bogdan & Biklen, 1992, p. 177) among the seven initially separate codes. For example, *copying names and making lists* and *reading* became, *literacy activities: copying names and making lists* and *literacy activities: reading*. This eventually yielded 21 codes. By reexamining the codes in this way, I was able to see the emergence of categories from this data. For example, major codes such as *environmental influences* and *literacy activities* became categories to further sort the data.

After data were coded, I organized the data into categories (Lincoln & Guba, 1985). I reexamined the codes and developed propositional statements to characterize each set of data. For example, the propositional statement regarding the environmental influences set of data reads: "This category is a collection of codes that describes the aspects of everyday life in this kindergarten classroom that influence children's participation in literacy activities."

Then I devised an inclusion rule or set of rules (Lincoln and Guba, 1985). I stated the set of rules as a list of questions that related to the properties of each category. For example, questions related to the *environmental influences* category included: Were children given time to read, write, or talk to one another during unstructured play? Was unstructured play time consistently available for reading, writing, and talking or was this time interrupted? Were there literacy props in the room that contributed to children's participation in literacy activities? In what ways did Ms. Casey influence children's participation in literacy activities? I used my set of questions to reexamine the data and see if what I had identified as environmental influences fit the criteria established in my set of questions. Propositional statements and inclusion rules were generated for each category. Four categories were developed to organize the data: (1) environmental influences, (2) literacy activities, (3) oral language in literacy activities, and (4) social interaction in literacy activities.

## Findings

Interactions among children at play are familiar, everyday events. However, in this study, interactions among kindergarten children at play were examined to clarify understandings about emergent literacy, specifically the social nature of literacy development. The findings will be presented as they relate to the four categories developed during data analysis.

### Environmental Influences

The *environmental influences* category describes physical and social aspects of everyday life in Ms. Casey's kindergarten classroom that influence children's participation in literacy activities. Specific physical environmental influences in Ms. Casey's kindergarten classroom either facilitated or inhibited children's participation in literacy activities during unstructured play. For example, the children in Ms. Casey's classroom sat in groups of eight or nine at three work tables rather than individual student desks during classroom instruction and work time. As a result, the children had opportunities throughout the day to interact with one another as they worked. During unstructured play, some children participated in literacy activities as they played at the work tables. They wrote letters, drew pictures, labeled their drawings, and wrote lists.

In addition to the physical arrangement of the classroom, Ms. Casey made literacy props available during unstructured play. Literacy props are reading and publishing materials, such as paper, pencils, and markers. Although the availability of some literacy props did facilitate children's participation in literacy activities during unstructured play, the lack of easy access to literacy props in this classroom inhibited children's participation in literacy activities during unstructured play.

Another part of the physical environment that influenced children's participation in literacy activities was environmental print. Environmental print refers to printed text that is available in the classroom. In Ms. Casey's classroom, examples of environmental print included an alphabet frieze posted above the chalkboard, children's name tags taped to the work tables, and a chart that outlined children's work stations in the computer lab. The children participated in literacy activities as they read letter names from the alphabet frieze and copied their classmates' names. However, the lack of environmental print, specifically children's writing, inhibited children's participation in literacy activities.

In addition to these physical environmental influences, social environmental influences either facilitated or inhibited children's participation in literacy activities during unstructured play. Ms. Casey continually encouraged her students to form communities and interact together during unstructured play. The social environment that Ms. Casey created facilitated children's participation in literacy activities because she routinely observed children to ensure they were playing together.

Interruptions, however, inhibited children's participation in literacy activities during unstructured play. I observed four kinds of interruptions during children's participation in literacy activities. First, Ms. Casey sometimes interrupted a child's play to give individual tutoring. Second, children were interrupted as groups of children were sent to a Chapter I reading resource teacher for additional reading instruction. At other times, the schedule for unstructured play was interrupted so that the children could participate in special activities, such as launching red balloons for drug awareness week or to allow for additional achievement test practice. Finally, children's unstructured play was sometimes interrupted by other children. On occasion, children might interrupt scenarios or take props away from other children. Likewise, children sometimes interrupted literacy activities by using aggressive behavior, such as hitting or kicking.

### *Literacy Activities*

The *literacy activities* category describes instances when children used language, including reading, writing, and speaking, to construct and communicate meaning. Children often participated in literacy activities during unstructured play when they read together. The availability of literacy props, particularly the children's library books, facilitated children's participation in literacy activities. In some instances, the children read together for pleasure, while in other instances, the children read together to gain information.

In addition to the literacy activities that involved reading, children participated in literacy activities that involved constructing and communicating meaning through their own writing. Children used pretend writing as part of their unstructured play. In addition, children used more conventional writing in literacy activities during unstructured play to rehearse handwriting skills, write lists, and write letters to people outside of their classroom.

Children also participated in literacy activities as they enacted scenarios. Children used oral language and social interaction to transform meanings for objects and establish roles to facilitate their scenarios during unstructured play. For the purposes of this paper, I will offer as an example, two specific scenarios the children established during unstructured play: the phone book scenario and library scenario.

**The Phone Book Scenario.** On one particular day of participant observation, I brought in literacy props, specifically an outdated local phone book and a small note pad. I placed these literacy props in the kitchen center. In the following excerpt from the data, Elizabeth and Katie interact as they pretend they are constructing a phone book. The data excerpt illustrates ways that Katie and Elizabeth use oral language and social interaction to establish a scenario and participate in literacy activities: in this instance, construct and communicate meanings about real world events.

Katie: I know my phone number.
Elizabeth: I can . . . I can . . . (she begins to write) 7 - 3 - 6 25 - 60.

(Elizabeth and Katie begin to look up and circle phone numbers in the phone book.)

    Katie: 2 - 2 - 4 - 6

(Hannah enters the kitchen center.)

  Elizabeth: (Speaking in a formal, crisp tone) What's your name?

  Hannah: Hannah.

  Elizabeth: What's your number?

  Hannah: 7 - 3 - 6 - 1 - 5 - 1 - 7.

  Elizabeth: (reciting as she is writing) 7 - 3 - 6 - 1 - 5 - 1 - 7.

    Katie: Let's look for Miss Casey's phone number.

(Elizabeth and Katie circle a phone number. Elizabeth and Katie leave the kitchen center to join Garrison and Steven on the floor in the open area at the front of the classroom.)

  Elizabeth: (Speaking in a crisp, formal tone) What is your address?

(Elizabeth takes notes. Katie continues to look through the phone book and circle phone numbers. Katie mouths words without speaking. She writes as she speaks on the phone. As she finishes each line of text, she sweeps her pencil above the paper as if to add a flourish to her script.)

  Elizabeth: (To Katie) Katie, Katie, Katie . . . I'm calling you.

(Elizabeth "dials" Katie's number and then begins to write.)

  Elizabeth: I'm writing, "I need to talk to you."

    Katie: (Into the phone) OK.

Katie and Elizabeth construct and communicate meanings about using a phone book, working together, and gathering information. As Katie and Elizabeth ask for phone numbers they change their tone of speech to affect a more formal tone. Elizabeth clips her words and uses a higher pitch as she asks for Hannah's phone number. When Elizabeth recites and writes Hannah's phone number, each digit is pronounced with crisp efficiency. Following Elizabeth's example, Katie affects the same crisp tone and high pitch as she pretends to work in the office. As Katie and Elizabeth become more and more involved in their phone book scenario, their language and actions become more adult-like and they communicate and interact as colleagues in the work place. Without formal discussion, Elizabeth and Katie construct and communicate meanings about the ways that adults communicate through oral and written discourse in a professional setting.

    **The Library Scenario.** The library scenario began in last week of March and continued through May. In early May, during the peak of the library scenario, the kitchen, computer, and blocks centers were transformed into physical spaces for the library. Children at play in kitchen center routinely went to their library (the computer center) to check out books and then returned to the kitchen center to read. Children at play in their library (computer center) used the sink from the kitchen center to clean their books. Hannah, Katie, and Shauna created an office scenario in the blocks center to publish books for the library. Wooden trucks from the blocks center were moved to the computer center so that they could be used as delivery trucks for library books. Additional blocks and construction toys (a plastic carpenter's plane and toy skill saw) were moved from the blocks center to the computer and kitchen centers and used to clean books prior to delivery. Ms. Casey's teacher's editions, which were stored in a student desk in the computer center, were used as operating manuals for the head librarians. The children's library books (from the school library) were collected in the wooden trucks each day during unstructured play and moved to the computer center so that other children could participate in the library scenario and check out real books.

In the library scenario, children transformed meanings of objects through social interaction as they interacted in a way that was appropriate to the newly assigned meanings for the objects. Sometimes children used oral language to communicate as they interacted and at other times their actions communicated as they interacted. In the following excerpt, Francisco and Dylan liberate a toy carpenter's plane from the blocks center and use it to scan and "clean" the books in their library. Neither Francisco nor Dylan announce that the toy carpenter's plane has been transformed from a toy carpenter's tool into a library scanner or book cleaning device, however, their oral language and social interaction is appropriate for the meaning they assigned to the toy carpenter's plane.

Francisco: Wanna play? We're stamping the books. Where's those stamps. Here.

Billy: Ya'll playing library?

Francisco: Here's the stamps. Dylan said he's doing it too.

Billy: Well, I'm stamping now. He let me stamp . . . um . . .

Francisco: No. You gotta do this first (Francisco demonstrates scanning the books with the toy carpenter's plane).

Billy: Yeah.

Francisco: Yeah . . . You're supposed to make 'em like . . . (Francisco is demonstrating how to clean the books). I'm gonna do that.

Throughout the library scenario, the children use social interaction to construct and communicate meanings about realistic activities they associate with running a busy library. The children who participated in this study had varied and somewhat limited experiences with libraries, especially working behind the scenes at a library. However, the children who participated in the library scenario used oral language and social interaction to transform objects in their environment while constructing and communicating a set of meanings associated with running a busy library.

### Oral Language in Literacy Activities

The *oral language* category describes ways children used oral language in literacy activities during unstructured play. Although each category in this study involves children's use of oral language, what distinguishes this category is the emphasis on children's specific uses of oral language as they participated in literacy activities during unstructured play. Children in this study used oral language specifically to direct their own actions. In addition, children used oral language to direct the activities of others as they participated in literacy activities. Finally, children used oral language to sing or recite nursery rhymes as they participated in literacy activities during unstructured play.

### Social Interaction in Literacy Activities

The *social interaction in literacy activities* category describes ways that the children in this study acted together as they participated in literacy activities during unstructured play. Although each category in this study includes ways that children used social interaction in literacy activities during unstructured play, what distinguishes the *social interaction* category is the emphasis on children's specific uses of social interaction as they participated in literacy activities during unstructured play. Children in this study used social interaction specifically to establish scenarios, participate in shared literacy activities, and form literacy partnerships to further participate in shared literacy activities.

The phone book and library scenarios illustrate ways that children form communities to establish and enact scenarios during unstructured play. The communities formed during unstructured play to create scenarios were short-lived, or formed and reformed each day. In addition to the communities formed during unstructured play, the children formed micro-communities, or literacy partnerships (between two children), as they engaged in shared literacy activities. For example, as Katie and Hannah played, they developed a list of their classmates' names by copying names from desk tags. One would call letters as the other wrote the list. Additional examples of literacy partnerships include Elizabeth spontaneously reciting the alphabet to the researcher in her classroom, Elizabeth and Brittany reading together, and Steven and Garrison rehearsing known literacy concepts. The following excerpt illustrates a literacy partnership between Steven and Garrison. They use social interaction to form a literacy partnership and use known literacy concepts, e.g., rhyming words, as they participate in a shared literacy activity.

Steven: Sat. Sat. Write sat.
Garrison: (Reading his list) Cat . . . fat . . . rat . . . sat
Steven: Lat! (Laughing) Lat . . . nat . . .
Garrison: (Garrison writes the new words and reads his list again.)
Cat . . . fat . . . rat . . . sat . . . lat . . . nat.
Steven and Garrison laugh.

Thus, Steven and Garrison form a micro-community and participate in a shared literacy activity as they construct their list of rhyming words. Steven develops a partnership with Garrison when he adds to Garrison's list of rhyming words. They have developed understandings about rhyming words and create an opportunity during unstructured play to participate in a shared literacy activity.

It appears that when these children participated in larger communities (i.e., three or more children), their participation in literacy activities included varied opportunities to rehearse constructing and communicating meaning among members of a community. They were able to engage in representational competence (Pellegrini, Galda, Dresden, & Cox, 1991) by transforming objects and establishing roles to facilitate participation in play scenarios. However, it also appears that when these children participated in literacy partnerships, i.e., between two children, their participation in shared literacy activities included more traditionally recognized forms of literacy activities, such as reading and writing together. Further research is warranted to determine if this finding is unique to this particular study.

## Conclusions

The importance of literacy development and the role of the school in developing literacy in children are recognized as vital issues in education.

When considering ways children's uses of oral language are displayed, oral language cannot be separated from literacy. Oral language and literacy are interrelated processes; development in one area influences development in the other. These findings suggest that literacy development is as natural a process as oral language development. It follows then, that literacy development should be thought of in much the same way as oral language development. Children develop oral language through observation, interaction, and imitation. Those who work with young children should take advantage of every opportunity to model effective oral discourse forms and engage children in conversation. Further, children's uses of oral language should be encouraged throughout the school day.

Literacy is also a social phenomenon developed through meaningful interactions with others. The findings from this study imply that traditional literacy programs which focus on individual achievement and the sequential acquisition of isolated bits of knowledge may not offer adequate opportunities for children to develop understandings about ways that people express their ideas to one another. The relationships among children's use of oral language, social interaction, and literacy activities are built from the understandings that children develop about the communicative nature of literacy. Three key understandings about the communicative nature of literacy were further developed and refined as children used oral language and social interaction in literacy activities during unstructured play in this study.

First, children further developed existing understandings about the communicative nature of oral language. They used oral language to talk to themselves when they directed their own literacy activities during unstructured play. In addition, they used oral language to communicate with others when they directed the literacy activities of others during unstructured play. The children further refined their understandings about the communicative nature of oral language as they approximated real world events to pretend they were adults communicating in offices and libraries.

Second, children further developed understandings about the communicative nature of reading. While the children came into kindergarten with similar understandings about the communicative nature of oral language, their understandings about the communicative nature of written language were not as clearly displayed. Children developed understandings that the printed symbols on the page communicate ideas, just as their oral language communicates ideas.

Finally, children displayed understandings about the communicative nature of their own writing and the role of audience in their writing. For example, when children share their writing, they talk about what their writing says. They demonstrate understandings about the relationship between communication and their own writing.

Overall, literacy activities can be defined as children's purposeful use of oral and written language to communicate ideas to others. Further, children's participation in literacy activities is an approximation of ways they have observed that adults use language to construct and communicate messages. The notion that children purposefully use language to construct and communicate ideas implies that although children naturally engage in literacy activities, this participation is a planned thoughtful process. Brief periods of uninterrupted play may not provide adequate time for children to plan meaningful ways to use their language. Extended periods of unstructured play with easy access to literacy props are required to facilitate children's purposeful use of oral and written language to construct and communicate meanings to others.

## References

Andersen, E. S. (1984). The acquisition of sociolinguistic knowledge: Some evidence from children's verbal role-play. *Western Journal of Speech Communication, 48,* 125-144.

Bogdan, R., & Biklen, S. (1992). *Qualitative research for education: An introduction to theory and methods* (2nd ed.). Boston: Allyn and Bacon.

Clay, M. (1966). *Emergent reading behaviour.* Unpublished doctoral dissertation, University of Auckland, Auckland, New Zealand.

Clay, M. (1986). Constructive practices: Talking, reading, writing, art, and craft. *Reading Teacher, 39,* 764-770.

Dyson, A. (1993). From invention to social action in early childhood literacy: A reconceptualization through dialogue about difference. *Early Childhood Research Quarterly, 8,* 409-425.

Erickson, F. (1986). Qualitative methods in research on teaching. In M. C. Wittrock (Ed.), *Handbook of research on teaching* (pp. 139 - 145). New York: Macmillan.

Goodman, Y. (1984). The development of initial literacy. In H. Goelman, A. Oberg, & F. Smith (Eds.), *Awaking to literacy* (pp. 102-109). Exeter, NH: Heinemann.

Green, J., & Wallet, C. (1988). Mapping instructional conversations—A sociolinguistic ethnography. In J. Green & C. Wallet (Eds.), *Ethnography and language in educational settings* (pp. 161-175). Norwood, NJ: Ablex.

Grugeon, E. (1988). Children's oral culture: A transitional experience. In M. MacLure, T. Phillips, & A. Wilkinson (Eds.), *Oracy matters* (pp. 159-173). Philadelphia, PA: Open University Press.

Guthrie, J., & Greaney, V. (1991). Literacy acts. In R. Barr, M. Kamil, P. B. Mosenthal, & P. D. Pearson (Eds.), *Handbook of reading research* (pp. 68-96). White Plains, NY: Longman.

Hall, N. (1987). *The emergence of literacy.* Portsmouth, NH: Heinemann.

Harste, J. C. (1985). Portrait of a new paradigm: Reading comprehension research. In A. Crismore & J. Harste (Eds.), *Landscapes: A state-of-the-art assessment of reading comprehension research, 1974-1984* (Final Report USDE C-300-83-0130). Bloomington: Indiana University, Language Education Department.

Hatch, J. A. (1988, February). *Young children as informants in classroom studies.* Paper presented at the meeting of the Ethnography in Educational Research Forum, Philadelphia, PA.

Heath, S. B. (1991). The sense of being literate: Historical and cross-cultural features. In R. Barr, M. Kamil, P. B. Mosenthal, & P. D. Pearson (Eds.), *Handbook of reading research* (pp. 3-25). White Plains, NY: Longman.

Isenberg, J., & Jacob, E. (1985). Playful literacy activities and learning: Preliminary observations. In J. L. Frost & S. Sunderlin (Eds.), *When children play* (pp. 17-21). Wheaton, MD: Association for Childhood Education International.

Jacob, E. (1984). Learning literacy through play: Puerto Rican kindergarten children. In H. Goelman, A. Oberg, & F. Smith (Eds.) *Awakening to literacy* (pp. 73-83). Exeter, NH: Heinemann.

Lincoln, Y., & Guba, E. (1985). *Naturalistic inquiry.* London: Sage.

Morrow, L. M., & Smith, (1990). Forward. In L. M. Morrow & J. K. Smith (Eds.), *Assessment for instruction in early literacy* (pp. xi-xii). Englewood Cliffs, NJ: Prentice Hall.

Neuman, S., & Roskos, K. (1990). Play, print, and purpose: Enriching play environments for literacy development. *The Reading Teacher, 44,* 214-221.

Neuman, S., & Roskos, K. (1992). Literacy objects as cultural tools: Effects on children's literacy behaviors in play. *Reading Research Quarterly, 27,* 203-225.

Nieto, S. (1992). *Affirming diversity: The sociopolitical context of multicultural education.* While Plains, NY: Longman.

Pearson, P. D. (1992). Reading. In M. C. Alkin (Ed.) *Encyclopedia of educational research* (pp. 1075-1085). New York: Macmillan.

Pearson, P. D. (1993). Teaching and learning reading: A research perspective. *Language Arts, 70,* 502-511.

Pellegrini, A. D. (1985). Relations between preschool children's symbolic play and literate behavior. In L. Galda & A. D. Pellegrini (Eds.), *Play, language, and stories: The development of children's literate behavior* (pp. 79-98). Norwood, NJ: Ablex.

Pellegrini, A. D., Galda, L., Dresden, J., & Cox, S. (1991). A longitudinal study of predictive relations among symbolic play, linguistic verbs, and early literacy. *Research in the Teaching of English, 25,* 219-235.

Pellegrini, A. D., Galda, L., & Rubin, D. (1984). Context in text: The development of oral and written language in two genres. *Child Development, 55,* 1549-1555.

Roskos, K. (1991). An inventory of literate behavior in the pretend play episodes of eight preschoolers. *Reading Research and Instruction, 30,* 39-52.

Rowe, D. W. (1989). Author/audience interaction in the preschool: The role of social interaction in literacy learning. *Journal of Reading Behavior, 21,* 311-349.

Schober-Peterson, D., & Johnson, C. J. (1989). Conversational topics of 4-year-olds. *Journal of Speech and Hearing Research, 32,* 857-870.

Schober-Peterson, D., & Johnson, C. J. (1991). Non-Dialogue speech during preschool interactions. *Journal of Child Language, 18,* 153-170.

Strickland, D., & Morrow, L. (1988). Reading, writing, and oral language. *The Reading Teacher, 42,* 240-241.

Sulzby, E., & Teale, W. (1991). Emergent literacy. In R. Barr, M. Kamil, P. B. Mosenthal, & P. D. Pearson (Eds.), *Handbook of reading research* (pp. 727-757). White Plains, NY: Longman.

Teale, W., & Sulzby, E. (1986). Introduction: Emergent literacy as a perspective for examining how young children become writers and readers. In W. Teale & E. Sulzby (Eds.), *Emergent literacy: writing and reading* (pp. vii-xix). Norwood, NJ: Ablex.

Thomas, K., Rinehart, S., & Wampler, S. (1992). Oral language, literacy and schooling: Kindergarten years. *Reading Horizons, 33,* 149-166.

Vygotsky, L. S. (1967). Play and its role in the mental development of the child. *Soviet Psychology, 5,* 6-18.

Vygotsky, L. S. (1978). *Mind in society.* Cambridge: Harvard University Press.

# Influences on Grade-Five Students' Decisions to Read: An Exploratory Study of Leisure Reading Behavior

## Patricia Whitney
### Heritage College

## Abstract

*The purpose of this study was to explore why a child who is a capable reader either elects to read or not to read during out-of-school leisure time. Fifty-three grade-five students from a school district outside a major metropolitan area in Canada provided information about their out-of-school activities for a 17 day period. Measures administered were the comprehension section of the Gates-MacGinitie Reading Test, the Children's Nowicki-Strickland Internal-External Control Scale, and the recreational reading subscale of the Elementary Reading Attitude Survey. Subjects, their parents, and their teachers were interviewed. Descriptive analyses were conducted for out-of-school activities, amount of reading, and affective beliefs and values. Significant effects were found for gender, attitude toward recreational reading, teacher behavior during Undisturbed Sustained Silent Reading, reading behavior of siblings and parents, and provision of a space for reading in the home.*

Aliteracy, the ability to read but choosing not to, seems to be a growing concern in American society (Decker, 1985). George Steiner (1985) believes that the "classical age of reading" is diminishing and that we know astonishingly little about the feelings individuals have about reading. The current research-base focuses more on the cognitive side of reading than on the affective side (Alverman, 1987). Knowing the factors that affect why readers choose to read or not to read is significant if the goal of parents and educators is to create life-long readers.

When most children start school, they look forward to learning to read or are already reading (Durkin, 1960/61). Most young children are intrinsically interested in acquiring this skill (Condry & Koslowski, 1979; Deci, 1975; Farris

& Kaczmarski, 1988), find looking at books enchanting, and quickly warm to a person who will take the time to read to them. As children progress through the elementary grades, this intrinsic interest begins to change (Kohn, 1987).

Some students at various grade levels testify either that they hate reading, or that they do not enjoy it (Shapiro & White, 1991); some teachers testify that their students do not like to read (Whitney, 1986), or that their students rarely read for pleasure (Chisom, 1989). This trend seems to be getting worse (Elley, 1992; Foertsch, 1992). Overall, many students who can read choose not to (Alvermann & Guthrie, 1993). It appears that something happens to some of these readers between the points in time when they are intrinsically interested and when they hate reading. This shift may have something to do with a misconception on the part of some librarians and educators as to what motivates a student to read.

The purpose of this study is to investigate why a child who can read either elects to read or not to read during out-of-school leisure time. This investigation was conducted at the grade-five level because studies have found that at this grade, students are still reading (Duggins, 1989; Greaney, 1980; Lamme, 1976; Maxwell, 1977; Neuman, 1980; Whitehead, Capey, Maddren, & Wellings, 1977). Since this was an exploratory study, the purpose was to generate questions and examine various answers in order to document the reasons for not reading during time out of school. The questions guiding this study were as follows:

- Do capable readers read out of school only when intrinsic reasons are present?
- How does locus of control affect leisure reading?
- How does attitude affect one's decision to spend time reading for leisure?
- Are there similarities and differences in classroom and home practices around leisure reading for frequent and infrequent readers?

## Method

This problem was investigated through an exploratory study using a survey design. The group measured was a sample of grade-five students selected from four classrooms who had volunteered to participate in the study. The method of data collection included closed diaries, available measuring instruments, and personal interviews.

### Subjects

The subjects were students selected from four grade-five classrooms in three different schools that served families with similar economic backgrounds in a suburban area of British Columbia, Canada. Fifty-six percent of the fathers worked in the trades; 23% worked in service, sales, and clerical occupations; 19% worked in managerial positions; and 2% were not classified. Twenty-five percent of the mothers worked as homemakers; 42% were clerical workers; 17% worked in managerial positions; 15% worked in sales or service occupations, and 1% worked in the trades.

The enrollment for the participating school district was approximately 17,000 students. The three schools, which had enrollments between 380 and 540 students, were no further than eight blocks apart and had overlapping attendance areas. They enrolled students in kindergarten through grade seven.

One hundred and five children in the four classrooms were invited to participate in this voluntary study. Sixty-nine students volunteered to participate. Since the study was designed to investigate only capable readers, ten students were eliminated from the sample group because both teacher judgement and the comprehension scores from the *Gates-MacGinitie Reading Test* (1992) found them to be low on their reading ability. An additional six students were eliminated for reasons such as illness or no interview.Consequently, the final sample group was reduced to 53 students (21 boys and 32 girls).

The mean age for this sample was 10 years and six months. The ethnic origins were Caucasian (83%), Asian (13%), Aboriginal (2%), and undecided (2%). The educational levels of the fathers ranged from professional degrees (MD, JD, DDS), to less than high school; for the mothers, educational levels ranged from a masters degree to less than high school.

## *Measures*

To help students account for their time out of school, *Clock Sheets* were developed. There were clock sheets allotted for an after school day (Figure 1), a weekend day (Figure 2), and a weekend night (Figure 3). Activities, expanded from Anderson, Wilson and Fielding (1988), were grouped under several categories namely, "I played," "I did," "I watched/listened," "I . . . ," "What else did I do," and "I went to."

Three protocols were developed by the researcher. The *Student Interview* probed what reinforcements or rewards each student derived from his/her most frequent leisure activities, and what values he/she attached to these rewards. Reading classroom practices and home reading practices were also discussed.

The *Teacher Interview* probed for classroom reading practices that could impact out-of-school student activities. Questions focused on the reading program, materials, and activities within the classroom as well as the personal reading habits of each teacher.

The *Parent Interview* probed for support and encouragement that students might receive in the home for the activities that they chose to do out of school. Questions centered on the parents' leisure activities, parental activities that

## Figure 1. After School Day Clock-Sheet

This is what I did out-of-school on_____

Code #_____

### Instructions

1. Check off the boxes indicating what you did yesterday out-of-school.
2. Think about the time you did them and place the code which is next to that activity into the circles of the clock at the appropriate time. Each circle equals about 15 minutes.
3. Some activities need to be completed with information.
4. Here are some special codes:

    B (bathing)    D (dressing)    E (eating)

    S (sleeping)    T (transportation)

*I Played*

A1 ❑ with my friends at _____ this is what we did _____.

A1 ❑ with my friends at _____ this is what we did _____.

A2 ❑ talked on the phone

A3 ❑ a sport called _____.

A3 ❑ a sport called _____.

A3 ❑ a sport called _____.

A4 ❑ a game called _____.

A4 ❑ a game called _____.

A4 ❑ a game called _____.

A5 ❑ a video game (Nintendo or other)

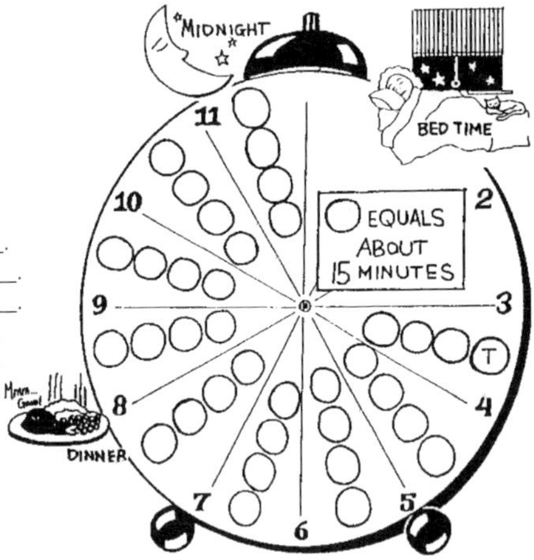

*I Did*

B1 ❑ my homework

B2 ❑ help around the house _____.

B3 ❑ work on a hobby called _____.

B3 ❑ work on a hobby called _____.

B4 ❑ a (practice/lesson) for _____.

B4 ❑ a (practice/lesson) for _____.

*I Watched/Listened*

C1 ❑ to a movie video

C1 ❑ to television

C1 ❑ to (radio, records, tapes, CDs)

*I . . .*

D1 ❑ read mail from _____.

D2 ❑ wrote a letter NOT for school to _____.

D3 ❑ read a newspaper NOT for school about _____.

D3 ❑ read a newspaper NOT for school about _____.

D4 ❑ read a magazine NOT for school about _____.

D5 ❑ read a book NOT for school about _____.

D5 ❑ read a book NOT for school about _____.

D6 ❑ wrote something NOT for school (diary, journal, story, poetry)

D7 ❑ read comic books called _____.

*What Else Did I Do?*

E1 ❑ _____

E2 ❑ _____

E3 ❑ _____

E4 ❑ _____

*I Went To*

F1 ❑ the library

F2 ❑ the store

# Figure 2. Weekend Day Clock-Sheet

This is what I did out-of-school on_____
Code #_____

## Instructions
1. Check off the boxes indicating what you did yesterday out-of-school.
2. Think about the time you did them and place the code which is next to that activity into the circles of the clock at the appropriate time. Each circle equals about 15 minutes.
3. Some activities need to be completed with information.
4. Here are some special codes:
   B (bathing)   D (dressing)   E (eating)
   S (sleeping)   T (transportation)

*I Played*
A1 ☐ with my friends at _____ this is what we did _____.
A1 ☐ with my friends at _____ this is what we did _____.
A2 ☐ talked on the phone
A3 ☐ a sport called _____.
A3 ☐ a sport called _____.
A3 ☐ a sport called _____.
A4 ☐ a game called _____.
A4 ☐ a game called _____.
A4 ☐ a game called _____.
A5 ☐ a video game (Nintendo or other)

*I Did*
B1 ☐ my homework
B2 ☐ help around the house _____.
B3 ☐ work on a hobby called _____.
B3 ☐ work on a hobby called _____.
B4 ☐ a (practice/lesson) for _____.
B4 ☐ a (practice/lesson) for _____.

*I Watched/Listened*
C1 ☐ to a movie video
C1 ☐ to television
C1 ☐ to (radio, records, tapes, CDs)

*I . . .*
D1 ☐ read mail from _____.
D2 ☐ wrote a letter NOT for school to _____.
D3 ☐ read a newspaper NOT for school about _____.
D3 ☐ read a newspaper NOT for school about _____.
D4 ☐ read a magazine NOT for school about _____.
D5 ☐ read a book NOT for school about _____.
D5 ☐ read a book NOT for school about _____.
D6 ☐ wrote something NOT for school (diary, journal, story, poetry)
D7 ☐ read comic books called _____.

*What Else Did I Do?*
E1 ☐ _____
E2 ☐ _____
E3 ☐ _____
E4 ☐ _____

*I Went To*
F1 ☐ the library
F2 ☐ the store

## Figure 3. Weekend Night Clock-Sheet

This is what I did out-of-school on_____
Code #_____

### Instructions
1. Check off the boxes indicating what you did yesterday out-of-school.
2. Think about the time you did them and place the code which is next to that activity into the circles of the clock at the appropriate time. Each circle equals about 15 minutes.
3. Some activities need to be completed with information.
4. Here are some special codes:
   B (bathing)   D (dressing)   E (eating)
   S (sleeping)   T (transportation)

*I Played*
A1 ❐ with my friends at _____ this is what we did _____.
A1 ❐ with my friends at _____ this is what we did _____.
A2 ❐ talked on the phone
A3 ❐ a sport called _____.
A3 ❐ a sport called _____.
A3 ❐ a sport called _____.
A4 ❐ a game called _____.
A4 ❐ a game called _____.
A4 ❐ a game called _____.
A5 ❐ a video game (Nintendo or other)

*I Did*
B1 ❐ my homework
B2 ❐ help around the house _____.
B3 ❐ work on a hobby called _____.
B3 ❐ work on a hobby called _____.
B4 ❐ a (practice/lesson) for _____.
B4 ❐ a (practice/lesson) for _____.

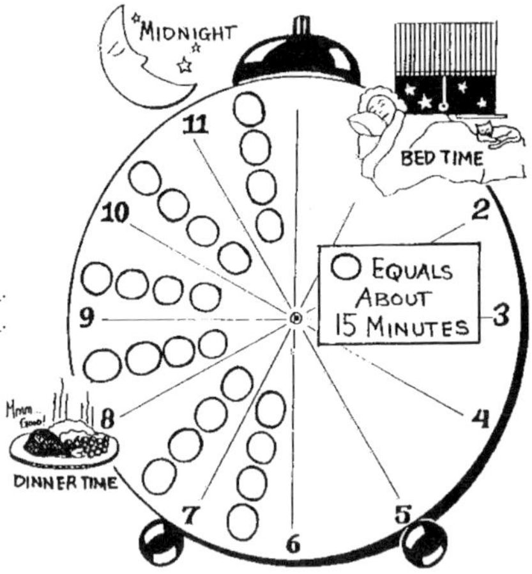

*I Watched/Listened*
C1 ❐ to a movie video
C1 ❐ to television
C1 ❐ to (radio, records, tapes, CDs)

*I . . .*
D1 ❐ read mail from _____.
D2 ❐ wrote a letter NOT for school to _____.
D3 ❐ read a newspaper NOT for school about _____.
D3 ❐ read a newspaper NOT for school about _____.
D4 ❐ read a magazine NOT for school about _____.
D5 ❐ read a book NOT for school about _____.
D5 ❐ read a book NOT for school about _____.
D6 ❐ wrote something NOT for school (diary, journal, story, poetry)
D7 ❐ read comic books called _____.

*What Else Did I Do?*
E1 ❐ _____
E2 ❐ _____
E3 ❐ _____
E4 ❐ _____

*I Went To*
F1 ❐ the library
F2 ❐ the store

were similar to the student's, reading in the home, reading at school, and family background. The *Children's Nowicki-Strickland Internal-External Control Scale* (Nowicki & Strickland, 1973) was used to measure locus of control, and the *Elementary Reading Attitude Survey* (McKenna, & Kear, 1990), was used to measure attitude toward recreational reading.

### Procedure

So as not to bias this study, participants were told that the researcher's interest was to document out-of-school activities, i.e., what students spend their time doing out of school, and why they choose to participate in these activities. Prior to beginning the study, details were given as to what was involved, i.e., filling in clock-sheets and taking part in an interview. Students were reminded that their participation was voluntary, would have no impact on their grades, and that they could withdraw from the project at any time. Confidentiality was stressed to students, that is, they would be assigned code numbers and that no one but the researcher would have access to the data. Assurances were given that if they were chosen to be interviewed, how they spent their time out of school would not be revealed to their parents, and that the purpose of the parent interview was to find out how they, the parent, spent some of their leisure time.

On the day the study began, students were given a pocket-folder marked with their names and assigned code numbers, which contained the clock-sheets. Students were provided with time in school to complete the clock-sheets on a daily basis for three weeks. Students could take a clock-sheet home during the week if they desired. On Friday, all students took sheets home.

Initially, students were given instructions on how to complete the clock-sheets. After the demonstration and guided practice the researcher collected and reviewed the forms. The next day the researcher met each class to clarify the procedure and to help students with problems that they had filling out their clock-sheet for the first day of the study. The students filled out a clock-sheet on a daily basis for three weeks. Five to ten minutes were allotted each morning for filling out and collecting these forms. The clock-sheets were collected each day and checked by the researcher for any omissions. The researcher clarified responses by questioning individual pupils privately.

On designated days during this three week period, the locus of control scale and the *Gates-MacGinitie Reading Test* (MacGinitie & MacGinitie, 1992) were administered to all participating students. Results from the comprehension section and teacher judgment were used to determine whether or not a student was reading at the level of his/her grade-five peers.

After all clock-sheets had been completed, collected, and analyzed for the amounts of time spent on different activities, all students participated in individual interviews. The interviews were conducted at the schools in rooms set aside by the principal. All student interviews were completed within a two week period and were recorded on audio tape. After students had been interviewed, parents were interviewed over the telephone, and the teachers were interviewed at school.

Once interviews were completed, a recreational reading attitude survey, a subscale of the *Elementary Reading Attitude Survey* (McKenna & Kear, 1990) was given to all students. This instrument, because of its reading nature, was given after all other data had been collected so as not to bias any responses given for other items and instruments. The scale was administered by the researcher in each classroom.

## Results

Students who were part of this study reported spending between zero and 19% of their out-of-school time reading for leisure. The leisure reading material included books, magazines, newspapers, comic books, and mail. A median split was made at 5%, creating a group of 27 frequent readers, 11 boys and 16 girls, who spent at least 5% of their out-of-school time (averaging 34 minutes per day) reading for leisure, and a group of 26 infrequent readers, 10 boys and 16 girls, who spent 4% or less of their out-of-school time (averaging 6 minutes per day) reading for leisure. Limiting reading material to books only, the study shows that frequent readers read an average of 23 minutes per day, and infrequent readers read an average of four minutes per day.

No significant relationships ($p$=.05) were found between locus of control and socioeconomic status, ability, minutes spent book reading, total minutes spent reading all materials, percentage of leisure time spent book reading, percentage of leisure time spent reading all materials, attitude toward recreational reading, gender, and ethnicity. Of the following variables: gender, socioeconomic status (SES), ethnicity, and ability, only gender showed a significant effect on leisure reading. The gender effect was for minutes spent book reading ($F_{1,52}$=5.26, $p$=.03), percentage of leisure time spent book reading ($F_{1,52}$=9.43, $p$=.00), and percentage of leisure time spent reading all materials ($F_{1,52}$=4.42, $p$=.04). Overall, girls spent more time reading for leisure than boys.

Significant positive correlations were found between minutes spent book reading (.28, $p$=.02), total minutes spent reading all materials (.46, $p$=.00), and student attitude toward reading. Students with a positive recreational reading attitude spent more time reading for leisure. Only two independent variables had a significant effect on the dependent variable, attitude toward recreational reading. Analyses of variance found a significant effect between seeing parents read and attitude toward recreational reading ($F_{2,52}$=4.52, $p$=.02). T-tests also found a significant difference between observing one's parents reading newspapers and attitudes toward recreational reading ($t$=2.55, $p$.01).

Students who observed their parents reading seemed to have a better attitude toward recreational reading.

Influences that the classroom may have had on spending time reading for leisure for these students were investigated. Significant differences were found between seeing the teacher read during Undisturbed Sustained Silent Reading and minutes spent reading books ($t$=2.01, $p$=.05), total minutes spent reading all materials ($t$=2.27, $p$=.02), and percentage of leisure time spent reading all materials ($t$=2.27, $p$=.03). Thus, students who observed their teacher reading during leisure reading time at school spent more time out of school reading for leisure.

Influences that the home may have had on the leisure reading time for these students were analyzed with 40 independent variables. Significant effects included students' observations of siblings' use of various reading materials ($t$=4.71, $p$=.00), and the parents' report of provision of a space for reading in the home ($F_{3,51}$=3.30, $p$=.03). Thus, students who observed siblings reading at home and students who had a place to read at home spent more time reading out of school for leisure.

## Conclusions

In this study, most children who had the ability to read did so out of school when intrinsic reasons were present; some children read for other reasons. Intrinsic reasons are defined as feelings of competence, satisfaction, self-determination, delight, or other similar reinforcements. The reasons for leisure reading given by students designated as frequent readers included statements which were categorized as "enjoyment" (59%), "learning" (26%), "relief from boredom" (30%), "encouragement" (11%), "other" (7%), and "availability" (11%). "Relief from boredom" and "availability" would not be intrinsic; "encouragement" and "other" might be considered intrinsic depending on the reasoning. Intrinsic reasons were therefore present for 85% of the frequent readers, but there were also other reasons. Fifteen percent of the frequent readers were not reading for intrinsic reasons. Thus, reading for intrinsic reasons did seem to impact frequent readers even though these were not the only reasons for spending leisure time reading.

Locus of control apparently had no effect on the time spent reading for leisure with this group of students. One explanation is that students by this age do not have to rely on generalized expectancy or beliefs about their behaviors and rewards when it comes to leisure reading. Fifth-grade students have already had a fair amount of experience with leisure reading and probably make their decisions based on that experience.

Recreational reading attitude had an effect on time spent reading for leisure with frequent readers. A positive attitude correlated significantly with time spent reading (number of minutes and percentage of leisure time) regardless of the reading material. Thus a positive attitude and spending time reading seemed to go together. "Which comes first?" is a question for further study.

The only classroom practice influencing leisure reading for these frequent and infrequent readers indicated was having a teacher that read during USSR. At home, having siblings that read books and comic books, and parents providing a space for reading appeared to make a significant difference in the amount of time spent reading. As one infrequent reader commented when asked "What, if anything, would get you to spend more time reading for leisure?"

> I guess if I was the kind of person who liked to read like my Mom and Dad. My Mom zips through a book about this thick in one day. I used to not even look at a book. But now I'm getting slowly more into it.

Students need to actually observe reading behavior. Talking about spending time reading, and assigning time for reading does not seem to be the answer. Parents reading at home also had a significant positive effect on student attitude toward recreational reading. Thus, there is considerable evidence that children need role models.

### Implications

Leisure reading behavior can be a fairly sensitive topic because teachers, librarians, parents, and grandparents have good intentions and would like to do "what's right" to encourage reading. This study described intentions and practices that impact leisure reading behavior in fifth-grade students. Practices that had no effect at this age may come as surprises to many.

Classroom practices that had no effect in this study included reading aloud to students, use of school and classroom libraries, and use of rewards for leisure reading. In the homes, practices that had no effect included parents encouraging their child to read; reading together; listening to their child read; talking with them about leisure materials; reading aloud to their child; providing materials; use of the library (parents' membership, or taking the child to the library at this age); use of rewards for leisure reading; distance of the home from the library; education levels of parents; languages used in the home; number of playmates of the child; size of the family; or birth order position. Thus, assumptions on how to increase leisure reading behavior may be based on research related to achievement, attitude, motivation, and participation rather than actual leisure reading behavior.

This study has also provided evidence for what grade-five students want from their reading materials. Students were asked "What would make reading more fun?" Often students had more than one response, but most responses fell into the category of content. Content refers to style, characters, or plot. For example, some of the students made generalized statements,

such as having materials that were more exciting, funny or interesting. Others were more specific about the materials themselves:
> "If in the comic books, they had more jokes and riddles, and stuff like that. Like funner activities." "Like magazines when they talk about a person, if they like give more information on that person rather than a little bit."

Some students had specific advice for authors:
> "If the authors would cut out the boring parts." "If they had lots of detail. Like more about the person or place. I like reading stuff because it's really interesting, and if it's not interesting then I don't read at all." "More action. Like every bit is action!" "I like it when a boat is going to fall over, and then you jump into the land and stuff. Or saving yourself, or like your friend is going to fall off the cliff, and you save them."

One infrequent reader explained what it was that made a book boring.
> "Well, they just talk. Like there's usually three chapters, and they just talking and talking; no where in particular that just talking about what happened straight in the day. Nothing interesting. The book I'm reading now, the boring story: buy the girl a Christmas present, a puppy. She buys him a pizza."

Others mention what they would particularly like to read about:
> "thoroughbred books," "hockey," " murder books or else dying books," "books about my favorite TV shows," and "right now I'm reading a skiing book; and one time I was reading a hockey book, and before that I was reading a novel book about motorcycles."

The researcher asked this particular student if he would rather read books that tell the reader how to do things or stories about those things. The student answered "stories." One student mentioned that the one thing that would make reading more fun for them is
> "If Roald Dahl never died because I like his books."

There were several results in this study that were not statistically significant but indicate trends that may be worth investigating further with a larger sample size. Some examples of these are effect of actual amounts of time given for USSR, effect of books being available in the classroom for leisure reading, and effect of using materials for teaching reading such as a reading series or technical materials. Trends in the analyses indicated these variables might be interacting with the amount of time spent reading. Other influences that may be fruitful for further investigation regarding students' attitude toward recreational reading were teacher behavior during USSR, silent reading programs that have students reading for pleasure in school and at home each night, and having a classroom library.

---

# References

Alvermann, D. E. (1987). Developing lifetime readers. In D. E. Alvermann, D. W. Moore, & M.W. Conely (Eds.), *Research within reach: Secondary school reading; A research guided response to concerns of reading educators* (25-36). Newark, DE: International Reading Association.

Alvermann, D. E., & Guthrie, J. T. (1993). *Themes and directions of the National Reading Research Center* (Perspectives in reading research, No. 1). Athens: University of Georgia and College Park: University of Maryland, National Reading Research Center.

Anderson, R. C., Wilson, P. T., & Fielding, L. G. (1988). Growth in reading and how children spend their time outside of school. *Reading Research Quarterly, 23,* 285-303.

Chisom, Y. L.( 1989). *Increasing literature appreciation and recreational reading behavior of intermediate grade students.* Unpublished doctoral dissertation, Nova University, Fort Lauderale, Florida. (ERIC Document Reproduction Service No. 308 494)

Condry, J., & Koslowski, B. (1979). Can education be made "intrinsically interesting" to children? In L. G. Katz (Ed.), *Current topics in early childhood education: Vol.11* (pp.227-260). Norwood,NJ: Ablex.

Deci, E. L. (1975). *Intrinsic motivation.* New York: Plenum Press.

Decker, B. C. (1985, November). *Aliteracy: What teachers can do to keep Johnny reading.* Paper presented at the meetings of Louisiana State University's Education Forum, Shreveport,LA. and at the Southeastern Regional Conference of the International Reading Association, Nashville,TN. (ERIC Document Reproduction Service No. 265 528)

Duggins, J. (1989,May). *Middle school students' interest in reading and reading ability.* Paper presented the 34th convention of the International Reading Association, New Orleans,LA.

Durkin, D. (1960/61). Children who read before grade one. *The Reading Teacher, 14,* 163-166.

Elley, W. B. (1992). *How in the world do students read?: IEA study of reading literacy.* The Hague: The International Association for the Evaluation of Educational Achievement.

Farris, P. J., & Kaczmarski, D. (1988). Whole language,a closer look. *Contemporary Education,59(2),*77-81.

Foertsch, M. A.(1992). *Reading in and out of school: Factors influencing the literacy achievement of American students in grades 4, 8, and 12, in 1988 and 1990.* Washington,DC: U.S. Government Printing Office.

Greaney, V. (1980). Factors related to amount and type of leisure time reading. *Reading Research Quarterly,* 15 (3), 337-357.

Kohn, A. (1987). Art for art's sake. *Psychology Today, 21* (9), 52-57.

Lamme, L. (1976). Are reading habits and abilities related? *The Reading Teacher, 30* (1), 21-27.

MacGinitie, W. H., & MacGinitie, R. K. (1992). *Gates-MacGinitie Reading Tests*(2nd Canadian ed.). Scarbough,Ontario: Nelson Canada.

Maxwell, J. (1977). *Reading progress from 8 to 15.* Windsor,Berks.: NFER Publishing Co.

McKenna, M. C., & Kear, D. J. (1990). Measuring attitude toward reading: A new tool for teachers. *The Reading Teacher,43* (9), 626-639.

Neuman, S. B. (1980). Why children read: A functional approach. *Journal of Reading Behavior, 12* (4), 333-336.

Nowicki, S., & Strickland, B. (1973). A locus of control scale for children. *Journal of Consulting & Clinical Psychology, 40* (1), 148-154.

Shapiro, J., & White, W. (1991). Reading attitude and perceptions in traditional and nontraditional reading programs. *Reading, Research, & Instruction, 30* (4), 52-66.

Steiner, G. (1985). Books in an age of post-literacy. *Publishers Weekly, 227* (21), 44-48.

Whitehead, F., Capey, A. C., Maddren, W., & Wellings, A. (1977). *Children and their books*. London: Macmillan Education.

Whitney, P. (1986). *Children's locus of control and intrinsically motivated reading*. Unpublished master's thesis, San Francisco State University.

# The Influence of Developmentally Appropriate Spelling Instruction on the Achievement of First Grade Students

**Linda B. Hunter**

Pennsylvania State University
at Harrisburg

## Abstract

*This study was conducted to determine whether first grade students, instructed in small groups according to appropriate developmental levels, would achieve significantly greater spelling gains than a control group receiving whole group, uniform grade level instruction. Thirty-eight first grade students in a suburban school district participated in the 28-week study.*

*Schlagal's Qualitative Inventory of Word Knowledge (Schlagal, 1986) was administered to the experimental group to determine appropriate instructional levels. A teacher-constructed pretest/posttest instrument was used to measure spelling gains. Results of an ANCOVA showed no significant difference between the control and experimental groups on teacher-constructed pre and posttests. However, the qualitative analysis of writing samples revealed advantages in developmental stage progression for the experimental group.*

With the growth of the whole language approach, the use of invented spellings has become a common practice in children's writing. Two decades of research on children's invented spelling has established that learning how to spell is a developmental process (Read, 1975; Beers & Henderson, 1977; Gentry, 1977; Zutell, 1979). Current spelling instruction, however, frequently consists of children in a given classroom studying the same words at the same time as their classmates, in spite of the fact that they may be at different stages of development. Schlagal (1986) calls uniform spelling instruction for an entire class "problematic." Students with a weak base of word knowledge will struggle with grade level instruction, while those with superior word knowledge study already-mastered concepts.

The call for changes in spelling instruction is a result of the implications of research by Read (1971, 1975), Beers & Henderson (1977) and Zutell (1979). They discovered that children's attempts to spell were neither random nor haphazard. Instead, the attempts seemed to progress predictably as students experimented with writing and began to assimilate increasing knowledge of English orthography (Beers & Henderson, 1977).

Read (1971) sought to explain children's invented spellings by showing that they were based on an unconscious knowledge of English phonology. He proposed that preschool children brought this knowledge to their first experiences with reading and writing. He further hypothesized that invented spellings were dependent on children's perception and organization of spoken forms (Read, 1971). In Read's second study (1975), he included formal experiments to identify the specific characteristics that influence children's categorization of speech sounds. Their categorizations, he concluded, are unexpected, but phonetically justified. In addition, the changes observed seemed to follow predictable patterns, reflecting levels of phonological knowledge (Beers & Henderson. 1977). Zutell's study showed that the types of errors children made changed as they developed more sophisticated strategies for inventing spellings (Zutell, 1979).

Because of this research, as well as subsequent studies by Henderson and his colleagues, five levels or stages of spelling knowledge have been identified. *Precommunicative stage* spellings show a familiarity with letters, with a preference for uppercase letters, but have no letter/sound correspondence. In the *semiphonetic stage,* spelling attempts display a recognition that letters represent sounds, though only some sound features are represented. Use of a "letter-name" strategy is evident (e.g., AT for eighty). The hallmark of the *phonetic spelling stage* is that all sounds are represented. Words are spelled as they sound (e.g., EGL for eagle). *Transitional stage* spelling represents what English sounds *and* looks like (e.g. YOUNIGHTED for united). A child at the *conventional spelling stage* accurately spells the corpus of words that a majority of grade level peers who are developmentally on target have mastered (Gentry & Gillet, 1993).

Many educators are calling for changes in spelling curricula to reflect the implications of developmental spelling research (Bean & Bouffler, 1987; Bloodgood, l99l; O'Flahavan & Blassberg, 1992; Routman, 1991; Wilde, 1990). Based on their action research with kindergarten, first and second grade children, Bean & Bouffler (1987) emphasize that reading and writing activities enable children to develop the spelling strategies needed to write with fluency. They believe that these activities should focus children's attention on words within the context of written texts in order to help children develop needed spelling strategies. Wilde (1990) supports a shift from the traditional, textbook-based approach to spelling instruction to an approach that first grows out of writing, with a focus on the children's developmental needs. Minilessons on spelling strategies and proofreading should become part of instruction as students mature and have further experiences with writing. Along the way, the classroom must provide an environment full of opportunities and resources that support the children's development as independent spellers. Bloodgood (1991) lists three important requirements of a new approach to spelling instruction: first, instruction is based on accurate assessment of children's spelling abilities; second, use of word-study groups and activities provides for individual needs; third, spelling instruction should be incorporated into reading and writing activities.

Morris, Nelson & Perney (1986) stress the need for small group spelling instruction in schools to provide spelling instruction that is appropriate for the differing developmental levels of students. They also point out that this type of instruction may be slow in coming because of insufficient empirical data to support this change.

Templeton (1991) asserts that students should be grouped according to similar abilities for spelling and word study. The words that children examine should be at their instructional level to insure that they will be truly learned, not misspelled after Friday's test. Zutell (1992) also states that when students examine words within their own developmental "grasp," they are much more likely to experience sustained spelling growth. Ehri (1992) has specifically called for studies that will verify that students taught at developmentally appropriate levels will achieve superior gains in spelling achievement.

One of Bloodgood's proposed changes was implemented in this study to determine how this type of instruction affects students' spelling achievement as compared to students who receive instruction at a uniform level. As Bloodgood (1991) recommends, small groups were created based on assessment of the children's spelling abilities, and instruction was incorporated into reading and writing activities. The study was also designed to respond to Ehri's call for research, by establishing a setting in which students were instructed in small groups at developmentally appropriate levels and by comparing their spelling achievement gains to those of students receiving whole group, uniform grade level instruction.

Thus, this study was conducted to answer the question "Is there a significant difference between the spelling pretest to posttest gains of first grade students instructed in small groups according to their developmental level and first grade students who received whole group instruction at one level?" Since the developmental nature of learning to spell has been demonstrated by much previous research, it was hypothesized that the experimental group would show significantly greater gains from pretest to posttest than the control group.

# Method

Two self-contained classrooms of first grade students in a suburban public school district participated in the study for 28 weeks. One class received the experimental treatment, while the other class served as a control group.

## Participants

The 38 students, aged six through seven years, came from a variety of socio-economic and ethnic groups, although the majority of families in the district were middle class. Twenty-five percent were minority students. The control and experimental classes were heterogeneously grouped. Each class was instructed by a teacher who was aided by an instructional assistant. There were 20 students in the control group and 18 students in the experimental group.

## Procedure

Prior to the start of the study, spelling instruction in both classes (as in the other first grade classrooms) during the first quarter focused on the recognition of initial and final consonant sounds and an introduction to short vowel sounds. The study was initiated at the beginning of the second quarter, when the use of word lists for study and weekly tests usually commenced. Typically, all first grade classes used the same set of word lists in spelling instruction from the second through fourth quarters.

The Grade One Spelling Word List (Appendix A) had been previously compiled by two first grade teachers in the school district. The majority of the list words were selected from the Dolch List (Dolch, 1939) and the Five Hundred Words Most Frequently Used in Children's Writing (Smith and Ingersoll, 1984). The lists were constructed to include the spelling patterns common in a first grade basal spelling book.

Schlagal's *Qualitative Inventory of Word Knowledge* or QIWK (1986) was administered to the experimental group to determine appropriate instructional levels and to form small groups for instruction at these levels. This inventory has six levels of word lists, I through VI, at increasing levels of difficulty.

Students in the experimental group completed Levels I and II. Each student's percentage of accurate spellings was calculated for Levels I and II. Frustration level was indicated by a score in the 0-69% range, instructional level by a score of 70-89% and independent level by a score of 90% or above.

In addition to each student's scores on the spelling inventory, types of misspellings were examined to observe the kinds of strategies the student used in his or her spelling attempts. Consistent error types helped to indicate the student's developmental stage of spelling growth (Gentry & Gillet, 1993) and were considered with the inventory scores to establish instructional groups.

Based on the number of students with the same instructional level on the QIWK and similar developmental stage characteristics, three small groups were formed for instruction. While the Grade One Spelling Word List was the basis for instruction in the control group and other first grade classrooms, instruction for the three small groups was modified or enriched, according to their instructional levels. Scores on pretests of the Grade One Spelling Word units given each week were also considered to allow flexibility in the grouping as needed.

The experimental group's spelling instruction took place in small groups each day during the morning Language Arts block. On the first day of the week, each of the groups with a word list had a brief lesson to introduce new words. Thereafter, direct instruction of one or two groups per day occurred while the other group(s) were involved in independent word study activities. In general, there was much emphasis on comparing and contrasting list words according to length, meaning, rhyming, and spelling patterns (such as consonant-vowel-consonant or consonant-vowel-consonant silent e). Activities such as word sorts were used regularly. Additional activities, specifically suited for each small group's developmental level, were implemented in each of the three groups as follows.

Instruction for the group of experimental students who scored at the *independent* level of the Level I list from Schlagal's inventory focused on more advanced spelling strategies than the other participants in the study. These students usually scored 100% on the pretest of the Grade One Word List unit for the week, so "enrichment" word lists were created each week for these students (see Appendix B). If a student in this group scored below 90% on a pretest, they worked with the group that was exploring the Grade One Spelling Word List unit that week. Spelling strategies such as doubling consonants, vowel pairs, and inflectional endings were studied. Also included on the enrichment list were words frequently misspelled by the students in their journals and creative writing.

Another advanced activity used for the independent level students was the creation of personal dictionaries. They made personal dictionaries in conjunction with the use of the Have-A-Go technique for correcting spellings as described in Routman's (1991) text. In Have-A-Go sessions, students selected misspelled words from their own writing to list on Have-A-Go sheets which were pasted onto several pages in the back of their composition books. Students worked in groups of four and were given clues to help them attempt several ways to spell the word. As correct spellings were reached, students studied and added them to their alphabetic listing in the front of their composition book. Have-A-Go sessions occurred once a week.

Experimental group students who scored at the *instructional* level of the Level I list of Schlagal's QIWK studied the Grade One Spelling List units. The difference for this small group in the experimental classroom, compared to students in the other classes, was that this level of instruction was appropriate for their developmental needs, not assigned arbitrarily to the whole class. Also, if a student scored 90% or more on a weekly pretest, he or she joined the group working at an enrichment level that week.

In addition to word sorting activities, these students frequently used manipulatives to form words. For instance, they used boxes of individual letter squares on small charts with ledges to "build" list words. Word "hunts" involved the students in a search for list words in classroom print (books, posters, signs, etc.). They also enjoyed doing spelling crossword puzzles and word search puzzles.

At the beginning of the study, those experimental group students determined to be at a *frustration* level on Schlagal's Level I inventory list were not assigned lists of words and had no weekly tests. The objective for this group was to develop greater phonemic awareness. Beginning activities for these students focused on the recognition of troublesome letter-sound correspondences, which were identified through an alphabet recognition checklist given to each child. Picture sorts were used to develop letter-sound associations, followed by the creation of letter/sound books made by the students with the help of the instructional aide. Letter-sound correspondences and phonemic awareness were also developed in the context of language experience stories and shared reading lessons with big books.

As these students' invented spelling attempts increased and improved, their instruction included the use of a teacher-constructed Modified Grade One Word List, which consisted of fewer words and simpler spelling patterns than the Grade One Word Lists (see Appendix C). The Modified List units had seven words instead of ten. Most words on the Modified List fit the consonant-vowel-consonant or consonant-vowel-consonant-vowel pattern, and there were fewer high frequency words.

Control group students received whole group instruction at a uniform grade level, using the Grade One Spelling Units previously mentioned. Although the study is limited by the fact that some instructional activities for the control and experimental groups were similar (such as word search and crossword puzzles), the small-group activities previously described were limited to the experimental group.

### Data Collection

A teacher-constructed pretest/posttest instrument was given to the control and experimental groups at the beginning and end of the study (see Appendix D). It was created by randomly selecting words from a stratified version of the Grade One Spelling Units. In developing the pretest/posttest instrument, the existing grade level lists were first examined to determine the types of words and common spelling patterns that were included. Of the

220 words on the Grade One Spelling List, words with long vowel sounds (most of which were spelled with the c-v-c-e pattern) accounted for 23% of the list words, words with short vowel sounds (particularly the c-v-c pattern) comprised 34% of the list, and 43% of the list words were high frequency sight words. The same percentages were used in selecting words for the pretest/posttest instrument.

In addition, samples of all students' writing were collected at three times, in December, March, and June, to allow enough time for noticeable progress in student's invented spellings to occur. The writing samples were taken from the children's journals during the same week of the months noted. The writing in the student journals was often shared orally, but not corrected. Anecdotal records were developed by noting changes in spelling error types from the first to the third sample for each child. This error analysis provided valuable qualitative evidence of the students' progress through developmental levels over the course of the study.

### *Data Analysis*

Scores on the teacher-developed pretest/posttest instrument were recorded for the control and experimental group students. A quantitative analysis was conducted using the scores on the teacher-developed pretest/posttest instrument. The adjusted pretest to posttest means of the control and experimental groups were tested for statistical significance of differences using analysis of covariance procedures. The .05 level of significance was used to evaluate the F ratios.

Writing samples were analyzed to chart the progression of students during the course of the study through the successive developmental stages of word knowledge. The analysis focused on the characteristics of the invented spelling evident in the writing samples by identifying the stage of development of each subject on each of their three writing samples according to the characteristics listed for the five stages in Gentry & Gillet (1993):

> *Precommunicative Stage Spelling*
> > familiarity with letters
> > no letter/sound correspondence
> > preference for uppercase letters
>
> *Semiphonetic Stage Spelling*
> > recognizes that letters represent sounds
> > spellings represent only some of the sound features
> > use of letter-name strategy evident
>
> *Phonetic Stage Spelling*
> > spelling represents all sounds ("total mapping")
> > letters are assigned strictly by sound
> > generally shows word segmentation and spatial orientation

*Transitional Stage Spelling*
>  represents what English sounds and looks like
>  vowels in every syllable
>  use of nasals before consonants (e.g. think not THIK)
>  uses vowels before syllabic r
>  silent e vowel marker used
>  inflectional endings and digraphs evident
>  greater number of correct words used

*Conventional Stage Spelling*
>  accurately spells the corpus of words that
>  a majority of grade level peers who are
>  developmentally on target have mastered.
>  growing accuracy in using silent consonants,
>  and doubling consonants appropriately.
>  accurate spelling of contractions and compound words

Writing samples of experimental group subjects also were examined for signs of transfer of learning to writing. A list of spelling patterns and strategies included in instruction was created for each small group within the class. Each list was divided into three periods of time to parallel the time between writing samples. As writing samples were examined, the appearance of correctly spelled words that had been included in classroom instruction prior to the writing was noted.

## Results and Discussion

The differences between the pretest and posttest mean scores seem to indicate that spelling gains occurred for both groups. When the posttest means were analyzed by an ANCOVA, with control of pretest scores, the differences between the means of the two groups were not statistically significant at the .05 level of significance, $F (1,37) = .77$, $p. = .386$.

Qualitative analysis of student writing samples, however, revealed information about differences in the spelling development of experimental group students compared to control group students. These differences were observed by recording the subjects' movement, from their first through third samples, through the developmental stages as described in Gentry & Gillet (1993). Movement from one stage to another, or a transition between two stages, from one writing sample to the next, was determined by evidence of the specific stage characteristics in the students' writing (see Table 1).

Examination of the movement of students through the developmental stages showed that 56% of the experimental group progressed to a new or transitional stage from Sample 1 to Sample 2 and Sample 2 to Sample 3, while only 35% of the control group students showed this type of progression. Thus

# Table 1. Stage Progression in Writing Samples.

**Experimental Group**

| | Pre | Semi | Phon | Trans | Conv |
|---|---|---|---|---|---|
| *Subj 1 | 1 | 2 | 3 | | |
| *Subj 2 | | 1 | 2 | 3 | |
| Subj 3 | | 1 | 2-3 | | |
| Subj 4 | | 1-2 | 3 | | |
| Subj 5 | | 1 | 2-3 | | |
| Subj 6 | | 1-2-3 | | | |
| *Subj 7 | | 1 | 2 | 3 | |
| *Subj 8 | | 1 | 2 | 3 | |
| *Subj 9 | | | 1 | 2 | 3 |
| *Subj 10 | | | 1 | 2 | 3 |
| Subj 11 | | | | 1-2 | 3 |
| Subj 12 | | | 1-2 | 3 | |
| *Subj 13 | | | 1 | 2 | 3 |
| *Subj 14 | | | 1 | 2 | 3 |
| *Subj 15 | | | 1 | 2 | 3 |
| *Subj 16 | | | 1 | 2 | 3 |
| Subj 17 | | | 1-2 | 3 | |
| Subj 18 | | | 1-2 | 3 | |

**Control Group**

| | Pre | Semi | Phon | Trans | Conv |
|---|---|---|---|---|---|
| *Subj 19 | | 1 | 2 | 3 | |
| *Subj 20 | 1 | 2 | 3 | | |
| Subj 21 | 1 | 2-3 | | | |
| Subj 22 | | 1 | 2-3 | | |
| †Subj 23 | 1 | 2 | | | |
| Subj 24 | | 1 | 2-3 | | |
| *Subj 25 | | 1 | 2 | 3 | |
| Subj 26 | | 1-2 | | | |
| Subj 27 | | | 1-2 | 3 | |
| Subj 28 | | 1 | 2-3 | | |
| Subj 29 | | | 1-2 | 3 | |
| *Subj 30 | | 1 | 2 | 3 | |
| *Subj 31 | | | 1 | 2 | 3 |
| Subj 32 | | | 1-2 | 3 | |
| Subj 33 | | | 1 | 2-3 | |
| Subj 34 | | | 1-2 | 3 | |
| *Subj 35 | | 1 | 2 | 3 | |
| Subj 36 | | | 1-2 | | |

Note: 1 = first sample; 2 = second sample; 3 = third sample.

Note: Pre = Precommunicative; Semi = Semiphonetic; Phon = Phonetic; Trans = Transitional; Conv = Conventional.

Note: * = Subject moved a stage on each sample.

Note: † = Subject 23 dropped, since a lack of Sample 3 prevents inclusion in percentages.

it appears that a greater percentage of the experimental group students demonstrated a progression to a new or transitional level with each writing sample. It seems possible that the focus of instruction at appropriate levels within small groups may have allowed more students to develop or refine sophisticated spelling strategies characteristic of the next developmental level.

Moreover, instruction at appropriate developmental levels seems to have favorably influenced the progress of the experimental group students instructed at an enrichment level. These students accounted for the greater number of experimental group students who reached the transitional level of spelling development by the end of the study, compared to control group students at that stage. Their instruction focused on more advanced spelling strategies which may have facilitated their progression to the higher stage.

Furthermore, anecdotal records showed that transfer of learning was more evident among experimental group students at the transitional spelling stage. This observation supports Gentry & Gillet's (1993) recommendation that formal spelling instruction begin at this developmental level.

Based solely on the results of the statistical analysis, one might conclude that spelling instruction in small groups according to developmental levels offers no appreciable advantage to whole group instruction at a uniform level. However, other variables in the study may have influenced the results. One of these variables may have been the pretest/posttest used. This testing instrument may not have been sensitive enough to measure accurately the gains of all subjects in the study. This seemed especially true for the more advanced spellers in the study, whose pretest scores were so high that there was less room for gain at the posttest.

Also, students who began the study at earlier stages of spelling development showed only small gains from pretest to posttest. Pretest to posttest scores only measured growth in the number of correct spellings. These scores did not reflect students' actual growth in the use of new spelling strategies. By contrast, the error analysis of spelling attempts in writing samples provided visual evidence of substantial growth in stage level for most students. For instance, an experimental group subject gained only two points from pretest to posttest. However, error analysis of his writing samples showed movement from the earliest developmental stage, precommunicative, to a transition level between the semiphonetic and phonetic stages. His first sample was one line, unreadable by the student or teacher. His final sample was seven lines long and indicated the development of strategies characteristic of the semiphonetic and even phonetic stages of spelling. He used conventional spellings (such as "to," "the," "and," "am," and "my") consistently in the final sample.

The use of a more challenging pretest/posttest for first grade students might allow for a more accurate measurement of student gains. Gentry's

Developmental Test (Gentry & Gillet, 1993) or Schlagal's QIWK (1986) could be more useful than the teacher designed pretest/posttest. Additionally, scores should be based on the quality of the spelling attempt, with point values assigned based on the number of sounds and features represented, with correct spellings receiving the highest point value. For example, a student who spells "like" as "LIK" would score higher than a student who spells "like" as "L" or "LK," since the former spelling reflects a higher level of spelling knowledge. Such an approach to scoring would account for differences in the types of strategies students use, while assigning a quantitative value to be measured.

The investigation for evidence of transfer of learning to writing among experimental group students showed that the greatest transfer occurred for students in the transitional spelling stage. For two of the three experimental small groups, the formal use of word lists and weekly tests may not have been as effective, since they had not reached the transitional level. This was a limitation of the study. For future research, this implies a need to devote more instructional time to word study activities in the context of the children's reading and writing, delaying the traditional weekly tests until they have reached the transitional stage. Error analysis of writing samples and periodic developmental spelling tests could be substituted to provide a means for assessment.

The statistical analysis of pretest to posttest gains in this study did not indicate that the use of small groups based on developmental levels for spelling instruction was either more or less effective than whole group spelling instruction at grade level. Yet, qualitative analysis of students' writing appeared to show benefits for each of the small groups. As previously indicated, a greater percentage of the experimental group students showed movement from one developmental spelling stage or transitional level to another at each quarter's end.

In addition, experimental students taught at an enrichment level accounted for a larger number of students reaching the transitional stage by the end of the study than those in the control group. This pattern appears to indicate an advantage to small group instruction at developmentally appropriate levels for these learners.

Small group instruction allowed the students with a grade one instructional level to explore words with manipulatives and activities specifically geared for students at the semiphonetic to phonetic spelling stages. Flexibility of groupings made it possible for students to work at an enrichment level when they demonstrated mastery of a spelling strategy at grade one level. Error analysis of their writing samples indicated a progression of more than one stage or transitional level, from the first to final writing sample, for four out of six students in this group.

The small group that scored at frustration level on the QIWK benefitted from small group instruction that provided a greater emphasis on the development of phonemic awareness, instead of memorizing words for weekly tests. This was an important instructional focus for this group, since children's learning strategies may become confused when they are forced to deal with words at too advanced a level (Schlagal, 1982 in Schlagal & Schlagal, 1992). Writing samples provided visual evidence of a progression of at least one developmental level for all of these students from the start to the end of the study.

## Conclusion

Since there was no disadvantage to spelling achievement with small group instruction at developmentally appropriate levels and the possibility of advantages were noted by qualitative analysis, a case can be made for using this approach in the classroom. While this approach falls between traditional, uniform grade level spelling instruction and the more individualized instruction proposed by educators such as Routman, it certainly provides a transitional approach for teachers looking for an alternative to the same instruction for all. Thus, the information gained in this study strongly supports the need for further experimental research in the use of flexible grouping or individualized instruction for developmentally appropriate spelling instruction.

## References

Beers, J. W., & Henderson, E. H. (1977). A study of developing orthographic concepts among first graders. *Research in the Teaching of English, 11,* 133-148.

Bean, W., & Bouffler, C. (1987). *Spell by Writing.* Rozelle, Australia: Primary English Teaching Association.

Bloodgood, J. W. (1991). A new approach to spelling instruction in language arts programs. *The Elementary School Journal, 92,* 203-211.

Dolch, E. W. (1939). *Manual for remedial reading.* Champaign, IL: Gerrard.

Ehri, L. (1992). Review and commentary: Stages of spelling development. In S. Templeton & D. B. Bear (Eds.), *Development of orthographic knowledge and the foundations of literacy: A memorial festschrift for Edmund H. Henderson* (pp. 307-322). Hillsdale, NJ: Erlbaum.

Gentry, J. R. (1977). *A study of the orthographic strategies of beginning readers.* Unpublished doctoral dissertation, University of Virginia, Charlottesville.

Gentry, J. R., & Gillet, J. W. (1993). *Teaching kids to spell.* Portsmouth, NH: Heinemann.

Morris, D., Nelson, L., & Perney, J. (1986). Exploring the concept of "spelling instructional level" through the analysis of error-types. *The Elementary School Journal, 87,* 181-200.

O'Flahavan, J. R., & Blassberg, R. (1992). Toward an embedded model of spelling instruction for emergent literates. *Language Arts, 69,* 409-417.

Read, C. (1971) Pre-school children's knowledge of English phonology. *Harvard Educational Review, 41,* 1-34.

Read, C. (1975) *Children's categorization of speech sounds in English.* Urbana, IL: National Council of Teachers of English. (ERIC Document Reproduction Service No. ED 112-426).

Routman, R. (1991). *Invitations: Changing as teachers and learners K-12.* Portsmouth, NH: Heinemann.

Schlagal, R. (1986) Informal and qualitative assessment of spelling. *The Pointer, 30,* 37-41.

Schlagal, R. C., & Schlagal, J. H. (1992). The integral character of spelling: Teaching strategies for multiple purposes. *Language Arts, 69,* 418-424.

Smith, C. B., & Ingersoll, G. M. (1984). Written vocabulary of elementary school pupils, Ages 6-14. *Monographs in Language and Reading Studies, 6,* 33-42.

Templeton, S. (1991). Teaching and learning the English spelling system: reconceptualizing method and purpose. *The Elementary School Journal, 92,* 185-201.

Wilde, S. (1990) A proposal for a new spelling curriculum. *The Elementary School Journal, 90,* 275-289.

Zutell, J. (1979). Spelling strategies of primary school children and their relationship to Piaget's concept of decentration. *Research in the Teaching of English, 13,* 69-80.

Zutell, J. (1992). An integrated view of word knowledge: correlational studies of the relationships among spelling, reading and conceptual development. In D. B. Bear & S. Templeton (Eds.) *Development of orthographic knowledge and the foundations of literacy: A memorial festschrift for Edmund H. Henderson.* (213-230.) Hillsdale, NJ: Erlbaum.

# Appendix A: Grade 1 Spelling List

| Unit 1 | Unit 2 | Unit 3 | Unit 4 | Unit 5 (review) | Unit 6 | Unit 7 | Unit 8 | Unit 9 |
|---|---|---|---|---|---|---|---|---|
| at | am | bed | let | and | in | big | hill | not |
| cat | ham | fed | met | man | chin | dig | will | got |
| hat | jam | led | wet | sat | pin | pig | still | spot |
| an | dad | feet | eat | mad | it | did | him | dog |
| can | had | tree | neat | ram | sit | hid | trim | log |
| ran | sad | need | wheat | tame | hit | lid | wish | hog |
| ate | came | she | hen | rate | bike | ride | fish | home |
| late | name | be | then | what | like | side | five | rope |
| date | same | we | ten | them | hike | hide | dive | nose |
| and | the | them | what | the | little | while | with | over |
|  |  |  |  | men |  |  |  |  |
|  |  |  |  | red |  |  |  |  |
|  |  |  |  | he |  |  |  |  |
|  |  |  |  | get |  |  |  |  |
|  |  |  |  | beat |  |  |  |  |

| Unit 10 | Unit 11 | Unit 12 | Unit 13 (review) | Unit 14 | Unit 15 | Unit 16 | Unit 17 | Unit 18 |
|---|---|---|---|---|---|---|---|---|
| go | to | book | him | but | bug | up | cry | after |
| no | do | cook | bike | cut | plug | cup | try | before |
| so | out | look | while | nut | snug | jump | fly | now |
| some | about | down | dish | shut | us | bump | why | soon |
| come | shout | now | slide | round | bus | under | by | where |
| would | brother | how | hope | sound | must | thunder | story | there |
| could | mother | boy | about | pound | fun | blue | baby | have |
| should | other | toy | with | cute | run | true | pretty | every |
| you | of | joy | should | tube | sun | put | many | saw |
| who | school | your | little | spring | funny | know | only | more |
|  |  |  | come |  |  |  |  |  |
|  |  |  | who |  |  |  |  |  |
|  |  |  | of |  |  |  |  |  |
|  |  |  | how |  |  |  |  |  |
|  |  |  | your |  |  |  |  |  |

| Unit 19 | Unit 20 (review) | Unit 21+ | Unit 22+ | Unit 23+ | Unit 24+ | Unit 25 (review) |
|---|---|---|---|---|---|---|
| red | know | one | father | all | help | which |
| blue | story | two | mother | ball | say | her |
| green | have | three | sister | tall | play | one |
| yellow | funny | four | brother | her | please | boy |
| purple | under | five | children | his | thank you | our |
| orange | many | six | house | mine | again | were |
| black | there | seven | family | their | want | again |
| brown | white | eight | love | our | think | please |
| white | black | nine | boy | they | which | children |
| color | soon | ten | girl | those | were | love |
|  | after |  |  |  |  | girl |
|  | saw |  |  |  |  | they |
|  | shut |  |  |  |  | those |
|  | found |  |  |  |  | family |
|  |  |  |  |  |  | color |
|  |  |  |  |  |  | want |

# Appendix B: Grade 1 Spelling List—Enrichment

| Unit 1+ | Unit 2+ | Unit 3+ | Unit 4+ | Unit 5 (review) | Unit 6+ | Unit 7+ | Unit 8+ | Unit 9+ |
|---------|---------|---------|---------|-----------------|---------|---------|---------|---------|
| ate | bag | best | ear | and | ship | kick | mix | boat |
| late | tag | them | hear | man | trip | pick | fix | coat |
| date | flag | sled | smear | sat | flip | quick | give | float |
| gate | back | head | eat | mad | write | trick | live | load |
| plate | pack | bread | neat | ram | kite | king | nice | road |
| fan | sack | thread | wheat | tame | bite | sing | price | toad |
| pan | flame | keep | clean | rate | night | thing | twice | stop |
| ran | came | week | peanut | what | right | bring | find | drop |
| man | frame | queen | leaves | them | light | smile | kind | chop |
| and | you | here | spread | the | little | while | mind | shop |
| | | | | men | | | | |
| | | | | red | | | | |
| | | | | he | | | | |
| | | | | get | | | | |
| | | | | beat | | | | |

| Unit 10+ | Unit 11+ | Unit 12+ | Unit 13 (review) | Unit 14+ | Unit 15+ | Unit 16+ | Unit 17+ | Unit 18+ |
|----------|----------|----------|------------------|----------|----------|----------|----------|----------|
| sock | noon | voice | him | use | car | new | happy | sight |
| rock | soon | choice | bike | huge | far | knew | angry | hear |
| clock | food | coin | while | tube | jar | grew | hungry | smell |
| song | done | join | dish | luck | star | flew | lonely | touch |
| long | none | door | slide | stuck | saw | chew | friendly | taste |
| wrong | glove | floor | hope | truck | paw | drew | money | eye |
| know | having | poor | about | getting | claw | crew | penny | ear |
| show | making | cried | with | running | draw | stew | nickel | nose |
| glow | coming | tried | should | skipped | yawn | news | dime | finger |
| throw | riding | fried | little | bigger | lawn | few | quarter | tongue |
| | | | come | | | | | |
| | | | who | | | | | |
| | | | of | | | | | |
| | | | how | | | | | |
| | | | your | | | | | |

| Unit 19+ | Unit 20 (review) | Unit 21+ | Unit 22+ | Unit 23+ | Unit 24+ | Unit 25 (review) |
|----------|------------------|----------|----------|----------|----------|------------------|
| time | know | won | began | all | help | which |
| minute | story | to | soup | ball | say | her |
| hour | have | too | enough | tall | play | one |
| o'clock | funny | for | rough | her | please | boy |
| month | under | count | smooth | his | thank you | our |
| idea | many | number | thick | mine | again | were |
| present | there | word | thin | their | want | again |
| birthday | white | again | sweet | our | think | please |
| open | black | knee | sour | they | which | children |
| sure | soon | knickknack | young | those | were | love |
| | after | | | | | girl |
| | saw | | | | | they |
| | shut | | | | | those |
| | found | | | | | family |
| | only | | | | | color |
| | | | | | | want |

# Appendix C: Modified Spelling List—Grade One

| *Unit 1* | *Unit 2* | *Unit 3* | *Unit 4* | *Unit 5* |
|----------|----------|----------|----------|----------|
| at | big | not | run | let |
| hat | pin | got | sun | get |
| can | him | hop | but | ten |
| ran | did | top | cup | when |
| had | will | box | hug | bed |
| dad | sit | fox | bus | fed |
| and | with | the | funny | them |

| *Unit 6* | *Unit 7* | *Unit 8* | *Unit 9* | *Unit 10* |
|----------|----------|----------|----------|-----------|
| came | feet | go | bike | cute |
| same | need | no | like | huge |
| ate | we | so | hide | use |
| late | me | home | ride | to |
| make | eat | rope | five | do |
| take | neat | nose | dive | you |
| what | please | over | while | who |

| *Unit 11* | *Unit 12* | *Unit 13 (Review)* |
|-----------|-----------|--------------------|
| my | one | and |
| by | two | them |
| fly | three | with |
| why | four | got |
| very | five | but |
| many | six | make |
| story | seven | need |
| | eight | home |
| | nine | like |
| | ten | you |

# Appendix D: Pretest/Posttest

| | | |
|---|---|---|
| 1. ran | 11. same | 21. jam |
| 2. fly | 12. brother | 22. who |
| 3. ball | 13. will | 23. snug |
| 4. met | 14. look | 24. tree |
| 5. hope | 15. not | 25. could |
| 6. after | 16. story | 26. wish |
| 7. chin | 17. five | 27. some |
| 8. wheat | 18. toy | 28. play |
| 9. our | 19. now | 29. them |
| 10. bus | 20. before | 30. jump |

# EARLY LEADERS
## IN LITERACY

# A Psychologist-Educator's Journey Through the Reading World

### Jules C. Abrams

Professor and Director
Institute for Graduate Clinical Psychology
Widener University, Chester, PA

*Jules C. Abrams received his Ph.D. in psychology from Temple University, Philadelphia, where he served as a graduate assistant to Emmett A. Betts. For many years, Dr. Abrams was a Professor in the Department of Mental Health Sciences of the Hahnemann Medical College and Hospital, Philadelphia, where he founded and directed the oldest accredited Doctor of Psychology (Psy.D.) program in the country. At the present time, Dr. Abrams is the director of the Institute for Graduate Clinical Psychology of Widener University, Chester, Pa. He is a past president of the College Reading Association and the recipient of both the Distinguished Service Award and the H. B. Herr*  *Award. He is the author of over 100 articles, many of which deal with reading disabilities and related learning disorders. Dr. Abrams' comments are followed with a personal reflection by Patricia M. Bricklin, Widener University.*

## In the Beginning

Each person finds his career path in rather idiosyncratic ways. I suspect that my becoming involved in the psychology of reading was quite different from many others in the field. I originally started out as an experimental psychologist; at least my master's degree was in that field. My research project was on the learning ability of the hamster. After a year at the University of Toronto in the graduate program leading to a Ph.D. in cognitive psychology, some urgent personal reasons made it necessary for me to return to my hometown of Philadelphia. Of course, in retrospect, I now believe that there were also some strong unconscious reasons behind this return.

In any event, I soon found myself enrolled in the graduate program at Temple University leading to a Ph.D. in general psychology. Since the program was not going to begin for six months (and because I desperately needed some financial help), I took a job at the Temple University Reading Clinic as a psychometrician. The clinic at that time was headed by Emmett A. Betts, one of the foremost figures in the field of reading. The clinic, itself, had an international reputation, as children and adults from all over the world went there for the diagnosis of their reading disabilities.

As a psychometrician, my job was to administer an individual intelligence test to each client. I found myself giving these tests to persons who were in a very real sense anonymous. I began to wonder what happened to these children and adults after I saw them. After all, they spent three days in the clinic being evaluated. What could be so complex about a reading disability that it required three days of psychodiagnostic and educational testing? Ultimately, I found myself asking that very question of Dr. Russell Stauffer, who was the Associate Director of the clinic. Within one hour I was whisked into the office of Dr. Betts (whom I had never met before). Little did I know at that time that this would be one of the most significant meetings of my life!

I spent approximately two hours with Betts that afternoon. By the time I left, I had been registered for seven courses in the Psychology of Reading. I remember them well because I was taking all of them in that one semester prior to my formally starting the doctoral program. They were as follows: Foundations of Reading Instruction, Reading Disabilities, Corrective Reading in the Secondary School, Psychophysiological Problems of Vision and Hearing, Advanced Vision Seminar, Diagnosis of Reading Disabilities, and Readings in Reading Research. One might say that I was saturated with the field of reading that semester! But I loved every moment of it. I found myself completely invested in the area and determined to learn everything I could about reading and particularly reading disabilities.

When the graduate program actually began in the Fall, I had the choice of three different assistantships. I was tempted to be a teaching assistant, because I truly enjoyed lecturing, and I had little experience to date in that area. I was also interested in working in the Psychological Clinic of the Department of Psychology because this would give me the opportunity to see a variety of clients with multifaceted disorders. However, I really did not hesitate to choose the third option: working as a clinician in the Diagnostic Division of the Reading Clinic. By that time, I was throughly intrigued by the many factors which could cause children and adults to experience difficulty in reading.

## Early Professional Influences

In the four years I spent in the Diagnostic Division (ultimately ending up as a supervisor), I gained tremendous experience under the tutelage of a number of very insightful reading specialists. At the risk of excluding others who also taught me a great deal, I would have to mention Betts, of course, who was unrelenting in his zealous attention to the neuropsychological factors in reading disability. Russ Stauffer taught me a great deal about directed reading activities and thinking; Roy Kress showed me how to write meaningful and helpful psychological-educational evaluations; and Marjorie Seddons Johnson taught me more about teaching kids than I could have learned from anyone else in a million years!

When I received my doctorate in psychology, while I felt that I had learned a great deal about reading and reading disabilities, I certainly was aware that there was much more to be explored. For example, I was not very satisfied with the instruments that were used in the Reading Clinic to evaluate the social and emotional status of individuals with reading problems. I was very curious about the relationship of reading disabilities to other types of learning disorders (the term "learning disabilities" had not yet come into vogue). I felt that there was much more to be learned about the neuropsychology of reading and related learning disabilities. Furthermore, I felt that we should not be conceptualizing these issues into dichotomous terms. It seemed to me that in each individual there was a unique interaction of both psychological and neurological factors.

## My Current Beliefs

In the last thirty years, I have devoted a considerable amount of my professional life to the search for some of these answers. Some have said that the incidence of severe reading disabilities is so small that we should not waste our efforts in that direction. Others have even argued that there is no such thing as reading disability or dyslexia, that all problems should be attributed to inappropriate or inadequate teaching. My research and clinical experience clearly indicate to me that dyslexia does exist even if it is limited to approximately 3-5% of the total school population. And we have an obligation to these unfortunate individuals, the majority of whom have average to very superior intelligence, and who must deal with the frustration of feeling different and ultimately equating this with being inferior. The emotional concomitants of reading and related learning disability are horrendous and a tragic burden for the individual to bear.

Freud once said that by studying the pathological we can learn much about what is normal. I am convinced that the study of severe reading disability can teach us much about how the average child learns to read. The more we can learn about the nature of the reading process, the more we can do by way of prevention of reading problems.

In the last analysis, the vast majority of reading difficulties are caused by a variety of factors, all of which may be highly interrelated. It is my view that the child with a reading disability has an intrinsic problem, presumably the result of some form of central nervous system dysfunction. But, at this time, we cannot say that even these types of severe disabilities are caused by faulty synaptic transmission per se. It is likely that a child born with some insult to the central nervous system is unable to develop important cognitive functions at the time that he or she should develop them. This may bring about an altered response from the environment that interferes with the mutuality phase of personality development. In turn, this may impair the ability to acquire higher order cognitive functions which are so important in learning to read. In essence, we should more accurately be speaking of a developmental disability rather than a learning disability. Furthermore, we should be speaking of habilitation rather than rehabilitation. Always, we should be focused on the unique interaction of psychological and organic factors.

## In Closing

Certainly the task of the reading professional is a formidable one. There is still so much more that we must know. God willing, I hope to spend at least the next fifteen years continuing to explore this most intriguing topic.

## *Reflections on Jules C. Abrams*
## *by Patricia M. Bricklin*

I have had the unique and very special experience of knowing and working with Dr. Jules C. Abrams throughout much of his very significant professional career. Today Dr. Abrams is a distinguished psychologist, specialist in reading and learning disorders, teacher, professional leader and innovator. It has been a delight for me to watch this happen.

When I first met him I was a beginning graduate student and he was an instructor and supervisor in the Temple University Reading Clinic and was completing his doctoral dissertation. I was struck by the fact that, even then, everyone consulted him on difficult diagnostic cases, especially where personality factors were involved. So I got in line to wait my turn for supervision and thus began a more than thirty-year mentoring relationship which still continues. Starting with those early years, each supervisory session was an exciting adventure in clinical detection work and demonstrated the considerable clinical skills for which he is known today.

From him I learned persistence, whether it was in reaching a goal, understanding a complex difficult case, or figuring out the meaning of a complex written passage. I can remember one 'several hour' conversation over the meaning of one paragraph on "specifically and non specifically deployed energies" in David Rapaport's volume, *Diagnostic Psychological Testing* (Rapaport, Gill, & Schafer, 1968).

As the "tag along" graduate student, I began to learn, through Dr. Abrams, about the potentials for integration of psychoanalytic, neuropsychological and reading theories and met some of the "greats" in each field. I did pick up a "bad" habit or two from my mentor—"late reports" and "doing too much." The former he is no longer guilty of. The latter is still his style.

As a teacher, Dr. Abrams is a "natural" both in class and out. He is popular, informed, and organized. There is no conference that he attends where people don't come up and say, "Oh Dr. Abrams, I was in your class at Temple [or Hahnemann or Johns Hopkins] and I remember what you said about - - - -. You were so clear." Personally, I can drop in on one of his courses today and always learn something new, or find a new way to look at something old.

Dr. Abrams is a leader and an innovator. Three of these innovations are the founding and development of the first Doctor of Psychology program in Pennsylvania, which is now the oldest American Psychological Association accredited Psy.D. program in the country; the founding of Parkway Day School, a learning therapeutic program for children with reading/learning disorders which represented the application of Dr. Abrams' views on the integration of psychology and education; and the founding of the Multi-Disciplinary Academy of Clinical Education, a group of professionals from a variety of disciplines who share his multiperspective on learning disorders. This group has membership throughout the country.

Despite the difficulties inherent in initiating these kinds of innovations, Dr. Abrams' persistence and ability to make things "look easy" shines through. As our careers separated and reconnected over the years it has always been exciting to find out what the next "Abrams first" would be and, where possible, to be part of it.

As a theoretician, Dr. Abrams' development and refinement of the dynamic developmental interaction approach to learning disorders is an impressive contribution to the fields of education and psychology. It integrates thinking from a number of disciplines, includes a way to manage the causality debate and provides a framework for understanding reading/learning difficulties (disabilities or problems) in the context of developmental interaction. It was this kind of thinking that contributed to the interorganizational definition of learning disabilities by the Joint Committee on Learning Disabilities, of which he was a member. As if integrated theoretical thinking, talented clinical practice, being a teacher and innovator were not enough Dr. Abrams was and continues to be a leader in professional organizations. His impact on any group is significant.

Dr. Abrams is all of these things professionally. He is a devoted family man and a good friend to many. He also is still my mentor and I'm still willing to wait in line for my turn for supervision.

---

## References

Rapaport, D., Gill, M. M., Schafer, R. (1968). *Diagnostic psychological testing.* (Holt, R. R., Ed.) (Rev. Ed.). New York: International Universities Press.

# FROM METRONOSCOPES
# TO MEGABYTES

### Richard L. Carner

Professor Emeritus
University of Miami

*Richard L. Carner is a native of central New York State. During World War II he served in the Air Force, mainly in the European Theater of Operations. He later completed the B.A., M.A., and Ph.D. degrees at Syracuse University. His professional experiences ranged from public school to the university level, and he also was active in professional organizations and as a consultant. At the University of Miami, Dr. Carner was Professor of Educational Psychology and directed the Reading Clinic for over twenty years. Following retirement in 1984, he has actively pursued hobbies such as photography, travel, writing, music, and reading. Dr. Carner's comments are followed with a personal reflection by Fritzi Chowning from The Reading Connection, Miami, Florida.*

## Briefly Noted

My lifelong interests have included astronomy, geology, art, music, travel, photography, and archeology—fascinations that sparked much reading and doing over a long span of years. It is entirely possible that I could have been content with tapping away at rock strata above and below the K-T boundary in an attempt to understand the great dinosaur extinction or spending cold, quiet nights at some observatory trying to fathom the mysteries that cloak our origins. However, serendipity played a role that allowed other interests to surface that ultimately dictated how I would spend my professional life.

## Early Influences

I suspect that one of the very earliest influences, from the very beginning of my school days, was that I did not experience any particular difficulty in establishing a "relationship" with printed words. When I was young, words became like old friends that I could readily recognize regardless of the endless guises their letters might assume—capitals, italics, cursive, Old English, or most any other stylized letters, hand written or printed—it didn't seem to matter. As a consequence, reading became a very important and pleasurable activity for me at a young age. Perhaps I was lucky that I became a reader during a time in our history when television was still on the far distant horizon. Unlike many passive young T.V. watchers of today, I learned to rely upon my own visual imagery and imagination, which transported me to the scenes and actions of all the wonderful stories I read.

I also vividly remember empathizing with my classmates who were often frustrated and embarrassed when called upon to read, and it seemed to me that there were always a certain few kids like this in every classroom I was ever in. In the days before labels such as "remedial," "dyslexia," or "learning disability," came into vogue, those having reading problems were often viewed as being "slow" or "dumb," primarily because they didn't perceive printed words as "old friends." I strongly suspect that the origins of my interest in reading as a complex processing behavior was an awareness that acquiring the ability to read seemed to come quite easily to some of my friends but only with great difficulty to others.

## Professional Influences

Like thousands of other veterans following World War II, I took advantage of the G.I. Bill and returned to college with only a vague notion about what my ultimate career would be. I eventually decided that I would concentrate on journalism, English, psychology, and education as major areas of interest. A requirement of the freshman English course was the obligatory term paper. Without any prior knowledge about reading as a distinct field of study, it became the topic of my first term paper. Although a rereading of the yellowed pages of this paper reflects great naiveté on my part, apparently my interest in the subject of reading had been in place all along.

I did the time-honored "practice teaching" stint during my senior year in English classes for 11th and 12th grade students. It was during this time that I once again became aware that a number of students, some of them obviously bright, had marked reading problems. My supervising teacher also expressed a concern about this problem but, like many secondary teachers, she conjectured that the real problem was at the elementary level where kids should have learned to read. "Passing the buck" apparently did not occur exclusively in the military sphere.

As a result of my experience during practice teaching, I took an elective course, "Reading At The Secondary Level," the following semester. Three things influenced me greatly at this time. First, the course was taught by William (Bill) Sheldon, whose enthusiasm for the field of reading education was most contagious and whose insights opened up whole new educational vistas for me. The second influence was the text used in the course, *Problems in the Improvement of Reading* by McCullough, Strang, and Traxler (1946), which made it clear that reading was indeed a worthy field of study and that something needed to be done to help children learn to read. The third factor was Bill Sheldon's encouragement to pursue the master's degree and his offer of an assistantship in the Reading Center at Syracuse University. The timing couldn't have been better since my G.I. benefits were about to run out.

My first assignment as an assistant was to teach a course called "Improvement of Learning." Others teaching in the same program at that time, who became of some note in the field of reading, were Len Braam, Cliff Bush, Lyman Hunt, and Larry Carrillo. We used the text, "Effective Study" by F.P. Robinson, which was the model for many of the subsequent texts published on how to improve reading and study skills. We soon had students SQ3R-ing and working on increasing their reading efficiency. It was encouraging to note that a number of students actually did seem to improve their grades and to increase their reading rate significantly.

It was during this time that I became acquainted with what in the computer age would appear to be antediluvian, a device called a *metronoscope*, designed by Guy Buswell to help students increase their reading rate. It had three clackety shutters which would open up sequentially to expose phrases printed on a kind of piano roll at a predetermined speed. My first attempt to use the machine was with an obviously brilliant electronics engineer who wanted to increase his reading rate. Bill Sheldon "assigned" him to me as a project and suggested that the gentleman might profit from using the metronoscope. The result was pure disaster. After several frustrating attempts to use the machine, my "student" declared emphatically that blinking at strange word phrases was not reading and, besides that, the machine was poorly engineered, too noisy, and actually slowed him down since it went more slowly than he could read already. As a result of this experience, for a long time to come, I regarded most machines with considerable suspicion.

Following the year of my master's degree program, I joined the staff at Utica College, at that time a branch of Syracuse University, to set up an "Improvement of Learning" program there, teach adult speed reading courses, and also serve as " Assistant Dean of Men." However, I soon felt the need for more experience at the public school level and accepted the invitation to join one of the early BOCES (Board of Cooperative Educational Services) as the Reading Supervisor in a school district in central New York State. After a number of years of invaluable experience in this position, I returned full time to Syracuse University to complete my doctoral program. During this period I directed the Syracuse University summer reading camp (Pinebrook) in the Adirondacks, supervised the "Improvement of Learning" program, taught adult reading classes and graduate extension courses, and was a consultant in a pioneering closed circuit reading program for the Cortland, New York area public schools.

Following completion of the doctorate, I spent a year as Director of the Charlotte-Mecklenburg reading program, after which I was invited to become Director of the University of Miami Reading Clinic and a member of the graduate faculty in the School of Education. My tenure there was for over twenty years, during which I had the opportunity to work with Emmett Betts, Arthur Traxler, Helen Smith, and others who had made important contributions to the field of reading.

## A Few Issues of Note

Over the years, on the broad canvas of Reading Education, many issues posing as "great debates" have, like Moby Dick, surfaced and retreated to the depths only to reappear again. Among them were, for example, issues such as "phonics" vs. "sight word" strategies and "individualized" reading vs. basal readers, both of which have been heatedly debated as though they were legitimate "either/or" arguments. During some periods, great interest (and controversy) arose in regard to various approaches in teaching reading such as the Initial Teaching Alphabet (ITA), "Linguistic" readers, Evelyn Wood's speed reading courses, and Orton-Gillingham vs. Fernald strategies in remediating severe reading disabilities or dyslexia. Learning disabilities and various manifestations also arrived on the scene with much debate over the implications for diagnosis and remediation. The concepts inherent in the "whole language" approach and the more recent idea of "inclusivity" in the classroom will probably continue to be debated for some time to come.

While the need continues for empirical evidence concerning the cognitive and perceptual nature of reading-learning processes, many educational issues across the country are local in nature. For example, in Miami (Dade County), native born, English-speaking people, who would constitute the majority in many other places around the country, are now in the minority. The flood of refugees continues to challenge local educators, who must establish teaching priorities to meet the needs of all the students, as well as society at large.

Old time aviators who know first hand about the Spad and the Jenny can only wonder about the quantum leaps in technology when they see a super-sonic plane like the Concord or watch a shuttle take off from Cape

Canaveral. In a sense, I am also quite amazed at the ever more rapidly evolving computer technology and programming in all areas of education, particularly when I compare the *megabytes* of today with the evolutionary dead-end of the *metronoscope* many decades ago. New technology also gives rise, however, to important new issues and questions. Will "surfing the net" ever really take the place of books, as has been suggested by some? Will we really need to know how to read in the traditional sense with computers capable of doing almost anything including listening, following oral directions, and talking back? What will the reading and education issues be in the future now that it is possible to place an entire set of encyclopedias or the Harvard Classics on a single disk which will fit into one's pocket? Surely, computers themselves will continue to become more and more efficient, and yet shrink in size. What will be the need for books in the coming millennium? It is commonplace now to talk about computer literacy and I truly suspect that anyone who does not have a working knowledge of computers will be "diagnosed" as having a new brand of learning disability (possibly called *disk*-lexia?). On the other hand, perhaps future computer programs, unlike that first (to me) important text of long ago, *Problems in the Improvement of Reading* (McCullough, et al., 1946), will have chronicled on pocket-sized disks for pocket-size computers all of the "Solutions in the Improvement of Reading." This will, perhaps, truly place us on the brink of universal literacy.

---

## References

McCullough, C. M., Strang, R.M., Traxler, A. E. (1946). *Problems in the improvement of reading*. New York: McGraw-Hill.

Robinson, F. P. (1946). *Effective Study*. NY: Harper.

### *Reflections on Richard Carner*
### *by Fritzi Chowning*

My early impressions of Dr. Richard Carner are as vivid now as they were when I was his student. To me he has always been a model scholar and trusted mentor with a mind as complex and fascinating as the topics he addressed. His lectures and assignments introduced me to the tools of the trade and sparked my fascination with the study of reading. Just as important, his own examples as a teacher suggested many methods for capturing students' attention.

Dr. Carner's never-failing sense of humor and professional expertise made his graduate classes fast-paced and spirited intellectual experiences. I developed more teaching strategies from his example than from any other source. I particularly appreciated his habit of beginning almost every session with a brief description of one or two professional books. These texts, both classics and notable new contributions, were not necessarily required reading but he "sold" them so well that I almost always went to the library immediately after class to investigate them further. To this day I also am thankful he required that we type our classnotes and hand them in at the end of each course. This and other assignments helped ensure the development of scholarly habits. During a recent move, I finally jettisoned most of the artifacts of my graduate education but I still couldn't part with my notes from Dick's classes.

Dick Carner taught his students that reading is much more than one of the language arts. We became familiar with neural mechanisms and psychological processes involved in language, reading, and learning. We learned about the special needs of those who have difficulty in learning and were taught to take into account the many interacting factors involved in their reading/learning difficulties. Through his obvious respect for the English language and the relationships among its forms, we also came to understand and appreciate the special roles that language and social factors play in learning and reading. His goal for his students was for them to become specialists in the diagnosis of reading problems as well as in the teaching of reading at all levels, to all types of learners.

As a counselor/advisor, Dr. Carner always seemed to know just how to elicit the best from his students. However, he was also careful to point out when they were attempting more than they should. With his characteristic wry humor he once suggested that I would be better off if I did not try to write the "War and Peace" of dissertations!

As Director of the University of Miami Reading Clinic for more than twenty years, Dick Carner provided many, many students with incomparable experiences in the diagnosing and teaching of children and adults with reading difficulties. His wise counsel and insightful comments after observing student performances in clinical and classroom settings helped them hone their skills and learn to match individuals and groups with appropriate modes of instruction. These contributions were not only invaluable to his students, but also made it possible for many children and adults with seemingly insurmountable problems to succeed in learning to read.

In later years, Dick expanded the scope of the Clinic by establishing the University of Miami Reading and Learning Skills Center (RLSC) to serve university students. I became Director of the RLSC, and during those years we collaborated on research projects and presented at professional meetings. When I came to know Dick as a friend and colleague, I learned that his life away from campus is as rich and varied as his teaching research. He is an accomplished musician (pianist and organist), expert photographer, amateur painter and astronomer, as well as an avid football fan!

Today I often meet with some of Dick's former students on both a personal and professional basis. I know they share my conviction that the preparation he provided us was instrumental in our professional development. The greatest bonus is that we will always have in him a valued friend and advocate.

# A Genuine Legacy

## M. Jerry Weiss

Distinguished Service Professor Emeritus
Jersey City State College

*M. Jerry Weiss received his Ed.D. from Teach-*
*ers College, Columbia University in New York in*
*1952. He taught English, language arts, and*
*reading in secondary schools and colleges in Vir-*
*ginia, New York, Pennsylvania and Ohio, and*
*has been a faculty member at Jersey City State*
*College for thirty-three years. Dr. Weiss also has*
*been actively involved in many professional or-*
*ganizations and received the Distinguished Ser-*
*vice Award (College Reading Association), the*
*Arbuthnot Award (International Reading Asso-*
*ciation), and the National Council of Teachers of*
*English Distinguished Service Award. Dr. Weiss*
*also has authored and edited many publications and articles related to read-*
*ing, writing, and literature instruction. His comments are followed with a*
*personal reflection by Janet K. Carsetti, past president of CRA and founder of*
*READ, Inc.*

D r. Ruth Strang at Teachers College, Columbia University, convinced me
that one of the most important characteristics of a good teacher is having time for each student and caring about each person. She was never too
busy in her schedule to deny students appointments; yet, she was constantly
writing, teaching, grading papers, reading, and doing research. But when a
student who had a particular problem with a child in the reading clinic asked
for help because nothing seemed to be working, Dr. Strang smiled gently and
kindly stated, "Why don't you try something new?" To me this made so much
sense. In the reading clinic we were free to try anything that might help a child
grow and develop in and through reading. Try something new.

Why is that so foreign for some classroom teachers? Putting children into reading groups, "Cardinals," "Canaries," "Crows," and basing the groupings on test scores always seemed alien to me. There's something wrong with the notion that children with a common test score all need help in the same skills at the same time. I've had enough clinical experience in my lifetime to know that children perform as they do in reading for a variety of reasons. Dr. Strang was quick to remind us that a problem might be related to physical and/or emotional reasons and that some children have a lack of interest or experiential background for the types of materials they are asked to read. Some children also come from environments in which reading is not held up as an activity of importance.

Let me give one good example of the latter. I was a secondary school reading teacher in New York City. I had a class of thirteen, mostly young men. When we spoke in class about different topics related to what I wanted them to read, they were quite savvy. They knew more than I expected, and they were comfortable in sharing their knowledge with others. Then I would ask them to read some material related to our discussion, and they did so. I followed this with some written work to check their vocabulary understandings as well their comprehension abilities. I was amazed at how poorly some of these students did. I would call each one in, and we would discuss the work. They nodded attentively, signifying to me they knew what they had gotten wrong. I persisted in trying to find out why they had done so poorly. The answer was easy: "I don't know." But I was convinced they did know. I kept hitting harder and harder. Finally, one student cracked. "Listen, teach, we aren't supposed to get good grades here. When we leave school, our leader is waiting at the subway to check our grades and our papers. If we get higher than a C, we're in trouble. So we have to make mistakes. It's as simple as all that."

I ached all over when I heard this. Reading is a game. It's a social process. People could get hurt for what they know.

About this time, Dr. Strang published an important book, *Gateways to Readable Books* (1966). It was an annotated list of books, classified under different subject headings. Once a teacher found out an interest of a student, the teacher could go to that book and find a listing of several titles that might be of interest to that student. I loved that book and found I was using it more than SRA Reading Kits, Controlled Readers, and workbooks. I began to find out the interests of my students and then would group them according to these interests. In any group, students might be reading the same book because they all wanted to read that book. The group interaction was terrific as they exchanged information about what they were reading. In fact, some students swapped books because of what others happened to say about particular books that piqued their interests. Skills were taught in conjunction with the readings and assignments were based on individual and group needs.

I changed my classroom grading system based on what I learned. I told them if they read six books in a marking period, they would get an A; five would get them a B; four books would get them a C+; three books would get them a C. The only requirement was that they had to convince me they had read the book. Some of this might be in a writing assignment; some of this might be through oral activities. These secondary students went along with the idea for a long time—until they had to have a report card. While many were getting B's and A's, they did not want these grades on their report cards. So I made up two sets of report cards for each student. The one they would show their leader was filled with C's and D's. They survived; I did also.

Try something different. I was hooked on books, not textbooks, workbooks, kits, or gimmicks. I became part of the paperback revolution and the trade book world, long before the Whole Language movement became strong. At College Reading Association meetings I arranged to have exhibits of many paperback books, trade titles, and professional books. Unfortunately, at that time few people would go into the exhibit area to look at these wonderful books.

I also remember promoting CRA sessions at which children's, young adult, and adult authors would make excellent presentations. Lois Lowry, Lloyd Alexander, Paula Danziger, to name a few, all came, and for awhile I was embarrassed by the small turnout at their sessions. Finally, a few program chairs decided to have an author speak at the annual banquet. This increased the attendance to hear authors, but many a board member had to have an arm twisted to buy a banquet ticket. I never figured out just who or what these people wanted to hear. All of the days were filled with sessions on all phases of the profession, including diagnostic techniques, research, new methods and materials, ESL, the exceptional students, and so forth. Why would an author be so out of place at a reading convention?

I served as chair of a committee on media and communications and literacy, including literature, and was allowed to have one spot on the annual program. When I finally gave up the chair, the memorable and remarkable Peg Cagney took over. I worked with her, and we made some wonderful program proposals. Then one program chair wrote to indicate that the guaranteed spot was no longer guaranteed, and rejected our proposal. He violated the understanding that there would be one slot for this committee's presentation. Dr. Cagney and I were very hurt. Phone calls made no dent in his plans. Peg died soon after. I quit coming to CRA.

Yet, when CRA needed money to buy a computer, I got a publisher, Bantam, to donate 100 copies of Jimmy Carter's book, and June Ewing, a close friend of President Carter, got him to autograph each copy. The organization sold the books to have money for the computer. This is not trivia. This is a question of what there is for those who are interested in literature and reading across the curriculum at an annual CRA meeting.

I was called last year to recommend an author for a general session, the breakfast. Suzanne Fisher Staples, who lives in Florida and is a good friend, was my suggestion. She came, spoke, and conquered the hearts of the breakfast attendees. She is a Newbery Honor Book Award recipient for *Shabanu* (1989). Her sequel *Haveli* (1993) is equally compelling. In a very short time after her presentation, all copies of her books were sold out, and there was a line still waiting to purchase the autographed editions of a Pakistan tale too incredible to be true. But the adventures and events are fictionalized truths of a way of life. CRA might create a division to satisfy the interests of those who want to know more about good and popular books and effective ways of using them in a well planned integrated language arts program.

Some will remember the lost bus trip in Philadelphia to see a private screening of *They Shoot Horses, Don't They?* Sydney Pollack, the director, Academy Award winner, spoke at the banquet. I should point out that this film is based on a novel about marathon dancers. It was a gripping evening. Today, in New Jersey, viewing the visual arts and media is considered an essential part of the state's core curricula for all students. A film such as this is extremely provocative and stimulates critical thinking, discussion and writing. Yes, the media are a part of the 20th and 21st century. See the amazing Dorling Kindersley book: *Chronicle of the Cinema: 100 Years of the Movies* (1995). This is cultural history at its best. How many lives have been affected by the films and video attractions now so plentiful before us? How has life been changed with the progress of all forms of technology? Isn't this a factor in literacy education?

At CRA I used to bring bibliographies of new books, and those who heard me awaited the distribution of those bibliographies. Of course, there were even more who would come up to me and say: "Jerry, I'm sorry I could not come to your session. I had to be elsewhere. But do you have any extra copies of your bibliographies?" At CRA we are family. I learned to bring lots of bibliographies with me. Did anyone use them? I don't know. I don't work for the CIA. But at Appalachian State University, Burt Price used them, and produced quite a few reading lists of his own. He would take groups of students who were admitted with reading deficiencies and use paperbacks and trade books as integral tools to whet the appetites of young men and women so that they would be stimulated to improve in their reading abilities. As he often said to me: "Jerry, how come so many don't see the relationship between books and reading?"

I also have come to realize there is a connection between reading and the arts. Many students turned off by traditional programs get turned on again when they can read materials in play form or through songs and chanting. I have high respect for Robert and Marlene McCracken and their excellent work with primary children and teachers. *Reading, Writing & Language: A Practi-*

*cal Guide for Primary Teachers* (Peguis Publishers, 1979) is filled with practical suggestions that inspire teacher initiative and enthusiasm on the part of teachers and learners. Jonathan Kozol, John Holt, Robert Coles, Nancy Larrick, Jeannette Veatch, Jim Trelease, George and Nell Murphy, Tony Amato, Roma Gans, Leland Jacobs, and Bill Martin, Jr., also have published many articles and books that deal with crucial issues affecting literacy in all segments of the United States. These are the kinds of professional books I have had my students read. Dr. Strang wrote in a similar way also. She also exposed me to Dr. Frances M. Wilson, Director of Guidance, New York City Board of Education, who in turn introduced me to some amazing students at the High School of Performing Arts, New York City. Here I learned a great deal about the arts and literacy education.

I have enjoyed learning about the many offerings that the different divisions in CRA provide. But now I feel I'm out of place in CRA. For IRA and NCTE, I have the dubious responsibility of working with program chairs to arrange for the many featured author strands at both national conventions. I am happy to say these sessions are well attended, and the publishers are thrilled. Teachers have written to thank me for the small part I play and to tell me of the joys children have found in reading books by authors the teachers have met at these national conventions. I even get invited to school districts to work on revising curricula so that more trade books are integrated into the content areas.

CRA is made up of many talented people. I appreciate the awards I have received on behalf of the organization. But I'm restless for breakthroughs. I'm sure there are many ways to explore the various dimensions of literacy, and I think that now is the time to grow through knowledge. When I read *Midnight in the Garden of Good and Evil* (Berendt, 1994), I realized that even in a small community there are many different and interesting personalities. As I read *Torn Away* (Heneghan, 1996), I realized that I had to get a better understanding of the impact of the disruption through the centuries in Ireland. When I read *Broken Bridge* (Banks, 1995) and *One More River* (Banks, 1973), I learned more about the Palestinian-Israel conflicts than the newspaper headlines were telling me. No, I didn't expect a panacea at CRA; I dared to expect something new.

Many years ago a poet, a most unusual professor, and I were invited by a friend to speak at the National Reading Conference. The three of us had never met or heard of one another. The program chair scheduled us for a late afternoon slot and called our session: "Way Out!" The poet spoke of his love of poetry as a way of developing literacy; the unusual professor talked about his research, using astrology as a means for diagnosing students' problems, and he had the overheads to prove it; I spoke about the relationship of books to reading. Although this was the cocktail hour, the room was packed.

Skeptics came in many forms; but a few left with smiles on their faces. Did we reach them all? No, but we tried something different. And that made it all worthwhile. Thank you, Dr. Strang.

## References

Banks, R. L. (1973). *One more river.* New York: Simon and Schuster.

Banks, R. L. (1995). *Broken bridge.* New York: Morrow Junior Books.

Berendt, J. (1994). *Midnight in the garden of good and evil: A story of Savannah.* New York: Random House.

Heneghan, J. (1994). *Torn away.* New York: Viking.

Karney, R. (Ed.). (1995). *Chronicle of the cinema.* London; New York: Dorling Kindersley.

McCracken, M. J., & McCracken, R. A. (1979). *Reading, writing, and language: A practical guide for primary teachers.* Winnipeg: Peguis.

Staples, S. F. (1989). *Shabanu: Daughter of the wind.* New York: Knopf.

Staples, S. F. (1993). *Haveli.* New York: Knopf.

Strang, R. M. (1966). *Gateways to Readable Books* (4th ed.). New York: H. W. Wilson.

## Reflections on M. Jerry Weiss
## by Janet K. Carsetti

Readers of this publication know M. Jerry Weiss the teacher, the former President of CRA, the writer, the patron of the arts, the humorist, and, as a man revered by all who meet him. Yet, few know the idiosyncrasies of M. Jerry . . . the man. Perhaps I can share some of those lesser known, but highly endearing qualities.

As an English major at Jersey City State College I never met M. Jerry until my senior year. Like everyone else, I heard about Jerry, then the chair of Special Education. My introduction to him was rather abrupt, a trait that became quite familiar. He summoned me to his office. "So you want to teach reading? Why?" I replied that I had tried to teach literature to a group of high school athletes and found it an exercise in futility. They couldn't read. They couldn't care less about great literature. If the students couldn't read, we needed to learn how to reach them. "Here," said Jerry, handing me a name and phone number, "They need a reading teacher in Teaneck [NJ]." "Well, that's great but I need to learn how to teach reading," I said. Without batting an eye, M. Jerry said, "you'll enroll in graduate school this summer, take 12 credits and then take two courses each semester while you're teaching and you'll get your Masters in Reading in two years." "And, where exactly am I going to do this," I said. "Here, at JCSC, I'm going to be the chair of the new Reading Department." Welcome, M. Jerry, the *mentor.*

During those next two years the many faces of M. Jerry Weiss surfaced. In class he could make you feel both angry and guilty. He could humiliate you for not solving the educational problems of the world, but, oddly enough, the next week you changed your teaching techniques . . . M. Jerry, the *radical.*

He introduced us to *stars* . . . those in the field of reading . . . and those on the stage. Summer reading institutes with hundreds of participants; trips to the World's Fair; tickets to Broadway; and, *bus trips.* Now, anyone who ever went to JCSC took busses every day, but no one really took a bus until she went on an M. Jerry expedition. CRA was a command performance trip. Who knew what it was or where we were going, but 13 hours to Rochester, New York, followed by sleeping in the hotel lobby because the great man forgot to make reservations for all of us, did not turn us against him (for more than a few hours). Instead, we met more of the reading stars and were introduced as "Jerry's gang." Some of us even joined CRA, and a few of us became President in our time, following in his footsteps . . . M. Jerry, the *star.*

While riding busses, attending conferences, going to the theater, reading volumes of prose for class, teaching in our respective jobs, and trying to have a life, those of us touched by M. Jerry learned that above all, he was our *friend*. He was there to encourage us to be radical in our teaching and loving to our students, and, to believe in ourselves. Who else could have encouraged me to teach with nothing but paperbacks; or to take my classes to *Hello Dolly;* or to cross the Mason-Dixon line and get my doctorate at the University of Maryland? Who else could introduce me to a summer reading institute as the "Sophia Loren of Reading" and not get punched out? Who else would take a bus to Washington, D.C. (Jerry never drove) to make sure I was going to finish my doctorate, or yell at me for actually suggesting that phonics did have a role in the teaching of reading? And, after leaving university teaching to work for the American Bar Association, who lectured me for hours on making a futile mistake, only to tell everyone . . . "she's teaching prisoners to read with paperbacks!" (Smirk!)

M. Jerry Weiss cornered the market on *role-modeling*. He taught us how to teach by teaching; how to write by writing funny, meaningful prose; how to enjoy the arts by taking us to the theater; and, how to change the world (or part of it) through self-fulfilling prophecy. At his retirement festivities, hundreds of former students and colleagues toasted the man who had changed so many lives. We listened as he responded to the roasting of Jerry. We laughed incessantly at the dry humor. My husband, who only knew Jerry socially, but had never seen him in action, quipped, "He's better than Jack Benny!" I'm still not sure who was being honored that night, Jerry or the audience! We know he's not finished teaching, writing, living, and loving the art of being M. Jerry Weiss.

High school drop-out, reader, writer, radical, traveler, humorist, star performer, humanitarian, teacher, husband, father, grandfather, colleague, professor emeritus, curmudgeon, role model, mentor and *friend* . . . M. Jerry Weiss, thank you!

# TEACHER BELIEFS
## AND LITERACY

# CONSTRUCTING TEACHER-GENERATED "AUTHENTIC" READING ASSESSMENTS

### Evangeline V. Newton
John Carroll University

## Abstract

*Many school districts that have adopted "whole language," "literature-based," or "process" approaches to literacy instruction find traditional standardized assessment tools inadequate indicators of their students' development as readers and writers. Attempts to design more effective evaluation measures have spawned the notion of "authentic assessments," which link curricular objectives and classroom instruction in a natural and developmentally appropriate way. This article shares one suburban school district's year-long effort to implement authentic assessment in order to determine whether students were developing competency as readers. Discussion includes a review of the overall project and an analysis of typical interactive patterns. Finally, opportunities for professional development generated by this collaborative process are explored.*

## Introduction

Assessing student reading skills is a continuous and fundamental process in American public education. School districts routinely administer standardized and norm-referenced tests to evaluate their students against those in other districts. Because such tests are decontextualized, however, they do not always measure district-generated curricular objectives. Similarly, they do not always represent classroom-based instructional practices. Consequently, traditional standardized assessments provide a limited portrait of reading development in specific school districts.

Recent calls for more "authentic" assessment tools emphasize the need for context-specific instruments that will reflect and evaluate local reading curricula and instructional practices. Valencia, Hiebert and Afflerbach (1994) believe this authentic assessment movement has mandated changes in three central aspects of assessment: (1) the assessment tasks and contexts in which they are performed; (2) the role of teachers and students in the process; and (3) the data needs of those who study results, e.g., administrators and classroom teachers (p. 288). Because these changes often challenge established beliefs about teaching and learning, the process of developing and implementing authentic assessments can become a powerful tool for professional growth.

As a university literacy educator, I was invited by one school district to guide teachers in the design and implementation of authentic reading assessments. This article will describe challenges of the year-long project in which district teachers constructed, administered and evaluated grade-level reading assessments to determine whether their students were achieving reading competency. A review of the overall project will be followed by discussion of typical interactive patterns. Finally, opportunities for professional development generated by this collaborative process will be explored.

## Background

Two years ago, the state of Ohio required each school district to demonstrate through annual examination that its students were "developing competency" as readers and writers. The form and content of this examination were left solely to individual districts.

Administrators in one greater Cleveland school district decided to use this mandate as a staff development opportunity. For some time, the elementary language arts program had been incorporating "whole language" practices; the reading curriculum was officially literature based. Teachers were offered incentives to become knowledgeable about new teaching strategies through in-service workshops and tuition rebates for graduate study. Although the district was officially moving in this direction, teachers were still free to make instructional choices based on their own belief systems. For example, basal readers were provided for those who wished to use them.

Teachers in this district were also encouraged to participate in curriculum development. In fact, some faculty members had spent a year developing Pupil Performance Objectives (PPO) for language arts that reflected current beliefs about literacy learning. Designing authentic assessments based on these pupil performance objectives would be, administrators reasoned, an additional step in this growth process.

Before developing concrete plans for the project, I met with fourteen members of the elementary language arts committee and later with the entire middle and high school language arts faculties. At these sessions, the Assistant Superintendent explained the state mandate and introduced the task of designing grade-level reading assessments as an opportunity for teachers to expand their role in curricular development. I asked teachers to share their own expectations, goals and concerns about teacher-generated assessments.

As a follow-up, all district teachers involved received a questionnaire asking them to share concerns and expectations about the new assessments we would be developing (Figure 1). For each grade I made a master list of all comments, noting significant patterns of response. Not surprisingly, patterns revealed marked differences in how teachers viewed assessment. One second grade teacher suggested that comprehension be measured by the Gates McGinite comprehension section while two others suggested the more whole language technique of "retelling." Differences appeared in the teacher's learning paradigms as well. One teacher asked at what "level" the assessment text would be while another asked for a measure that acknowledged developmental differences among children. Interestingly, patterns developed within grade levels, but those patterns were different across grade levels, possibly reflecting different instructional concerns.

**Figure 1. Development of Formal Assessment Tool for Reading Competency: Teacher Feedback**

1. Do any concepts in the PPO need clarification? If so, how? (Please be as specific as possible.)

2. Does any language in the PPO need to be more concretely defined?

3. Do you have any suggestions about the format or design of an instrument?

4. As a classroom teacher, what would be most useful to you in an assessment instrument?

5. Additional Comments:

From these first meetings and questionnaires, it became apparent that most elementary school teachers were in some stage of moving from traditional to whole language beliefs and practices. Conversely, only a handful of middle and high school language arts teachers were making this transition. In fact, it seemed that most were just beginning to understand the tenets and implications of the new practices. All teachers in this district were, however, anticipating significant professional changes in the next few years.

## Project Design

In planning a procedural strategy, I considered the task and teachers against this backdrop of educational innovation and change. The task appeared straightforward: to construct one assessment tool for each grade level that was "authentic," i.e., reflecting classroom instruction and compatible with principles of literature-based reading instruction.

The teachers' roles were more complex. Certainly many of them needed to augment and integrate their knowledge in light of current research on authentic assessment before they could develop a credible instrument. But they also needed opportunities to share their own experiences and beliefs about learning in order to synthesize new information. Moreover, understanding the link between assessment, curriculum and instructional practice is critical to authentic assessment. Such understanding, however, requires uncovering and analyzing assumptions behind current instructional practices.

The process of developing authentic assessments would, then, involve personal hurdles as teachers articulated their current beliefs, appraised new information, and shared their perceptions within a peer community. Bridges (1980) writes that transition is a "difficult process of letting go of an old situation, suffering the confusing nowhere of in-betweeness, and launching forth again in a new situation" (p. 5). I believed my role was to assist them through such a transition process by providing information about authentic assessment, responding to concerns, and negotiating differences. I also hoped to model interactive strategies that teachers could adapt to their own classrooms.

Elementary teachers formed grade-level teams to construct an assessment for all students in that grade. Teams met over a three-month period to draft assessments, which were then presented to grade-level colleagues for feedback before revision. All assessments were administered and scored in the spring. When the process had been completed, team members again solicited feedback from grade-level colleagues before meeting to revise assessments for the coming year.

Since most middle and high school language arts teachers had just started "letting go of an old situation," we believed they should begin by attending a series of workshops where they could explore new theories about reading and writing. These interactive workshops became catalysts for reviewing curricula and experiencing whole language instructional strategies. Because there were fewer language arts teachers in the middle and upper grades, all teachers participated in drafting their grade-level assessments. They also administered and scored assessments in the spring, and met later to review and revise.

## Drafting an Assessment

At each team's initial session, I outlined the procedure we would follow in developing the assessment (Figure 2). I began by introducing eight principles of authentic assessment (Cooper, 1993) that should be represented by the final instrument (Figure 3). These principles focused discussion and established guidelines consistent with authentic assessment. No team member resisted, although many sought clarification of particular statements. The instruction to "identify students' strengths," for example, concerned those teachers who saw the primary goal of assessment as identifying weakness. At this first meeting, I also circulated questionnaire responses to team members so that they were familiar with the concerns of their grade-level colleagues who were not present.

## Figure 2. Proposed Format for Constructing Reading Assessment Instrument (12/16/93): Grade Four

**Pupil Performance Objective:** Given a nonfiction text to read silently, the learner will demonstrate comprehension by summarizing the main idea and giving supporting details in writing.

**Steps in Construction Process:**

1. Review principles of effective assessment (handout)
2. Establish purpose/review key terms in PPO
3. Discuss format possibilities
4. Draft an instrument
   a. Review "feedback" sheets/address any concerns
5. Write a rationale
   a. Discusss key items on the instrument
   b. Include concrete examples of "successful" assessment
6. Make sure instrument indicates compatibility among curriculum (content/skill requirements), instructional approaches, and mode of assessment.

As each team worked its way through steps in the construction process, two patterns dominated their interactions. First, teachers held conflicting beliefs about what constituted an effective assessment. These beliefs concealed idiosyncratic theories about how children learn to read. These theories had to be probed, and often reconciled, before members could agree on assessment items whose underpinnings were bound to a particular view of the reading process. Second, regardless of where they fell on a continuum of educational change, all team members sought frequent reassurance that their current beliefs and practices were valid. Such reassurance seemed a prerequisite of risk-taking and, by extension, to growth and change.

## Figure 3. Principles to Guide Effective Assessment.

1. Continuous, ongoing process
2. Integral part of instruction
3. Authentic, reflecting "real" reading and writing
4. Collaborative, reflective process
5. Multidimensional
6. Developmentally and culturally appropriate
7. Identify students' strengths
8. Based on how students learn

## *A Fourth-Grade Scenario*

The drafting process of fourth-grade team members reflected both patterns. The three members of this team were typical of the district's elementary teachers: Sally was a recent graduate who had been immersed in whole language philosophy and was comfortable with it as practice; Janet was working on a graduate degree in reading. While committed to the new approach, Janet was struggling to implement it. Kathy was more traditional, interested but nervous about the process. All, however, were enthusiastic about the project.

I initiated discussion by asking each team member to list reading behaviors that would indicate their students were developing reading competency. All three agreed that since the goal of reading was comprehension, the assessment should evaluate comprehension skills. Moreover, according to their pupil performance objective, comprehension could be demonstrated by "summarizing the main idea and giving supporting details in writing." Consensus about what would be measured was achieved quickly.

Similarly, as they discussed what texts to use for this purpose, all three noted that reading tasks for their students involve both fiction and non-fiction. Since students come into the fourth grade with many experiences reading fictional narratives, learning how to read non-fiction was an important learning objective. I suggested choosing texts from both genres, but team members felt the state mandate could be met by assessing comprehension of one text. Fourth-grade students were also preparing for state-generated proficiency tests in reading, writing and citizenship; they felt another comprehensive reading assessment was superfluous. I suggested using a non-fiction narrative text and the team members agreed quickly.

The team's efforts to identify an actual text, however, were hampered by their conflicting notions of comprehension. Sally and Janet, both committed to a psycholinguistic view of reading, believed that a reader's comprehension is influenced by the schemata or prior knowledge he or she can access during the meaning construction process (Smith, 1988). From their perspective, text choice was significant not just for its "level" of difficulty in terms of vocabulary or syntax, but also for the familiarity of its content. Traditional assessments do not consider a reader's prior knowledge central to comprehension; Kathy insisted that a text for which all students had ample background knowledge would be invalid. Since an authentic assessment must be grounded in beliefs about "how students learn" (Figure 3), team members struggled to resolve this issue.

The teachers' discussion revealed critical differences in how they conceptualized reading and organized instruction in their classrooms. Although I personally favored Sally and Janet's perspective, I also recognized that Kathy represented many teachers who were either unprepared to move forward or struggling to reconcile quite different learning paradigms. As members articulated concerns, I tried to validate their feelings and suggest compromises that were consistent with the principles of authentic assessment, met task goals, and were still compatible with all their beliefs. In this case, a biography of Martin Luther King was selected as such a compromise. King's name was familiar to most students, and since February was "Black History" month some classroom attention would naturally be devoted to King. Sally and Janet were satisfied. Still, in this predominantly white and suburban school district, details of King's life would not be well-known to students. Kathy was reasonably comfortable as well.

Next, team members read and discussed the suitability of many pieces about King. Eventually, members agreed on one, *Happy Birthday, Martin Luther King* (Marzollo, 1993). They were anxious about the text's difficulty, however, because it was a picture book with no publisher's designation of reading "level." Team members decided to "pilot" the text choice by asking a few students in each of their classrooms to read the selection and informally retell it. Based on their impression of these retellings, they decided the King text was appropriate.

Once the text had been agreed upon, members had to consider how students would demonstrate that they had comprehended it. All team members agreed that the assessment should use a question-answer design because such a format would be familiar to their students. They were also comfortable with the popular view of comprehension as literal, interpretive, and applied levels of thinking (Vacca, Vacca & Gove, 1991, p. 199). But Sally, who was most committed to the psycholinguistic perspective, wanted the assessment to indicate that comprehension was also an idiosyncratic process in which readers drew on multiple schemata to extend and construct new meanings. She lobbied for a response-based question that invited students to draw on their own experiences and beliefs to construct new understandings. I supported her by bringing in articles about response and examples of response-based assessment models.

Both Janet and Kathy were skeptical. To them, response was a way of generating student interest by inviting personal opinion. And "opinion" had no parameters of right-or-wrong by which to evaluate comprehension. Again, at the heart of this debate were conflicting views of the reading process. I suggested developing criteria for evaluation by designing a rubric to grade this question. Team members had used rubrics to evaluate writing, but not reading. Again, I brought in models and encouraged them to generate their own criteria.

Finally, Sally did persuade her colleagues to develop a response-based question: "Select a sentence from the story that interests you or makes you think. Write the sentence on the lines below. . . . Now tell why you chose this sentence." As they constructed a rubric to score the question, Janet and Kathy grew in their understanding of Sally's perspective (Figure 4). And because team members had generated the criteria for scoring themselves, they had talked through their individual beliefs and began to understand the theoretical underpinnings of the response question. In addition, team members felt comfortable explaining both the assessment and criteria for scoring to their grade-level colleagues. Sally's persistence enabled me to scaffold what was, for these team members, a dramatic innovation. Curiously, it was also a compromise: on the assessment itself, the response question is designated as an "applied" level of thinking.

**Figure 4. Scoring Rubric for Interpretive and Response-Based Questions**

---

- Student will receive 3 points for an answer illustrating a developed understanding of the text with evidence of careful thought and thoroughness.
- Student will receive 2 points for an answer illustrating a superficial understanding of the text.
- Student will receive 1 point for an answer illustrating little evidence of construction of meaning.
- Student will receive 0 points for an answer illustrating no evidence of construction of meaning.

---

The assessment in Figure 5 was used with all district fourth grades, and teacher feedback was overwhelmingly positive. Most teachers saw a direct link between curricular objectives, classroom instruction, and the assessment instrument. Not all assessments, however, were as effective.

### Assessments in Other Grades

First and second grade teams adapted a Retelling format that was also quite successful. The third grade teachers constructed an instrument similar to this one. Some of the teachers thought the text team members had selected was too easy. They wanted a voice in text selection. One of the teachers urged use of a readability formula to indicate a text was at the third grade "level." A new passage was selected for the following year that was not, in fact, much different from the original text the team had selected. And, not surprisingly, students' performance was about the same as it had been with the original text.

In the middle grades, teachers constructed a conventional multiple choice instrument. Their sole innovation was using some kind of familiar text for which students had appropriate background knowledge. In grades 9 through 12, teachers developed assessments whose overall design was similar to that of the fourth grade. Each of the 9 through 12 teams had one or two members who had recently completed undergraduate or graduate degrees, were

**Figure 5. City Schools Reading Competency Assessment: Grade 4.**

**Pupil Performance Objective:** Given a nonfiction text to read silently, the learner will demonstrate comprehension by summarizing the main idea and giving supporting details in writing.

Name: _____    Date: _____

|  | Student Score | Total Possible Points |
|---|---|---|
| Part A—Literal Section | | |
| Question 1 | _____ | 1 |
| Question 2 | _____ | 1 |
| Question 3 | _____ | 1 |
| Part B—Interpretive Section | | |
| Question 1 | _____* | 3 |
| Question 2 | _____* | 3 |
| Part C—Response Question | _____* | 3 |
| (Applied Section) | | |
| Total | _____ | 12 |
| Comp. | _____ (yes/no)** | |

To be completed by Classroom Teacher Only: Assessment result appears to be a satisfactory indicator of this student's performance: _____(yes/no)

*See Scoring Rubric in Figure 4.*

**To pass a student must receive a score of 9 points or higher.*

comfortable with whole language practices, and who assumed leadership roles in the text construction process. Despite individual differences, all the final assessments reflected, I believe, a natural evolutionary step in the process of growth and change.

## Opportunities for Professional Development

Many school districts are undergoing similar changes as they bypass basal readers in favor of literature-based or "whole language" instruction. Belying this simple change in texts is a much deeper paradigm shift from a linear to a sociopsycholinguistic view of reading and, by extension, from a transmission to a constructivist view of instruction. As I look back on my experience with all grade-level teams, I believe that the process of designing and implementing assessments gave these teachers a rare opportunity to grasp—firsthand—the depth of these changes.

Currently, most districts offer teachers superficial preparation for educational innovations. They may invite university consultants to demonstrate new strategies at district in-service meetings. Similarly, they may send teachers to workshops conducted by "experts" and then ask those teachers to share new information with colleagues. Some districts do offer financial incentives for graduate education, but such districts are few. In fact, most teachers are not invited to wrestle with intricate issues of program implementation. This is distressing since the innovations we have asked them to undertake are more than cosmetic techniques. They are epistemological changes rooted in complex research findings about how children learn, findings which have generated new debate about how children are best taught.

Furthermore, teachers are often bewildered these days by cries for "accountability." Frequently they see little connection between the tests purported to measure accountability and their own concrete instructional objectives. Teachers in this district had a real purpose for learning: to produce an instrument that would assess their own students according to their own instructional objectives. In short, they had a voice in deciding how and for what they would be held accountable.

In the process, teachers were required to articulate beliefs and share experiences. They also acquired new information. All this was occurring in a social environment where cooperation—not competition—was needed in order to generate an instrument that represented everyone's beliefs and practices. Wildman and Niles (1987) see teacher collaboration as a way to abrogate the "psychological isolation from other adults that characterizes the teacher's workplace" (p. 8). In addition, it offers teachers "emotional support and encouragement" as they "cope with the risk" inherent in learning to teach well (Wildman & Niles, 1987, p. 8). And since learning for authentic purposes by sharing current and evolving knowledge within a peer community are fundamental tenets of whole language, these teachers were also experiencing firsthand the vitality of this instructional approach.

Hall and Loucks (1978) maintain that educators facing significant changes pass through predictable stages of concern. As the year progressed, I found that most teams were, in fact, passing through the stages delineated in the "Concerns Based Adoption Model." Team members moved from seeking information about authentic assessment to wondering how their own instruction would be affected. As they became more focused on the task, team members appeared anxious about how the assessment would be implemented, how it would impact students, and how it would be received by administrators and parents. They worried about presenting drafts to colleagues. Finally, recognizing that no assessment would be flawless, teachers administered revised drafts. When the process was over, most teams analyzed feedback, reflected on their experience, and made modifications for next year.

By inviting teachers to construct grade-level assessments, and supporting them in that process, these district administrators sustained ongoing dialogue about teaching and learning that resulted in professional growth for
much of their staff. And as their mentor through this process, I came to understand that true educational change cannot be mandated by mentors, administrators, politicians, or even parents. It must come from within, and it
sometimes comes as the result of many small compromises negotiated and
reviewed over time. Hall and Loucks (1978) note that change takes time, is
highly personal, and requires intervention that helps resolve current issues
and needs. I found this to be true.

These were difficult "truths" for me to learn. As an enthusiastic propo-
nent of authentic assessments that, ideally, reflect holistic literacy practices,
I had my own belief systems and goals. But I gradually realized that my primary
role in this process was to offer encouragement and support as teachers
struggled to share and understand. I also realized that, if assessments were
to be truly authentic, all the teachers' beliefs about learning and learners had
to be represented in the final assessments. Wildman and Niles (1987) write
that teachers' growth is "intimately tied to the ways in which they handle
confusion, ambiguity, and conflicting goals" (p. 6). It was from resolving their
differences through compromise that I believe most teachers were able to
grow. And ultimately, the final assessments were a synthesis of **their** beliefs
and practices at that moment in their professional lives.

---

## References

Bridges, W. (1980). *Transitions: Making sense of life's changes*. Reading, MA: Addison-
Wesley.

Cooper, J. D. (1993). *Literacy: Helping Children Construct Meaning* (Second Edition).
Boston: Houghton-Mifflin Co.

Hall, G. E. & Loucks, S. (1978). Teacher concerns as a basis for facilitating and per-
sonalizing staff development. *Teachers College Record, 80,* 36-53.

Marzollo, J. (1993). *Happy Birthday, Martin Luther King*. New York:Scholastic Inc.

Smith, F. (1988). *Understanding reading: A psycholinguistic analysis of reading and
learning to read* (4th ed.). Hillsdale, NJ: Lawrence Erlbaum Associates.

Vacca, J., Vacca, R. & Gove, M M. (1991). *Reading and learning to read* (Second
Edition). New York: Harper Collins Publishers.

Valencia, S. W., Hiebert, E.H. & Afflerbach, P. (Eds). (1994). *Authentic Reading Assessment: Practices and Possibilities*. Newark: International Reading Association.

Wildman, T. M. & Niles, J. A. (1987). Essentials of professional growth. *Educational
Leadership, 44*(5), 4-10.

# Teachers' Personal Comfort With Reading and Writing: Divergent Profiles in Planning Instruction

**Dora L. Bailey**

Youngstown State University

## Abstract

*How a teacher's comfort or discomfort with reading and writing affects the articulation of planning for learners' literacy experiences has not been carefully scrutinzed. This study shares the language of nineteen teachers as they talk about their own reading and writing comfort. Their level of comfort and discomfort with reading and writing is reflected as they talk about planning for learners to read and write. Two composite profiles represent the extremes of the discomfort-comfort continuum.*

Although the home is important in establishing literacy, teachers remain the prime movers in developing literacy. The recent emphasis on family literacy (Morrow et al., 1995; Morrow, 1995; U.S. Department of Education, 1996) continues to suggest that teachers initiate and maintain collaboration with families. This seems reasonable since teachers are educated in how to create a literate classroom community. However, can teachers who are not readers and writers themselves create a thriving literacy learning community?

The literacy issue for Americans became a major concern in the 1980s (*Becoming a Nation of Readers*, Anderson et al., 1985; National Commission on Excellence in Education, *A Nation at Risk*, 1983). After ten years of effort to increase literacy in America, it still remains a priority concern (Lehr & Osborn, 1994). In spite of changes to increase the nation's literacy, what happens in many classrooms is often the same as what happened in classrooms forty years ago (Goodlad, 1984; 1990). Although over the past 50 years the philosophy of the teaching and learning of reading and writing has gone from a predominately phonics driven approach, to a skills approach, to a holistic approach (Atwell, 1987; Goodman, 1986; Meek, 1982; Rasinski &

Padak, 1996; Weaver, 1988), some teachers still do not seem to be creating learning communities that are conducive to literacy development (Goodlad, 1984, 1990).

Theoretical bases for holistic, child centered, literacy-oriented classroom communities emerged during the 1970s and 1980s in a variety of disciplines: psycholinguistics (Neisser, 1976; Smith, 1993), sociolinguistics (Vygotsky, 1978; Halliday, 1978), medical science (Healy, 1985), and reading research (Chomsky, 1979; Clay, 1979, Duffy, 1991; Roehler & Duffy, 1986). Connecting the research in these fields builds literacy learning theory and practice that addresses the whole child (Rhodes & Shanklin, 1993), employs whole pieces of literature and text (Norton, 1995; Short & Pierce, 1990), and integrates speaking, listening, reading, writing and viewing (Standards for the English Language Arts, 1996).

Britzman (1986) contends that teachers' resistance to moving toward best literacy practice results from the development of personal philosophies of teaching that come from teachers' own past lives with schooling. Teachers all have a collection of ". . . well-worn and commonsensical images of the teachers' work. They bring [to their teaching] their implicit institutional biographies—the cumulative experience of school lives (p. 443)." Kagan (1992) found that these images about teaching are particularly resistant to change. The images have power because they were formed during impressionable stages in teachers' lives, their own childhood.

In spite of the reluctance of most teachers to change, some teachers have made the journey intuitively, by going through a deep reflection process, and some have chosen to be educated. Teachers' stories (Reason & Hawkins, 1988) can inform us about the change teachers are making. For example, Wuthrick (1995) interviewed three teachers:

> Sally made a commitment to learning more about holistic instruction through professional reading. Jane was involved in a graduate program for two years. Both demonstrated a solid understanding of the philosophical roots of holistic instruction and expressed confidence in their ability to incorporate skill instruction through authentic literature. Rose, on the other hand attended single-day workshop presentations that did not provide much opportunity to explore the philosophical belief systems that underlie holistic instruction. She is still unwilling to organize instruction without the framework of the teacher's manual. (p. 80)

Notice that both Sally and Jane embraced a change route that required reading. Rose, who does not change, will only read the teacher's manual.

In order to facilitate positive literacy attitudes in children, teachers need to model these attitudes. Excellent literacy teachers usually use their own literacy to form insights about learners' literate behaviors. They are enthusiastic about reading and writing; they read and write. Excellent literacy teachers are observers of students' nuances, kidwatchers (Goodman, 1985). They possess a core philosophy that allows for an infinite number of decision points.

Thus, there is a need to explore why teachers continue to "teach as they have been taught" (Goodlad, 1984). We do have conjectures supported by exploratory research (Duffy & Roehler, 1993). Johnson & Hoffman, in their research on conceptions of literacy development, make an interesting concluding observation: "In order to prepare teachers to confidently and competently implement the literacy instruction espoused in the research literature, we must continue to build our understanding of how preservice teachers' thinking about literacy and literacy development evolves" (1994, p. 83). An understanding of how inservice teachers' thinking about literacy and literacy development evolves is of equal importance, since inservice teachers serve as models for preservice teachers.

The current study asked how a teacher's comfort or discomfort with reading and writing affects the articulation of planning for learners' literacy experiences. Teachers were asked to share stories about reading and writing in their personal lives and to reflect on their reading and writing planning. This study attempts to address reading researchers' criticism of the lack of concern for the impact of affect on reading (Shapiro, 1993).

## Methodology
### *Informants*

The nineteen informant-participants in this study were enrolled in a Reading Master's Program (eighteen female, one male). Participants are considered informants when they are asked to report on their own lives (Spradley, 1979). The verbal strings and stories that are elicited are the information or data sought, as opposed to participants whose behaviors are observed, and the observations are reported or counted. Each informant was interviewed from 30-60 minutes.

### *Procedure*

An ethnographic (Guba, 1978) study employing interviews (Dexter, 1970; Merton et al, 1956; Spradley, 1979), was used to explore teachers' comfort in planning for literacy experiences. Interviews allowed the researcher to collect words and word clusters that informants consider relevant to the communication of their own stories about reading and writing (Reason & Hawkins, 1988). The kind of language a teacher uses provides a window from which to observe mental activity about literacy. The words and phrases teachers choose when discussing how they plan to interact with and guide learners indicate their level of literacy comfort. This study used the notion of pragmatics, "the study of the choices of language persons make . . ." (Harris & Hodges Eds., 1995 p. 230), to select pieces of language that describe levels of comfort and to compile profiles of the two extremes in the discomfort/ comfort continuum. Informants were given four requests:

I would like you to share with me your remembrance of your story of becoming a reader.

Share with me how you plan for your learners' reading experiences.

I would like you to share with me your remembrance of your story of becoming a writer.

Share with me how you plan for your learners' writing experiences.

These typical grand tour requests ask the informants to talk about the pattern of events (Spradley, 1979, p. 87) in their own words. It is important to elicit words that the informants consider relevant to the communication of their own story.

In this study when an informant began summarizing, as opposed to describing, probing questions were asked, such as:

You have described your reading in school, how about at home?

Describe how you think of yourself as a reader today.

What else do you think of as you plan for language activities?

Describe your writing activities at home.

Describe how you think of yourself as a writer today.

What other things do you plan for your learners to do with writing?

The informants' full use of oral language was encouraged through verbal recognition and positive body language. Thus, the interview attempted to elicit information about what guides teachers' explicit activities while planning for and implementing literacy instruction.

The teachers' verbal strings were massaged and analyzed by two researchers who read and reread the data with the help of *The Ethnograph* (Seidel et al., 1988). This computer program helps the researcher locate key concepts and supporting ideas across large amounts of prose material. In this way themes and semantic similarities within and among stories can surface. The two researchers compared their independently identified key concepts and supporting verbal strings to reach a concensus on the profiles.

## Results

In the majority of the stories, informants' comfort with reading clearly differed from their comfort with writing. There appears to be a discomfort/comfort continuum that ranges from total personal reading/writing discomfort and discomfort in articulating planning for literacy experiences, to total reading/ writing comfort and comfort in articulating planning for literacy experiences. Tables 1 and 2 show the frequency distribution of nineteen teachers' stories.

**Table 1. Reading Comfort and Discomfort Frequency.**

| Category | Number of Teachers |
|---|---|
| **Reading Comfort Total** | **8** |
| Could articulate planning for learners | 7 |
| Could not articulate planning for learners | 1 |
| **Reading Discomfort Total** | **15** |
| Could articulate planning for learners | 0 |
| Could not articulate planning for learners | 15 |

As shown in Table 1 all eight teachers who were comfortable with reading remembered home reading experiences. They made statements such as, "I was read to all the time" and "I have tons of books and I still buy books. I love to read, anything. I can't remember ever not reading." A further indication of comfort with reading is the mention of authors such as Eric Carle, Dr. Seuss, Judy Blume, Nancy Drew, Stephen King, Danielle Steele, John Grisham, Sue Grafton, and Robert Waller. All teachers who were comfortable with reading mentioned a positive teacher story about reading such as: "I had a sixth grade teacher who read to us for an extended period of time every day," and "In third grade we had Scholastic Books that we could buy and read in class." Although these teachers also had negative stories, these were always followed by a positive story. Those teachers who articulate planning for their learners included in their stories statements such as: "While reading my children decide what they would do if they were the main character," and "We do SSR daily, sometimes more often if we are doing a lot of reading in social studies or science." Some of these teachers mentioned specific books they would use in specific ways.

As shown in Table 1, the majority of the teachers were not comfortable with reading and none of these could articulate their planning for learners. These teachers indicated their discomfort in statements such as "I do not consider myself a reader. I seldom pick up a book and read for entertainment," "When I was little and even when I was in high school I didn't read too much," "I'm a lazy reader," "I only read things I have to read," and "I haven't read a whole book for years." These teachers usually included a negative story about school such as "I never really felt good about myself as a reader and I think it is related to the kinds of experiences I had in school," and "To this day I don't like reading because all I remember is the phonics workbooks when I was in third grade. I do not spell well." In telling their stories they could not go beyond vague references such as "I use the suggestions in the basal," and "I like to use a variety of techniques and books. I can't remember any specific ones now." None of these teachers mentioned specific books or authors.

Only four teachers were comfortable with writing (see Table 2). They made statements such as "I write all of the time. I have always kept a journal, like a diary," and "I love to write. I have written stories and poems, and still do. I have quite a collection." Of these four teachers only two could articulate planning for learners. They both told stories about modeling various writing for learners before and during their writing, referred to writing in relation to specific novels, mentioned several types of journals, and provided times for creative writing.

### Table 2. Writing Comfort and Discomfort Frequency.

| Category | Number of Teachers |
|---|---|
| **Writing Comfort Total** | **4** |
| Could articulate planning for learners | 2 |
| Could not articulate planning for learners | 2 |
| **Writing Discomfort Total** | **15** |
| Could articulate planning for learners | 0 |
| Could not articulate planning for learners | 15 |
| **Total Number of Teachers** | **19** |

Fifteen teachers demonstrated in their stories that they were not comfortable with writing (see Table 2). Comments such as the following were common: "I had a lot of trouble with writing. I still have a lot of trouble with writing," "I don't really remember doing that much writing at school," and "I remember doing my first report in fourth grade. I copied the whole thing from an encyclopedia and got an A; that's awful!" None of these teachers could articulate planning for learners. "We don't do a lot of writing, just the alphabet and the letter of the week. We haven't written any stories," was representative of teachers who teach younger children. Representative of teachers who teach older children was, "I try to help them make it their own, that's all," and "I'm trying to move towards allowing my students to make mistakes in grammar and to use invented spelling. I'm not very allowing yet. I'm still working on it."

It is interesting to note that only one teacher in this study was comfortable with both reading and writing and could articulate planning for learners in both areas. Of equal interest only one teacher, the male, while not being comfortable with reading and not being able to articulate planning for learners' reading development, was comfortable with writing and could articulate planning for learners' writing development.

## Composite Profiles

Below are two composite profiles that represent the extremes of the discomfort-comfort continuum. Profile 1 includes semantics and tones that reflect a discomfort with reading and writing. When telling of planning for reading, note that the composite profile moves quickly through reading. The planning for writing consists almost entirely of an explanation of process writing. The second profile represents the teachers who show comfort with reading and writing and an ability to plan appropriate literacy experiences. This composite teacher's story profile is full of positive semantics and tones. The account of a personal writing life is less enthusiastic but shows engagement. The whole story establishes a positive tone. Throughout the account of reading and writing, there are stories of individual plans and individual learners' successes. This profile is rich in the interweaving of plans, stories, and projections.

### *Profile 1: Discomfort with Reading and Writing*

My parents read to me when I asked them to but they didn't force it on me. When I was little I loved my parents to take me to the library to get books. That did not seem to last past my third grade year. One of my earliest memories of reading was of the only kid in my first grade class who could read. He used to read to us. And then in 4th or 5th grade, we had to do read-a-thons. I read over 70 books but many were pretty easy. I got third or second prize. If I wasn't being rewarded I wouldn't really read. I am not as good at reading as I would like to be. In high school I didn't really read. Every once in a while I will read something that is not for classes. It can't bore me like the classics do; it has to be interesting like Stephen King or Danielle Steele. If I get bored then I put it down.

I think it would be appropriate for young adolescents to read Greek Mythology. I also like the classics for my students. I don't have them read the whole book at one time because that is too hard for kids that age to do. I let them share together their ideas and thoughts on the first quarter of the book.

I have never considered myself a writer. I don't enjoy writing as much as I should for being an English teacher. I don't really write for pleasure. I should get into writing more. I can't remember much about my writing in school. I remember my junior year; it was all on the grammar.

I want my students to do a lot of writing experiences and I give them a lot of opportunity for it. I get them into groups. We start out with book reports. Then they write their own book. They get into groups and do student newspapers. There is an editor, a sports writer, and a person to do the weather. I don't stress grammar. In all their writing they do the prewriting stage, the drafting stage, and proof each others papers. When they edit and proof, their grammar gets better. I think they are learning without realizing it.

### Profile 2: Comfort With Reading and Writing

My parents were voracious readers so there was always reading going on in the house. My parents got all kinds of magazines. We always did the library route. It was something that was always around me and I have always been a reader. One of my favorite reading memories is Sunday comics. My brother, my sister and I would get up on Sunday morning and we would lay in the family room and take turns reading the funnies. At the end of first grade my teacher had me read to the kindergarten class. I think that is when I really remember, I could read because I had an audience listening to me read. Now I read just about anything I can get my hands on, at all levels. I love reading children's books; I love reading adult books whether they are trash novels or historical novels. I read *Sports Illustrated* because it gives me one more thing I can talk about with my male students.

My first action is to expose my students to as much literature as I can, on all different levels, all different styles, and all different authors. I try to teach the kids to transport themselves into the book. Sometimes I read to them; sometimes they read to themselves or sometimes they read to some group. They need to read, read, read. Even magazines or comic books work; it is just a different medium for them to work with. Vocabulary is one area where I see that the students really have problems. We do all kinds of context work to "guess" meaning.

My own writing still needs work. Sometimes I tend to use these 25 cent words when I could use a nickel word get my point across better. I would like to put the words together in such a way that they sway people's thinking. I am not as good as I would like to be. I remember in 6th grade my having nothing to say about the topic assigned. That remained a problem. Finally, I went to one of my college instructors and she showed me how to keep a journal. I still keep a journal today. When I introduce journals to the kids, I hear moans and groans. I whip out my journals and show them.

The writing has to be there on a daily basis. When I start out at the beginning of the year I get two sentences. By the end of the year they really carry on in their dialogue journals. There are some weekends where all I do is the dialogue journals. The students' growth makes it worth it for me. I like being very descriptive. I model my descriptive writing so that my students can see how to be descriptive. When they write for an assignment, I write as well. This helps me know what some of their problem spots may be. I had a student last year who patterned her writing after a book by Laualene McDaniel. There were a lot of grammatical errors but the idea of the story was great and she had gotten that from reading. Then we did a reading-writing workshop. It was like a light bulb went on and everybody got something out of it.

In order to learn how to teach reading and writing better, I asked a professor what I could read. I taught myself how to do this. My reading of Reading and English journals is what has gotten me to this point and I just can't imagine teaching any other way.

## Implications

Research indicates that children need teachers who transmit a love of reading and writing (Buchanan, 1980; Cochrane et al., 1984). The reading and writing discomfort-comfort continuum resulting from this study indicates that teachers who say they read and write with ease, frequency and enthusiasm are more able to articulate plans for their learners to read and write. These teachers see themselves as readers and authors and thus say they are able to model and plan for and enthuse learners to read and write.

Profile 2 expresses how naturally a teacher who reads and writes addresses the teaching of reading and writing. This composite voice represents a rich personal and school background in literacy as well as knowledge about how to translate that experience for learners' literacy development. Conversely, Profile 1 represents a teacher who rarely chooses to read or write and who vaguely addresses planning for encouraging learners to read and write. This composite voice represents a paucity of personal and schooling background.

These profiles raise a number of questions for the teachers who are not comfortable with reading and writing, for teacher educators, and for literacy researchers. For example, can people who do not value reading and writing in their own personal lives teach others to do so? Consider a teacher who says, "I only read things I have to read." How can such a person explore enough children's reading to *plan appropriate reading experiences* that encourage literate behavior? A teacher who remembers doing ". . . a report in fourth grade. I copied the whole thing from an encyclopedia . . ." is poorly equipped to articulate planning for writing experiences. She states, "I try to help them make it their own, that's all." Can someone who does not have *a love of reading and writing* teach others to love reading and writing? "I never really felt good about myself as a reader. . . ." "I have never considered myself a writer. I don't enjoy writing. . . ." The big question remains, how can teachers with these *attitudes* positively influence children's attitudes about reading and writing?

Further, teacher educators, as well as preservice and practicing teachers, need to consider if it is even possible to teach a love of reading and writing to teachers who have established records of discomfort with reading and/or writing. If such schemata are possible to change in the framework of teacher education, how do we go about it? If discomfort schemata are not changeable, do we continue to graduate teachers who are not comfortable with reading and writing themselves and who are poorly equipped to articulate plans for literate behavior in their children?

Further research is needed about male teachers' literacy comfort stories. There was only one male informant in this study and his story was unique. He was the only one uncomfortable with reading and comfortable with writing, both personally and in planning for learners. This may be indicative that males have significantly different stories to tell.

Although all of these questions are possible areas for further research, perhaps a place to begin is with teachers' personal literacy stories. Perhaps uncovering stories of teachers who love to read and write and who are able to provide a variety of reading and writing opportunities for their learners can illuminate the literacy journey for teachers who are currently not comfortable with reading and writing. It may be that we can uncover a variety of ways that teachers can make the journey to literacy that can be incorporated into preservice and inservice teacher education.

## References

Anderson, R. C., Hieber, E. H., Scott, J. A., & Wildenson, I. A. G. (1985). *Becoming a nation of readers: The report of the Commission on Reading.* Washington, DC: The National Institute of Education.

Atwell, N. (1987). *In the middle: writing, reading, and learning with adolescents.* Portsmouth, NH: Heinemann.

Britzman, D. P. (1986). Cultural myths in the making of a teacher: Biography and social structure in teacher education. *Harvard Educational Review, 56,* 442-456.

Buchanan, E., ed. (1980). *For the love of reading.* Winnipeg: Whole Language Consultants, Ltd.

Chomsky, C. (1979). Approaching reading through invented spelling. In L. B. Resnick & P. A. Weaver (Eds.), *Theory and practice of early reading,* Vol. 2. Hillsdale, NJ: Erlbaum.

Clay, M. M. (1979). *Reading: The patterning of complex behavior (2nd ed.).* Auckland, New Zealand: Heinemann Educational Books.

Cochrane, O., Cochrane, D., Scalena, S., & Buchanan, E. (1984). *Reading, writing, and caring.* New York: Richard C. Owens.

Dexter, L. A. (1970). *Elite and specialized interviewing.* Evanston, Illinois: Northwestern University Press.

Duffy, G. (1991) What counts in teacher education? Dilemmas in educating empowered teachers. In J. Zutell & S. McCormick (Eds.), *Learner factors/teacher factors: Issues in literacy research and instruction* (pp. 1-18) Chicago: National Reading Conference.

Duffy, G. B., & Roehler, L. (1993). *Improving classroom reading instruction (3rd ed.)*. New York: McGraw-Hill.

Goodlad, J. L. (1984). *A place called school*. New York: McGraw-Hill.

Goodlad, J. L. (1990). *Teachers for our nations schools*. San Francisco: Jossey-Bass.

Goodman, Y. (1985). Kidwaching: Observing children in the classroom. In A. Jaggar & M. T. Smith-Burke (Eds.), *Observing the Language Learner* (pp. 9-18). Urbana, IL and Newark, DE: National Council of Teaching of English and International Reading Association.

Goodman, K. S. (1986). *What's whole in whole language?* Ontario: Scholastic-TAB.

Guba, E. (1978). *Toward a methodology of naturalistic inquiry in educational evaluation*. Los Angeles:Centerr for the Study of Evaluation Monograph Series.

Halliday, M. A. K. (1978). *Language as social semiotic*. Baltimore: University Park Press.

Harris, T. L. and Hodges, R. E. (Ed.) (1995). *The literacy dictionary: the vocabulary of reading and writing*. Newark, Delaware: International Reading Association.

Healy, J. (1984). *Endangered Minds*. Portsmouth, NH: Heinemann.

Johnson. R., & Hoffman, N. E. (1994). Preservice teachers' efficacy beliefs, literacy definitions, and conceptions of literacy development. In Sturtevant, E. G., & Linek, W. M. (Ed.). *Pathways for literacy: Learners teach and teachers learn*. The College Reading Association.

Kagan, D. (1992). Professional growth among presevice and beginning teachers. *Review of Educational Research, 62*(2), 129-169.

Lehr, F. & Osborn, J. (Eds.) (1994). *Reading, language, and literacy: Instruction for the twenty-first century*. Hillsdale, NJ: Erlbaum.

Merton, R. K., Fiske, M., & Kendal, P. L. (1956) *The focused interview*. New York: Free Press.

Meek, M. (1982). *Learning to Read*. London: The Bodley Head.

Morrow,. L. M., (Ed.) (1995). *Family literacy: Connections in schools and communities*. Newark, Delaware: International Reading Association.

Morrow,. L. M., Tracey, D. H., & Maxwell, C. M. (Eds.) (1995). *A survey of family literacy in the United States*. Newark, Delaware: Interanational Reading Association.

National Commission on Excellence in Education. (1983). *A Nation at Risk*. Washington, D.C.: U.S. Government Printing Office.

Neisser, U. (1976). *Cognition and reality: Principles and implications of cognitive psychology*. San Francisco: Freeman.

Norton, D. E. (1995). Through the eyes of a child: An introduction to children's literature (*4th ed.*). Englewood Cliffs, NJ: Merrill/Prentice Hall.

Rasinski, T. & Padak, N. (1996). *Holistic reading srtategies*. Columbus, Ohio: Merrill/Prentic Hall.

Rhodes, L., & Shanklin, N. (1993). *Windows into literacy*. Portsmouth, NH: Heinemann.

Reason, P., & Hawkins, P. (1988). Storytelling as inquiry. In P. Reason (Ed), *Human inquiry in action: Demelopments in new paradigm research,* pp. 79-101. Beverly Hills, CA: Sage.

Roehler, L. R. & Duffy, G.G. (1986). What makes one teacher a better explainer than another. *Journal of Education for Teaching, 37(3), pp. 273-284.*

Seidel, J. V., Kjolseth, R., Seymour, E. (1988). *The ethnograph version 3.0* [computer program]. Littleton, CO: Qualis Research Associates.

Shapiro, J. (1993). Affective concerns and reading. In T.V. Rasinski & N.D. Padak (Eds.),

*Inquires in literacy learning and instruction* (pp. 107-114). College Reading Association Yearbook.

Short, K. G. & Rierce, K. M. (Eds.). (1990). *Talking about books: Creating literate communities.* Portsmouth, NH: Heinemann.

Smith, F. (1993). *Understanding reading, 3rd ed.* New York: Holt.

Spradley, J. (1979). *The ethnographic interview.* New York: Holt.

*Standards for the English Language Arts.* (1996). Newark DE: Interanational Reading Association & Urbana, IL: National Council fo Teachers of English.

U.S. Department of Education's Office of Educational Research. (1996). *Family literacy: Directions in research and implications for practice.* Washington, D.C.: U.S. Government Printing Office.

Vygotsky, L. S. (1978). *Mind in society: The development of higher phychological processes.* Ed. Michael Cole, Vera John-Steiner, Sylvia Scribner, and Ellen Souberman. Cambridge, Mass.: Harvard University Press.

Weaver, C. (1988). *Reading process and practice: From socio-psycholinguistics to whole language.* Portsmouth, NH: Heinemann Educational Books.

Wuthrick, M. A. (1995). Case studies of teacher change from conventional to holistic literacy instruction. In W. M. Linek & E. G. Sturtevant (Eds.), *Generations of Literacy.* Harrisonburg, Virginia: College Reading Association.

# Living in the "Real World" of Instructional Change in Literacy: One Fourth Grade Teacher and Educational Reform

**A. Lee Williams**

Slippery Rock University

## Abstract

*This study describes the influences on a fourth-grade teacher's ongoing change process in literacy instruction after administrative purchase of a new literature-based reading series. The study also describes the change process after a perceived understanding by the teachers that the administration wished them to adopt tenets of whole language instruction. The research literature suggests that whole language instructional change is belief-driven and affected by regular district or administrative support. Even then, other factors including credible advice, collegial support, student success and curricular congruence were varyingly influential for this teacher as he experienced ongoing instructional change.*

Public clamor for school reform is ongoing (Bracey, 1994), and the school reading program is a popular arena for much reform discourse and energy. Whole language as a philosophical foundation for literacy instruction has been a primary source of both contentious and concurring research (ie., it both works and doesn't) and practice in recent years (Willis, 1995) in terms of reformers' notions of its ability to fundamentally (or not) improve how children learn to read and write in school.

Initially, classrooms reflecting a whole language philosophy of literacy learning were often created by individual teachers because of their beliefs about teaching and learning without support from their district or administration. Hence, whole language has been termed a "grassroots movement" (Goodman, 1992; Martin, 1991). Teachers' belief in the philosophic underpinnings of whole language has been cited as a primary attribute of successful whole language instruction and corresponding changes in instruction (Weaver, 1992). However, as school administrators understand the possibilities of whole language for increasing students' reading success in school, districts have increasingly called on teachers to adopt this philosophy or components of this approach as the school sanctioned method for teaching reading (Kraus, 1992). Basal reading programs consisting of children's literature selections are often adopted by schools to encourage whole language instruction (Vacca, Vacca & Gove, 1995) although the teachers in such schools may not see a need to change their literacy instructional methods. Literature-based literacy teaching does not necessarily translate directly to whole language teaching (Hiebert & Colt, 1989).

Moving toward whole language by dictum rather than by choice sets up some fundamental difficulties for teachers. Whole language is a philosophy about how literacy is acquired and about the values and beliefs associated with literacy in society. It is not a methodology that can easily be adopted (Hoffman, 1992); rather it is a way of seeing the world and being in it. A philosophy is more useful as a guide for choosing why and how to use activities than as a recipe for teaching. District adoption of a basal reading program based on authentic children's literature selections does not necessarily mean that teachers will understand or hold a whole language philosophy for literacy instruction. Thus, a packaged whole language or literature-based reading program is like an oxymoron. Whole language may be difficult for teachers to implement if they do not share the underlying rationale of the whole language philosophy. Such teachers may find little reason to change years of practices they consider worthwhile and beneficial to student learning.

With all the conflicting demands for reform made on schools and especially on the literacy curriculum, how do teachers make choices about their role in literacy instruction? Can teachers change in response to administrative decree, or are teachers' practices immutable over time? What must administrators and educators responsible for preservice or inservice teacher education, including teachers themselves, understand in order to appropriately support individuals who are asked to or are interested in changing instructional practice within institutions?

## Purpose of the Study

I undertook the present study to understand what sustained the change efforts of an elementary school classroom teacher as he worked to define a new sense of the meaning of learning to read and write in school after his school district had adopted a new literature-based reading series and administrators had asked teachers to adopt a more holistic approach to reading and writing instruction. I investigated how initial motivation might change over time, as the teacher lived with instructional innovation for three years.

This study was not designed to examine the instructional effectiveness of a particular group of teaching practices, so it does not inform educators hoping to judge the efficacy of literature-based reading instruction or whole language. As a descriptive study, the results are generalizable to other teachers only in a heuristic sense, especially given that the perspective of this study is one of many possible and thus reconstructs a partial reality of the teacher's experiences. The researcher also recognizes that this teacher's experience may have been impacted by participating in the research process.

## The Teacher and the District

The elementary school in this study is located in a small mid-western town, part of a rural school district with a population of 17,000 within a 130 square mile area. This school is attended by 424 children in grades K-5. Thirty-five percent receive free or reduced lunch. Fewer than two percent of the students are children of color. The teacher, Mr. Green, has taught for 16 years in the district, and for 10 as a fourth grade teacher in this school.

The school district initiated a change toward holistic literacy instruction with the purchase of new literature anthologies, classroom literature sets, and the removal of workbooks from classrooms. The district provided two district-level one-day inservice programs and encouraged teachers to attend outside conferences or workshops, but did not provide the type of on-going support that has been identified as an important factor in successful change (Joyce & Showers, 1980).

## Data Collection and Analysis

As part of a larger study, the data for this investigation was gathered over a three-year period as I acted as a participant-observer weekly in the teacher's fourth-grade classroom. I interviewed Mr. Green formally at the beginning and ending of each school year, and informally during reading and writing workshops in my role as participant observer. I also interviewed administrators and students and shared insights from my observations and in-progress analyses of all interviews with Mr. Green. I began to form tentative hypotheses, and to organize and analyze data using the constant-comparison method (Strauss & Corbin, 1990). My data analysis involved coding data conceptually and then comparing each coded data section with others to determine patterns and to look for negative examples. The data from the teacher's comments about on-going analysis formed a further data source and a member check of preliminary data categories. In all, fifteen complete tape recorded interviews and sections of other interviews and tape recorded classroom observations were transcribed, coded, and analyzed.

## Influences on Instructional Change in Literacy Toward Whole Language

Four patterns of influence on Green's willingness to begin and to continue changed literacy instruction emerged: credible expert advice, support from colleagues, the responses of students to changed instruction and the district's existing course of study for reading and language arts.

### Credible Expert Advice

Mr. Green believed that, although advice concerning optimum literacy teaching was abundant, not all of it was equally useful or valid. The district-sponsored inservice workshops, led by a representative of the basal publisher, seemed to him to be a sales pitch to buy the accompanying workbooks and spelling program, a step backwards from the literature-focused literacy instruction he was trying to understand.

> The district inservice didn't mean a whole lot to anybody . . . no one was comforted because she [the company representative] talked about the journal, and we don't have that. And a spelling program, and a student journal that is like a workbook that we don't have. . . . But there is a feeling you could get bogged down with that. They're basalizing the literature, and that just takes so much away from it.

An inservice by a professor from a large state university was equally disappointing to Green.

> [He] talked about how you should set your classroom up, class size, and generally telling us how education should be when you know they've got auditoriums with hundreds of people sitting in them. They aren't practicing what they preach.

However, a two-day workshop featuring Carol Avery that Mr. Green attended on his own gave him a strong sense of the viability of literature based instruction and writing process instruction and how they might work in his classroom. He went to workshops featuring Avery twice in two years.

> She exposed me to the idea that it's okay to love reading, to do this in front of your kids, that you are a professional. You can justify what you do in a different way than a workbook page or a standardized test score.

Green found Avery credible because she had actually taught, because she had real classroom experience with the ideas she promulgated. He wanted to try what she suggested even though he was unsure how her suggestions fit into his existing beliefs about literacy instruction.

> I came back from those days with Carol Avery pumped up. She just sold me. I'm not sure I believe in everything I try to start with, but if

someone who has her experience says to me, "this is what I've seen, this is what works," even though it may be questionable to me, I think we need to try it.

### Support From Colleagues

As Green lived with literature-based reading instruction and experimented with writing workshop (an Avery suggestion), he found that he kept some of her ideas and suggestions, but that he learned to trust his own instincts. As Green first moved his practice toward whole language, he felt he needed to use every technique he learned from Avery. He chose activities more carefully as he gained experience with changed literacy instruction. In a particular lesson on using context to determine word meaning Green said,

"I've worked that lesson into everything we read . . . before I was going through a learning process . . ."

Green also changed from picturing his class in terms of his understanding of Avery's class to sharing questions and successes with his fellow fourth grade teachers. Their support seemed especially important since many teachers in the building did not share his sense of the need to change literacy instruction.

Negative comments [in the lounge] made me really evaluate what I'm doing. Is this going to hurt the kids? I really examined what I was doing. With the other fourth grade teachers there is a rapport that is really enjoyable. We have gotten comfortable sharing with each other. It isn't competitive, that we want to do better than the others, but to help each other do better and to make it. If somebody has something good we share it. This is good; this works. Working with other people causes you to reassess what you're doing . . . I . . . watch and see what I can use in my room.

### Responses of Children to Changed Instruction

Green found that students' positive responses to his changed instruction and the increase in their proficiency in reading and writing for meaning gave him the energy he needed to sustain the uncertainty that accompanied change. His focused shifted from "are students really learning?" to "how can I help them learn?" While at first he assigned worksheets "to make sure they were learning," by his third year with the new reading program he stated,

"I don't need the worksheet to evaluate that they're learning. I choose worksheets carefully now, ones to help students gain an understanding of the process that goes into [the answer]."

Additionally, he began his third year by immediately reading aloud to the class supplementary high interest books by favorite authors like Gary Paulsen.

"I didn't used to get into reading orally to the children as early as I do now. Paulsen's books motivated a group of boys who didn't particularly care to read to where they are choosing his books on their own."

Green saw that children chose to pursue independent reading after he read aloud in class; however, he was disheartened that every fall he had to start anew selling students on reading and writing, as other teachers did not encourage self-selected reading or writing for self-expression.

"It's frustrating; I want to get started, to get the kids comfortable . . . the longer they do it, the more at ease they're going to be. Or else they never understand it; they never see the purpose."

Green's past experiences helped him stick with his goals for students to read and write for meaning since

"I remember the better work I've seen from past years."

Green noted that previously the students completed worksheets correctly but could not use the skills in actual writing

"for most of them, worksheets and writing are two separate things."

However, the students' abilities to demonstrate mastery of punctuation skills in actual writing motivated him to continue his attempts to have students write every day for

"bigger projects, lengthier things. It's more difficult, but I'm more comfortable with it than I was a couple of years ago. A few years ago, when I started, I was comfortable with giving students only the basic requirements. Now I have requirements, but they are open-ended and involve choices."

Thus, he continued to refine his literacy instruction.

### *The School District's Planned Course of Study in Reading and Writing*

Green was troubled that the district and the teachers never rewrote the planned course of study for reading and language arts when the new textbooks were purchased. Thus, the curriculum as written remained focused on the separate phonics-only textbook and the typical scope and sequence basal published in 1963 that the district had previously used.

Other teachers question this, "Why don't you use worksheets?" I don't do the things that are typically done, and if change is what the administration really wants us to do, it would be a lot more comforting to be able to say, "Yes, it is different, but that's the way it's written in the curriculum. This is the way it is supposed to be done."

Some of the other teachers, according to Green, interpreted the unchanged curriculum to mean that using the old books and the old phonics program was appropriate.

"If it's not written in the curriculum, it makes others say, 'Then why are you telling us to do it that way?'"

Talk in the teachers' lounge, according to Green, centered on the district's previous success with phonics-based reading instruction and the purported failures of literature-based reading in other districts. Additionally, Green reported that the teachers used the older curriculum as justification for not changing their practice. However, Green reported his own experiences with his changing instruction as positive. He dismissed the idea that he would revert to his previous way of teaching, no matter what future course the district might take.

> I don't think I could go back to the way I did things before. Kids enjoy reading so much now. It's not a task, but enjoyment for them. If you can make someone a lifelong reader, that's so much more meaningful than sounding words out. We are moving away from recalling so many literal facts to getting into the personality of the characters, evaluating opinions and feelings. Writing is no longer just getting out a correct sentence in as few words as possible, doing the least the teacher will accept, but really expressing thoughts and ideas.

## Conclusions and Implications

Reform in education seems elusive because change must correspond to teachers' belief systems, change must be supported by extensive, on-going inservice, and change must come from teachers to be successful, not from administrative dictum. However, with little explicit district support, Mr. Green was able to change his literacy instruction. A classroom that had almost no writing instruction, a separate phonics program and a traditional basal reader became a classroom focused on extended project-based writing, writing workshop and reading instruction with a literature anthology and self-selected children's literature.

### *Using Inservice Wisely: Experts Who Help Teachers Suspend Initial Disbelief*

While the district did not provide satisfactory inservice, according to Green, the two workshops on whole language he attended were beneficial because the advice was credible. Even if he did not fully believe Avery, she "sold him" on the possibilities of her approach. I remember from my undergraduate studies that Samuel Taylor Coleridge suggested that good literature encourages the reader's willing suspension of disbelief. It was Avery's stories of her success that allowed Green to suspend his initial disbelief. Avery gave Green both concrete suggestions and cheerleading so that he went back to his classroom with a renewed sense of his professional ability to make wise choices about instruction and with ways to imagine himself teaching and evaluating reading and writing without worksheets. Providing teachers with the means to see themselves and their students in new roles and showing them how others have made these new roles work makes advice acceptable and credible for teachers. Thus, it seems that we need to examine both preservice and inservice teaching. Do college professors and consultants provide the kinds of details and the necessary information that will help our students "see" themselves successfully doing what we describe in our classrooms? Have we encouraged the willing suspension of disbelief?

### *Realistic Timeframes for Change:*
### *Understanding the Slowness of the Change Process*

Additionally, Green moved slowly through the change process. He kept Avery as an image of what could be possible until he could substitute his own successful teaching memories to support him as he planned instruction. Student success was essential to Green's willingness to continue instructional change. As he saw that his new teaching strategies worked, he focused his teaching energy less on how he was doing and more on encouraging his students to read and write for meaning. Seeing student success motivated Green so that he found it difficult to imagine going back to his former way of teaching, a sign that his instructional change was deeply rooted. Teachers who try literature-based reading or writing workshops and do not experience student success are probably bound to dismiss them. Encouraging teachers to start slowly and to work through uncertainty until instructional change and student success are linked is vital. Ensuring that teachers have strategies for dealing with the messiness of new practice and have other strategies for adapting it as they become proficient helps ensure they will stay with an innovation long enough to see if it is truly useful for student learning.

### *The Importance of Collegial Support for Changed Practice*

Green depended on his colleagues as important advocates with him for good teaching. Without criticism, they shared, talked, watched each other, and learned together about what helped the children become literate. Theirs was not a mentor/mentee relationship, but rather one of equals, reflecting together on how to make teaching and learning work. A mindset of reflection, experimentation, and creation of an atmosphere that enabled sharing among peers supported Green's growth as a reading and writing teacher. It seems important, then, to encourage teachers to seek each other out in a spirit of collaboration and to help teachers develop a spirit of inquiry regarding their practice. Such collegial support was essential to Green when listening to other colleagues' attempts to dismiss his change efforts as less effective when compared with their established practices. Evidence of children's progress as readers/writers and grade four collegial support helped Green through criticism with a determination to continue struggling with the uncertainty of change.

### *Reflecting on Children's Progress to Inform Instruction*

Both Green and his colleagues measured their success as literacy teachers with the response of the children in their classrooms and their own changed sense of what it meant to be literate. This ability to think past the status quo, envision new definitions of literacy, and risk employing new instructional techniques, seems to be necessary for lasting change. Mr. Green and the teachers who criticized him held different definitions of success in reading. He moved from just expecting students to have the skills of reading to wanting them to love reading and to write to express important ideas.

### *The Importance of Supporting a New Curriculum With a New Planned Course of Study*

The curriculum document in schools is often relegated to a dusty shelf in the principal's office. However, Green attributed to it symbolic value as potential vindication for his change efforts in the face of resistance to change among other teachers in the building. He wondered, did the administration want the teachers to fundamentally change or not? The unspoken tension between the old curriculum that supported systematic phonics instruction separate from reading, low level skill/drill in reading and writing instruction, and his own efforts to grow as a reading and writing teacher, disturbed Green. The negative talk about the new reading series in the teachers lounge coupled with the administration's lack of explicit support in the form of an appropriate curriculum document was a strong counterbalance to the positive change Green believed he made with his students. Over time, as Green became more sure of how the instructional changes he made impacted positively on students, he perceived the unchanged curriculum document as an unspoken acceptance of teachers who did not change. It seems unlikely that the administration wished to create such tension among teachers, dividing them into the "changers" and the "stay-the-sames." Each group found support for their efforts—one group by the books in use and the other by the curriculum. Such divisiveness is counterproductive to the school's educational mission, and teachers and administrators would be wise to examine the goals and objectives of the planned course of study when the literacy program is changed.

## Revising Our Understanding of Meaningful Change in Literacy Instruction

Perhaps there is some good news about the efficacy of teachers' unsupported change efforts. While educational reform on the whole is not viewed as successful by the public, the press, or educators themselves, teachers do indeed attempt to change their practice with and without institutional support. The difficult-to-attain ideal conditions for change are well documented; however, this study shows that other-than-ideal conditions can still support change.

Further studies that explore teachers who change instructional practice with little or no administrative support could lend further insight into the influence of expert advice, collegial support and student response to change. Additionally, the role of administrative decree and teacher change and the corresponding sense teachers have of their expected response needs to be more fully explored. If research can help determine best practice in literacy instruction, yet teachers learn to ignore administrative efforts to institute these research-based instructional choices because imposed reform efforts come with mixed messages, it will be difficult or impossible to improve the literacy education in our schools. Teachers are the key link between educational research and the educational reform that most believe is necessary for the success of students in our schools. Thus, understanding teachers' responses to change is essential.

---

# References

Bracey, G. W. (1994). The fourth Bracey Report on the condition of public education. *Phi Delta Kappan, 76* (2), 115-127.

Cuban, L. (1992). Curriculum stability and change. In P. W. Jackson ( Ed.), *Handbook of research on curriculum* (pp. 216-247). New York: Macmillan.

Goodman, K. (1992). Whole language is today's agenda. *Language Arts, 69,* 354-363.

Hiebert, E. H., & Colt, J. (1989). Patterns of literature-based reading instruction. *The Reading Teacher, 43,* 14-20.

Hoffman, J. (1992). Am I whole yet? Are you? *Language Arts, 69,* 366-371.

Joyce, B., & Showers, B. (1980). Improving inservice training: The message of research. *Educational Leadership, 37,* 379-385.

Kraus, C. (1992). Changes in primary teachers' instructional practices after year 1 of a collaborative whole language project. In N. Padak, T. Rasinski, & J. Logan, (Eds.), *Literacy research and practice: Foundations for the year 2000* (pp. 50-67). Fourteenth yearbook of the College Reading Association. Provo, UT: College Reading Association.

Martin, R. (1991). *Empowering teachers to break the basal habit.* (ERIC Educational Document Reproduction Service No. ED 334 568)

Strauss, A. L., & Corbin, J. (1990). *Basis of qualitative research: Grounded theory procedures and techniques.* Newbury, CA: Sage.

Tyak, D., & Tobin, W. (1994). The "grammar" of schooling" Why has it been so hard to change? *American Educational Research Journal, 31,* 453-479.

Vacca, R. L., Vacca, J. L., & Gove, M. (1995). *Reading and learning to read.* (3rd ed.). New York: HarperCollins.

Weaver, C. (1992). A whole language belief system and its implications for teacher and institutional change. In C. Weaver & L. Henke (Eds.), *Supporting whole language: Stories of teacher and institutional change* (pp. 3-23). Portsmouth, NH: Heinemann.

Willis, S. (1995, Fall).Whole language: Finding the surest way to literacy. *ASCD Curriculum Update,* p. 1.

# TEACHER EDUCATION AND LITERACY

# CONCEPTUAL CHANGES: PRESERVICE TEACHERS' PATHWAYS TO PROVIDING LITERACY INSTRUCTION

**Victoria J. Risko**
**Jeanne Ann Peter**
**Dena McAllister**
Vanderbilt University

## Abstract

*This study was designed to trace how preservice teachers develop and use their knowledge of literacy instruction to guide their instruction of diverse learners. Descriptive case studies of these preservice teachers are presented to discuss how teachers develop and change their conceptions of literacy instruction. Implications for using video-based case methodology and its effect on the learning of future teachers also are presented.*

During the last decade, teacher education scholars (Merseth, 1991; Shulman, L. 1995) have argued that teacher preparation programs often fail to prepare future teachers to use information presented in college classes in their own teaching. They suggest that future teachers often view theory and pedagogical principles learned in college classes as far removed from classroom dilemmas they will face in their careers. Unfortunately, theory and pedagogical content are sometimes taught in lecture-based formats that are decontextualized and that require little or no application to instructional practice. Such instruction can oversimplify complex information and inhibit future teachers' ability to respond to real world, complex problems.

Several teacher educators have investigated the design and use of cases as one instructional method for helping future and practicing teachers apply theory and research to the interpretation of complex teaching situations. These cases, written in a narrative form, describe realities of classroom events and invite reflection (Kleinfeld, 1995; Merseth, 1991; Shulman, J., 1995; Silverman

& Welty, 1995). They also are designed to provide an indepth study of teaching issues and build problem-based learning.

At Vanderbilt University, we have been interested in the potential benefits of case methodology for instruction in our preservice reading methodology courses for several years. Prior to beginning our case project, we observed that students made good progress gaining an understanding of literacy development and procedures for implementing instruction. It seemed they were developing knowledge about "how to do things," but not an ability to determine "when or why things should be done." When we observed our preservice teachers in teaching situations, we noticed that they were inflexible when trying to respond to problems they encountered, seemed unable to adapt instruction when necessary, and seemed to have a limited repertoire of alternate strategies for times when instruction didn't go as expected. We also learned that our students entered our courses with naive concepts about teaching and children and that these conceptions were difficult to change.

We subsequently developed a set of cases and have been examining their effects on our preservice teachers' learning (Risko & Kinzer, 1991). Our cases are produced on videodiscs with the scenes accessed by menu-driven computer software. As we have discussed in previous papers (see, for example, Risko, 1995), we have produced 8 cases that contain various forms of naturally occurring classroom situations that demonstrate multiple layers of activities (e.g., teacher-student interactions, peer tutoring, teacher and peer questioning, student participation in various reading and writing activities) that are associated with the complexities embedded in reading instruction. These video cases were recorded in grades 2, 4, 6, resource, and Chapter 1 classrooms in elementary schools. Each case focuses on one classroom and presents the daily happenings across a unit of instruction. The units were developed by the respective classroom teacher around conceptual themes or identified instructional goals. The classrooms are located in urban, suburban, or rural settings and involve children of different SES levels and cultural backgrounds.

Each case is one-hour in length and begins with a connected video story about the teacher, students, classroom organization, and instruction. The remainder of the video material contains supplementary classroom scenes, student-teacher conferences, and interviews with parents, teachers, principals, and commentators who provide their perspectives on the literacy instruction. Four cases display classroom reading instruction and are used in our developmental reading methodology course. The other four cases focus on literacy instruction (within classrooms and pull-out programs) for diverse learners and are used within our remedial reading methodology course. These cases are supplemented by related text readings and case information (e.g., teachers' lesson plans, children's writing, and assessment protocols) in our college classes to provide our students with a comprehensive set of information.

Our cases are designed to situate preservice teachers' learning in realistic problem-solving experiences. Our students study the literacy instruction that occurs within the classrooms highlighted by the cases. They analyze the teachers' decision-making, choice of materials and curriculum goals, and the students' literacy abilities and problems. They are involved in rich discussions and cooperative learning activities within our college classrooms as they draw on multiple resources to understand and respond to the teaching dilemmas embedded in the cases. The videodisc cases are open-ended as the problems are not identified by the narrator and they are not resolved. The cases are sufficiently complex to allow for sustained problem solving over multiple episodes. Students are encouraged to examine the case information from multiple perspectives which allows them to form methods for applying their newly acquired knowledge in flexible and appropriate ways. Asking students to think of alternative solutions for the case problems helps their expectations move beyond a "one right answer" approach to problem solving.

In previous papers we have reported on various phases of a research program designed to examine the effectiveness of our case methodology. In a few studies, we examined the effect of our cases on classroom discourse (e.g., Risko, 1992; Risko, Yount, & McAllister, 1992). Some studies helped us reflect on the design of our cases (Risko, 1992); while others have guided our thinking about the effects of these cases on our students' ability to apply what they were learning to their own teaching (Risko, McAllister, Peter, & Bigenho, 1994; Risko, 1995). Overall, our former work suggests that our case methodology enhances the quality of discussions in our college classes. Additionally, we have observed substantial progress in our preservice teachers' ability to analyze classroom problems from multiple perspectives and to draw on multiple sources of information to respond to instructional problems they identify within our video cases.

## Purpose of the Study

The current study was designed to extend our previous investigations by tracing systematically how our preservice teachers acquire new knowledge about literacy instruction and how they use this knowledge to guide their instructional decisions in a practicum setting. For this study, we focused on three preservice teachers enrolled in the remedial reading methodology course in which our videodisc-based cases were implemented. We describe how these teachers developed and changed their conceptions of literacy instruction for diverse learners and we identify and interpret factors that may have contributed to this development.

# Methodology

Qualitative research methods were used to develop descriptive case studies for each of the three preservice teachers in the study. Two criteria guided our participant selection. Mario, Elizabeth, and Tammy (all fictional names) were typical *and* their selection represents maximum variation sampling (Lincoln & Guba, 1985). That is, we selected three participants, who while typical on several dimensions were different in background and experiences. This provided us with a sample that represented a broad range of information about each participant. The three participants were typical of students in undergraduate education programs in that they were all undergraduates working toward teacher certification. These participants also were representative of the range of majors enrolled in the course and the number of previous practicum experiences the students had prior to the course. All students previously or concurrently completed a developmental reading and language arts methodology course and an accompanying practicum. Other factors differentiated these three participants, as we describe in the following section.

## *Participants*

Mario, an African-American senior, was experiencing his first semester of education courses. He was enrolled during the same semester in both the language arts and developmental reading methods courses. His major was human growth and development and he stated that his career goals were "teaching, coaching and counseling." Mario was very talkative in class and his comments during class often inspired rich discussion. He was inquisitive and often asked for advice from the instructors or practicum supervisors. Occasionally, Mario struggled to make it to the class or the practicum on time because he had an unreliable car which he could not afford to have repaired. He was a football player and was often away on weekends. At times he seemed burdened by the demands of college life, yet he told us that he wanted to do well in his tutoring for the sake of his practicum student.

Elizabeth, a European-American senior majoring in elementary education, had completed two practica prior to entering the course and was planning to student teach the following semester. On the course information card, Elizabeth stated that she hoped the course would help her "become a better problem-solver for students having reading difficulties" and said her career goal was to "become an effective K-4 teacher." Elizabeth seemed to be a very focused, conscientious student, whose questions, comments, and participation in class were always measured and serious. She talked about her inexperience with remedial readers upon entering the course and she often asked for clarification of a comment or something she had read. She planned her activities carefully on a schedule and wanted everything to be clear and concise.

Tammy, also a European-American female senior, had a double major in special education and elementary education. She entered the course with experience in five practica. She had two part-time jobs during the evenings and weekends and she was frequently tired during class. Journal entries revealed that she perceived herself to be different from most other people in her courses because she went to a high school that was not highly acclaimed and she made average grades and scores on standardized test. She seldom spoke out in whole group discussions and noted in her journal that she felt more comfortable in small groups because people didn't "look at you like you were stupid when you made a comment." However, within one-on-one situations with the instructor or her practicum student, Tammy was vivacious, comfortable, and relaxed.

### *Setting*

The remedial reading methodology course is structured so that preservice teachers are in a university setting for the first half of the semester. Class sessions are devoted to the analysis of the videodisc cases and discussion of related content. During the semester under study, the preservice teachers analyzed videodisc cases focusing on three different children: Tericka, Emily, and Crystal. Hereafter these cases will be referred to by the children's names. After seven weeks in the college class, the preservice teachers were assigned to a practicum setting in a local elementary school. For the last seven weeks of the course, they developed and implemented literacy lessons for students experiencing reading problems.

### *Data source*

The data were collected from individual interviews, pre-and post-test data, journals, transcripts of class dialogue, lesson plans and evaluations, and case reports.

**Interviews.** Interviews were conducted three times throughout the semester: at the beginning of the course in August; in October prior to going out into the school to teach; at the end of the course in December. These 15-30 minute interviews were conducted by either the instructor or practicum supervisor. Prior to the interview, students were provided with questions to guide their reflections.

**Pre-post tests**. Pre-and post-tests were created using videocases. The preservice teachers were asked to view two different but matched cases and answer questions about the instruction observed.

**Journals**. The preservice teachers began keeping dialogue journals on the first day of class and continued until they began their teaching. Instructors read and responded to journals approximately every two weeks. Students responded to both assigned questions and other issues raised by students or the instructor.

**Class discourse**. The practicum supervisor began meeting with the class on the first day in order to familiarize herself with the students, course content, and expectations. In addition, the supervisor took extensive notes throughout the class sessions, documenting as much of the discourse as possible.

**Lesson plans and evaluations**. The preservice teachers were required to submit a lesson plan and self-evaluation each week during the tutoring.

**Case reports**. The final assignment for each preservice teacher was a case report on the student they had tutored. These reports included information concerning home background, interests and any information learned in an informal interview with the student; assessment information; instructional goals for the student; methods used that either worked well or did not work well; materials used in teaching; and any recommendations that the tutor might have for the classroom teacher or parents.

### Data Analysis

We conducted a multiple case study because of the potential, through cross-case analysis, for generating greater explanation of the findings in the study. The constant comparative method (Bogdan & Bilken, 1982) and cross-case pattern analysis were used.

We followed two stages of data analysis. First, each of us analyzed the data from each individual case study. We examined carefully the transcriptions, observational notes, and all written documents. Coding was used to categorize similar events and behaviors. Sections of the data that appeared to be similar were studied in relation to the context where we collected the data to determine a range of meanings that could be assigned to the data. Second, we completed a crosscase analysis to identify shared patterns and to develop our interpretations and explanations. Hypotheses were developed, changed, and abandoned throughout our process. Additional data continued to be examined and compared to previous data throughout our process until we were able to conclude that sufficient data were examined to answer our research questions. Triangulation was used to establish credibility of the data analysis (Bogdan & Bilken, 1982; Lincoln & Guba, 1985).

## Findings

We identified four main phases for the learning of the preservice teachers. These phases are presented in a sequential order representing how our students progressed throughout the semester. Phase 1, "undimensional conceptions," identifies as the point when students began the course. Phase 2, "conceptual changes," characterizes a shift in the preservice teacher's perspectives that allowed a wider range of theory and practice to influence their thinking. Phase 3, "problem identification," depicts the learning that occurred when the preservice teachers entered a practicum teaching experience and were forced to reconsider the information they learned in the college course. Phase 4, "problem resolution," describes the preservice teachers' progress with solving their teaching problems. Sample preservice teacher comments will be used throughout this section. We note that all three progressed through these stages within a similar time frame and shared global characteristics that allowed us to make some generalizations and observations. However, each preservice teacher's experience and performance across these phases was qualitatively different and we do not rule out the possibility that preservice teachers would move though these stages at different rates.

### Phase 1: "Undimensional Conceptions"

The preservice teachers entered the course with different experiential backgrounds yet they shared a similar perspective concerning the focus of literacy instruction. All three students indicated that meaning was the key to reading and writing. They verbalized their initial beliefs in the following manner:

> "The meaning behind the print should be emphasized during literacy lessons for poor readers." (Elizabeth, interview 1)

> ". . . students being able to gather meaning from what is read." (Tammy, interview 1)

> "I would proceed to teach the child with a holistic approach—stressing comprehension and clarity of what s/he reads or writes." (Mario, interview 1)

This shared emphasis on meaning was also apparent in the preservice teachers' analysis of the pretest case study. Mario tried to connect ideas about remedial readers to his ideas about whole language, a concept that he was studying in the language arts and developmental reading methodology block. This influenced his reaction to the case student, Tericka, and her instruction. He reacted more positively toward the Chapter 1 teacher's approach (which was more holistic) than he did to the regular classroom teacher, whom he said emphasized word recognition. Elizabeth and Tammy also interpreted the Chapter 1 teacher's methodology as more focused on communication and meaning, which they supported. Elizabeth wrote that the Chapter 1 teacher "seems to be more interested in the ideas communicated" than the regular teacher who "seems to think of reading as correctly naming the words on the page rather than the ideas behind them." Tammy agreed that meaning is more important than reading all the words correctly, and explained that the Chapter 1 teacher "wants their reading to have meaning and show them that it is not a rote process."

Although all three students were able to clearly define their perspective concerning literacy instruction, it was more difficult for them to identify the difficulties that the case student (Tericka) was experiencing and more difficult still for them to make recommendations for future instruction. Elizabeth and Tammy thought that Tericka "reads the words but does not really know what they are saying." Mario had trouble identifying a reading problem for Tericka. In trying to describe instructional recommendations that would help Tericka, Elizabeth noted "I don't know of a strategy but more encouragement. I would try to get her (Tericka) to attach her own meaning to a story, would free her not to read for correctness or fear of failing, but for enjoyment and understanding of the meaning." Tammy also had very global notions about instruction and stated "I know how to get started but what am I to do after the interview [with my student]?"

These three preservice teachers shared a comparable focus on meaning as the key to literacy development but had only inexperienced, global notions of how to evaluate, plan, and provide instruction for children experiencing reading difficulties. Instruction, however, was an important issue for them and they began the course with particular lenses that guided their goals and thinking about instruction. These lenses, however, were narrowly conceived, as we describe below. These lenses became apparent from the very first class and continued to influence their thinking about materials, students, and instruction throughout the course.

Elizabeth said in her first interview that learning about strategies for instruction was her goal because "it is the key to effective teaching." During class discussions of each case, she consistently asked others for advice in this area. For example, during a small group session in which students were reacting to a set of readings, Elizabeth asked a more experienced peer for strategies to teach poetry. Prior to the last class session before the practicum began, the preservice teachers were asked to write questions or topics on notecards that they wanted addressed in the last class. Elizabeth suggested that class members brainstorm every instructional strategy that they could think of so they would have a comprehensive list prior to beginning their tutoring. She seemed to filter all class experiences through this search for effective methods or strategies and how they should be used in instruction.

During the course, Tammy relied heavily on her previous experiences as a learner or a teacher. She seemed to measure experiences based on her feelings of whether something was enjoyable for her and whether or not it would be enjoyable for a child in a classroom. As mentioned in the earlier description of Tammy, she was very conscious of her social role in the college classroom and of the perceptions that others might have of her. She seemed to feel insecure in asking for help in front of others or even participating in a larger group because of preconceived reactions to her comments by her peers. However, she had a great deal of experience in a variety of teaching situations and when she did participate in class, it was in order to share an experience she had in her teaching or that she had experienced as a student. Most often, these comments illustrated her concern for students' comfort level and enjoyment. For example, when a peer asked the question in class, "what do you do with an older non-reader?" Tammy volunteered that she tried a lot of repeated readings so the student felt good about his reading. On another occasion, when watching Tericka engaged in a reading group she noted that "if it were me, I would not want to read in front of anyone either." This viewpoint continued to be prominent during class discussions.

Mario's approach to children experiencing reading difficulties centered on learning more about the child's background (personal experience, school background and scores, and instruction received by the child). His perspective seemed focused on this information in order to provide an instructional situation in which a child could feel comfortable. He explained that examining school files was important because they tell about family and race. In his reaction to Tericka, Mario commented about her violent home environment (the neighborhood) and her supportive mother. He remained sensitive to children's background and children's feelings throughout the course.

In summary, the prospective teachers' naive conceptions of literacy development for diverse learners guided their initial thinking about the first case that we explored in class. Their limited knowledge of the subject contributed to their one-dimensional view of the content.

### *Phase 2: Conceptual Changes (Adopting More Perspectives)*

A few weeks into the course, the students began reading articles as they continued to examine case content. It was at this point that we began to notice the preservice teachers' initial focus on meaning and the shift of individual lenses, (described above), as they recognized that connections needed to be made across students, materials, and instructional methods. Their comments showed a broader awareness of the multiple factors related to an instructional situation as they encountered the rich case examples. As they progressed through the course, the preservice teachers viewed two additional video cases. One case focused on a second grade student, Crystal, who was described by her teacher as a "non-reader," and the other on Emily, another second grade student described as "struggling in her regular classroom." The following comments illustrate the range of factors that our prospective teachers began to notice as they continued their readings and class discussions, and as they watched the instruction of these children on the videodiscs.

Tammy stated,

> with Crystal, I believe the repeated readings will help her a lot in connecting words to print. She seemed to have a good vocabulary but never really connected what was spoken to the written word. . . . While Crystal

was a non-reader starting at the beginning, Emily was impressive. This child has a bigger vocabulary than I do and I wonder why she could not read well since she has such knowledge. . . . Helping Emily with strategies for comprehension was what was needed and they worked. I like the way the semantic web helped to trigger her background knowledge and build her vocabulary some more." (Tammy, journal)

Mario stated,

I felt the teacher handled [Crystal] very well. He worked on her sight words, vocabulary, and reading fluency simultaneously. When she made mistakes he would ask her if it made sense. She would then go back and check. This teaches her self-monitoring and comprehension skills. When she continually missed a word, he had her write meaningful sentences with the words' proper use and context. I felt the techniques he used were both appropriate and effective. (Mario, journal)

The preservice teachers' involvement in the analysis of these cases served as a marker for us to notice that they were beginning to take on more perspectives. As they completed the third case, there was a noticeable shift in their ability to adopt additional ways to think about the cases beyond their initial focus. We noted that their involvement in this case analysis helped the preservice teachers frame and analyze problems from different perspectives at a stage even earlier than we would have anticipated. This finding is one that we reported previously (Risko, 1995), and is in direct contrast with an hypothesis generated by Doyle (1985) who suggested that flexible thinking about complex problems may not occur until prospective teachers are placed in actual teaching situations. We believe that involving future teachers in case analysis can provide a challenge similar to that of actual teaching situations because it requires them to make connections across multiple domains. When asked to analyze authentic cases, our preservice teachers found reasons for using the information they were learning.

During this time, we noticed major changes in the preservice teachers' conceptions about teaching. The cases posed problems requiring analysis, reflection, and resolutions. To respond to the case issues the preservice teachers reorganized their existing schemata, adopted new perspectives, and in the process advanced their thinking beyond their earlier naive conceptions. This progression of development is compatible with descriptions of how conceptual change occurs (Hynd & Guzzetti, 1993). These teachers began to embrace more complex understandings of concepts embedded in the cases and as they reorganized their understanding of these concepts they began to integrate and apply simultaneously different sets of information (e.g., information about students, materials, and so on) to respond to complicated issues. We believe they were developing what Richardson (1990, p.12) described as "knowledge that interacts with the particular context and class-room situation in which the knowledge is transformed into action." Involving these teachers in sustained opportunities to examine multiple aspects of concepts embedded in the cases helped them integrate information across sources needed for problem analysis and problem resolution.

### *Phase 3: Problem Identification*

We characterize the next phase as a period of "cognitive disarray" be-cause our preservice teachers' transition from the college class to the practicum setting was problematic. Asking these teachers to apply newly acquired knowledge to a new context—their own teaching in the practicum—pre-sented a challenge for them. The preservice teachers had difficulty coordi-nating all that they had learned about students, materials, and their role as a teacher as they attempted to develop instruction for their students. We visu-alize what occurred at this stage as similar to a symbol we borrowed from computer programming: the horizontal lightning bolt that symbolizes a com-munication link across multiple sources of information. Before entering the practicum the preservice teachers had a model, albeit a theoretical one, for how their instruction should progress during tutoring. When they began teaching they encountered unexpected situations as they learned character-istics of the children and the instructional setting. The preservice teachers were forced to reprocess information they had learned as they tried to rec-oncile the situation. The communication link symbolizes this reprocessing as the students took steps to try to begin accessing other sources of data, both old and new, to try to generate a model for instruction that could be successful for them and their student. They examined old sources of data by meeting with the instructor and supervisors who reminded the preservice teachers of readings, methods, or video cases that could help them approach their difficulties. They searched for new sources of information by asking their peers who were experiencing similar difficulties how they were ap-proaching their problems. Communication links between these old and new sources during this period of cognitive reprocessing required them to re-solve conflicts they were experiencing and allowed for the transfer of what the preservice teachers knew in one system (the college classroom) to an-other system (the teaching situation).

As these teachers began to reprocess information needed for their teach-ing, they relied heavily on the problem solving process they had learned when they analyzed our cases in the college class. During this phase, the students carefully articulated their difficulties and generated specific reasons for these. They stated:

> "Santana become discouraged during her Reading Miscue Inventory [(RMI) (Goodman, Watson, & Burke, 1987)] because it was so hard for

her and she struggled, so I want to be sure to give her a positive read-ing experience." (Elizabeth, lesson evaluation)

"I think that the book might have been too hard but he said he still enjoyed it." (Tammy, lesson evaluation)

"I'm not sure if my student had a bad day. I only got two words out of him. He didn't want to write. The material was difficult." (Mario, class discourse)

The students' ability to frame problems based on multiple sources of information was noticeably different from how they approached problems at the beginning of the course. Similar to an idea advanced by Copeland and colleagues (1994), these preservice teachers by now had shifted from vague notions of instruction to specific causal relations between teaching, materials, and text. In her evaluation of her fourth lesson, Elizabeth writes, "I have got to do something about the way my student deals with unknown words. I was very dissatisfied with the focus of the lesson—it doesn't focus on something she needs."

These preservice teachers drew on their experience with case analysis to describe their struggles and to carefully plan ways to resolve their difficul-ties. Their solutions were not random. Instead, they focused directly on spe-cific problems they identified in the teaching situation. And, similar to their experience with case-based discussions in the college class, these prospec-tive teachers sought support for their developing notions. Elizabeth arranged for a meeting with her instructor during which she outlined specific ideas and suggestions to get her on a successful track. Tammy carpooled with another student and reported that she asked her peer for advice because she was having similar struggles with her student. Mario had lengthy conversa-tions with his professor and the practicum supervisor, in addition to sharing his struggles with the class and asking for suggestions. The support that was available from a variety of sources served as a very important "scaffold" and appeared to make a difference in the students' ability to reprocess and move on with their teaching. Consistent with the findings of Guzzetti, Snyder, Glass, & Gamas (1993), discussions that mediated their thinking contributed to the growth of these future teachers. Collaboration and dialogue with the course instructors and their peers mediated their thinking; change was influenced by knowledge that was constructed socially through these encounters.

In addition to being aware of their problems, these teachers seemed to feel comfortable with the difficulties they were experiencing. Their history with case analysis seemed to prepare them to expect problems and dilem-mas. As a consequence of this awareness, the preservice teachers were per-ceptive about what in their lessons required a change and what did not. They didn't abandon total lessons, but instead adjusted those elements that they believed were unsatisfactory. These prospective teachers were not complete novices upon entering the practicum because they were able to examine carefully the impact of teaching strategies on the children's learning. All three preservice teachers mentioned that the materials that they used initially with their students were too difficult. All three of them generated goals for correcting the problem. They did not allow their difficulties to completely overwhelm them. Their history with case methodology seemed to boost their confidence in their ability to resolve their problems.

### *Phase 4: Problem Resolution*

By about their sixth lesson, each preservice teacher's struggle with instructional problems began to turn around. It was at this point that they began to feel that they were moving forward in their instruction. Being able to examine their problems more broadly helped them to return to the behavior we had observed earlier in the class in which they incorporated multiple factors to examine the cases. That is, they were able to connect several factors during their planning which contributed to successful teaching in the practicum. The following quotes illustrate this resolution phase:

"What influenced me most was my meeting with Jeanne [the instructor], one-on-one, specifically about my child. She referred me to the video with Emily and Joann and it was most helpful. It influenced all other lessons, which were very successful." (Elizabeth, interview 3)

"I really feel like Drashean was making progress today, especially with his vocabulary. He really did well." ( Tammy, lesson evaluation)

"Today was a good instruction day . . . His [the student's] confidence is high and his comprehension of the book is sound." (Mario, lesson evaluation)

The preservice teachers' ability to connect ideas to respond to their problems signaled another way in which their understandings about literacy instruction moved forward. These teachers achieved success on a variety of separate problems (e.g., problems with difficult texts, problems with word recognition strategies, and so on) and reflected on factors contributing to these successes. This reflection helped them remember what they had expressed earlier in the course when they analyzed the video cases: multiple factors need to be considered simultaneously when trying to resolve complex problems. The growth in their ability to integrate multiple sources of information for problem solving may be explained by a phenomenon described by Karmiloff-Smith (1984), a researcher interested in how conceptual changes occur. He proposed that once students have successfully solved a set of separate, related problems, they are able to reflect on these and integrate them into a unifying and more complex framework. Hence, conceptual change occurs as the students learn how to draw on multiple resources to think about complex events. Earlier in the course, these preservice teachers learned to integrate multiple sources of information during case analysis. This ability was reinforced and extended when they followed the same process to resolve their teaching conflicts during tutoring.

As the preservice teachers became more flexible in their ability to resolve their own teaching problems, they learned what many experienced teachers have learned—lesson planning is not a fixed entity, but instead requires many adjustments during implementation. A major breakthrough in the teachers' development was documented in their final lesson plans and case report. Here the prospective teachers indicated that their lesson adjustments were an important part of their growth as teachers. For example, Elizabeth noted that her "thinking changed from one of complete bewilderment— I had no idea how to help them—to one of greater self-assurance. I have learned about different strategies to help such children and how to reflect on how to use such strategies in my classroom." Further, Elizabeth said that she continued to ask questions and make adjustments based on new information concerning her student and that she "was able to make great progress by the end of the teaching experience." Tammy indicated that there were times when she held on to her lesson plans "against my expert judgement" and when this occurred the instruction was "not my best." When Mario began to see a resolution to his struggles, he said that his change in lesson plans helped not only the students but himself as a teacher, as he now "was learning how to teach!"

Perry (1993) draws an important distinction between strategic planning and strategic improvising. We rely on this distinction to help us interpret our preservice teachers' ability to think more flexibly about their teaching. Perry describes strategic planning as linear, a process that stops when action begins and starts again when action is finished and a new plan is required. The implication is that strategic planning is lockstep and linear, and proceeds unchanged through a planning cycle. Strategic improvising, in contrast, is much more open-ended and involves continuous learning, adjustments, and changes. Here lesson development is viewed as an interactive decision-making process with changes occurring based on feedback from lesson events. These two concepts help us think about the development of these preservice teachers. We believe that the prospective teachers' initial inability to adjust lesson plans and to think flexibly about instruction is the result of a confusion between what we are describing as strategic planning and strategic improvising. Throughout the study of cases in our college classes, our students learned that experienced teachers made many adjustments in their own teaching, for good reasons. The notion of moving from a linear, strategic planning process to that of more flexible planning illustrates for us development of "strategic improvising." These prospective teachers became more prepared to respond to unexpected events by generating thoughtful and effective instructional strategies.

## Discussion

We conclude by noting the progress made by these three preservice teachers and summarizing some factors contributing to this progress. These teachers' initial naive concepts about literacy instruction changed as they added new perspectives to guide their thinking and as they were forced to draw on this newly-formed knowledge to resolve their own teaching conflicts. Involvement in the analysis of complex, authentic teaching cases required these future teachers to frame problems from different perspectives and adopt new ways of approaching and resolving these problems. The sustained use of different perspectives to analyze cases during the college classes provided a rich knowledge base and a method for referring to this information when they were asked to identify and resolve problems they were experiencing in their own teaching. In the practicum, our prospective teachers experienced a predictable phenomenon—newly learned information was not easily applied to a novel context. These preservice teachers, however, were able to self-evaluate their instructional problems with surprising accuracy. They made discriminating choices about what areas of instruction should be changed and they drew on multiple resources (peers, instructors, readings) to help them make good decisions about changes. Overall, this line of research provides a way to specify more precisely some learning phases of preservice teachers and characteristics of a learning environment that can help them access relevant information when it is needed for teaching.

## References

Bogdan, R., & Biklen, S. (1982). *Qualitative research for education*. Boston, MA: Allyn & Bacon.

Copeland, W. D., Birmingham, C., DeMeulle, L., D'Emidio-Caston, M., & Natal, D. (1994). Making meaning in classrooms: An investigation of cognitive processes in aspiring teachers, experienced teachers, and their peers. *American Educational Research Journal, 31,* 166-196.

Doyle, W. (1985, January-February). Learning to teach: An emerging direction in preservice. *Journal of Teacher Education, 36,* 31-32.

Goodman, Y., Watson, D. J., & Burke, C. L. (1987). *Reading miscue inventory*. NY: Richard C. Owen Publishers.

Guzzetti, B. J., Snyder, T. E., Glass, G.V., & Gamas, W.S. (1993). Meta-analysis of instructional interventions from reading education and science education to promote conceptual change in science. *Reading Research Quarterly, 28,* 116-161.

Hynd, C. R., & Guzzetti, B. J. (1993). Exploring issues in conceptual change. In D. J.

Leu, & C. K. Kinzer (Eds.), *Examining central issues in literacy research, theory, and practice.* (pp. 375-381). Chicago: The National Reading Conference.

Karmiloff-Smith, A. (1984). Children's problem solving. In M. E. Lamb, A. L. Brown, & B. Rogoff (Eds.), *Advances in developmental psychology* (pp. 39-89). Hillside, NJ: Erlbaum.

Kleinfield, J. (1995). Our hero comes of age: What students learn from case writing in student teaching. In J. A. Colbert, P. Desberg, & K. Trimble (Eds.), *The case of education.* (pp. 79-97). Boston: Allyn & Bacon.

Lincoln, Y. S., & Guba, E. G. (1985). *Naturalistic inquiry.* Beverly Hills, CA: Sage Publications.

Merseth, K. (1991). *The case for cases in teacher education.* Washington, DC: American Association of Colleges of Teacher Education and American Association of Higher Education.

Perry, L. T. (1993). *Real time strategy.* NY: John Wiley & Sons.

Richardson, V. (1990). Significant and worthwhile change in teaching practice. *Educational Researcher, 19,* 10-18.

Risko, V. J. (1992). Developing problem-solving environments to prepare teachers for instruction of diverse learners. In B. Hayes & K. Camperell (Eds.), *Developing lifelong readers: Policies, procedures, and programs.* Logan, UT: Utah State Press.

Risko, V. J. (1995). Using videodisc-based cases to promote preservice teachers' problem solving and mental model building. In W. M. Linek & E. G. Sturtevant (Eds.), *Generations of literacy* (pp. 173-187). Pittsburg, KS: College Reading Association.

Risko, V. J., & Kinzer, C. K. (1991). *Improving undergraduate teacher education with technology and case-based instruction.* Fund for Improvement of Postsecondary Education.

Risko. V. J., McAllister, D., Peter, J., & Bigenho, F. (1994). Using technology in support of preservice teachers' generative learning. In E.G. Sturtevant & W. M. Linek (Eds.), *Pathways for literacy: Learners teach and teachers learn.* Pittsburg, KS: College Reading Association.

Risko V. J., Yount, D., & McAllister, D. (1992). Preparing preservice teachers for remedial instruction: Teaching problem solving and use of content and pedagogical knowledge. In N. Padak, T.V. Rasinski, & J. Logan (Eds.), *Inquiries in literacy learning and instruction.* (pp. 179-189). Pittsburg, KS: College Reading Association.

Shulman, L. S. (1995). Just in case: Reflections on learning from experience. In J. A. Colbert, P. Desberg, & K. Trimble (Eds.), *The case of education.* (pp. 197-217). Boston: Allyn & Bacon.

Shulman, J. H. (1995). Tender feelings, hidden thoughts: Confronting bias, innocence, and racism through case discussion. In J. A. Colbert, P. Desberg, & K. Trimble (Eds.), *The case of education.* (pp. 137-158). Boston: Allyn & Bacon.

Silverman, R., & Welty, W. M. (1995). Teaching without a net: using cases in teacher education. In J. A. Colbert, P. Desberg, & K. Trimble (Eds.), *The case of education.* (pp. 159171). Boston: Allyn & Bacon.

# Using Reflective Portfolios in Preservice Teacher Education Programs

**Kathleen Oropallo**
**Susan Gomez**
University of South Florida

## Abstract

*Research has contributed to the discussion of teacher education and situated knowledge by illuminating the importance of reflective thought as an integral characteristic in teacher education. Results of this study demonstrate that reflective portfolios are powerful tools that facilitate the development of prospective teachers by providing one means of bringing situated experiences into the university setting and engaging prospective teachers in a reflective process that responds to issues of pedagogy, literacy, and multicultural education. This paper focuses on the category of "portfolio construction," one of three broad categories that emerged from a larger study.*

## Introduction

Teacher-educators are faced with the dilemma of bringing classroom-situated experiences of teaching and schooling to prospective teachers. At each university setting in colleges of education, there are unique conditions that influence the types and models of teacher education programs (Howey & Zimpher, 1989). Other research has illuminated the importance of reflective thought on teaching and learning as an integral part of teacher preparation (Grimmett & Erickson, 1988).

The research reported here is part of a larger study that describes how portfolios can function as a reflective tool (Oropallo, 1994). This paper examines the decisions of prospective teachers and their instructors as they construct and use reflective portfolios in a multicultural education and language arts course. The role portfolio construction and discourse played in relation to classroom interaction with peers, instructor, pedagogy, and self was also investigated. Results of this study reveal three broad categories: managing port-folios and pedagogy, portfolio construction, and curricular dimensions (Oro-pallo, 1994). The remainder of this paper focuses on the category of portfo-lio construction and discusses three main assertions related to this category.

## Reflective Portfolios

Although teachers may assume that all portfolios are alike, in actuality they vary according to their purpose, stance, and design (Belanoff & Dickson, 1991; Collins, 1991; Graves & Sunstein, 1992). The reflective portfolio is a vehicle that guides prospective teachers' examinations of themselves as readers/writers/learners/teachers, and introduces them to the kinds of reflective prac-tices necessary to examine their roles as future agents of multiculturalism, literacy, and pedagogical understanding. Portfolio discourse functions as a medium for classroom exchange and interaction as prospective teachers and their instructors mutually explore pedagogy, course curriculum, and literacy development. The reflective portfolio model used in this research was adapted from the literacy portfolio of the Manchester Portfolio Project at the Univer-sity of New Hampshire. The Manchester Portfolio Project uses the literacy port-folio as a tool for examining literacy development from kindergarten through twelfth grade (Hansen, 1992).

For the purpose of this research, reflective portfolios functioned as me-diating tools that prospective teachers use to conversed with peers and their instructor, sharing unique experiences held both in and out of a university classroom. Reflective portfolios also functioned as autobiographical narra-tives. The portfolio became a representation of self that students construct through examination of intrapersonal context, they were the way in which students saw themselves and their lives (Butt, Raymond, & Yamagishi, 1988; Carter, 1993).

Reflective portfolios can also be characterized by what Sheridan (1993) calls "layered autobiographies." When examined collectively and holistically, they can represent an overall portrait of the portfolio keeper's (one who con-structs a portfolio) collective experiences. For this study, these collective ex-periences were conceptualized as *conduits* (see Figure 1), which functioned as both general themes and organizational schema through which prospec-tive teachers filter the contents of their portfolio.

Another aspect of reflective portfolios addresses the relationship between portfolio keepers (prospective teachers) and portfolio managers (course in-structors). Seger (1992) describes three possible stances which represent the relationship of portfolio keepers to portfolio content. When portfolio keep-ers are *"standing outside,"* portfolio management is based on external crite-ria and focuses on instructor assessment. When portfolio keepers *"stand on*

**Figure 1. The Portfolio Conduit.**

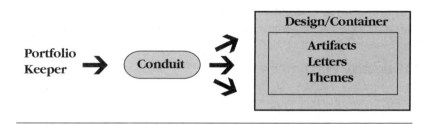

*the side,"* portfolio keepers produce materials for the portfolio but management still resides with the instructor. In the *"central stance,"* portfolio keepers participate collaboratively with instructors in decisions about criteria and management.

### *The Method of Investigation*

This study was a naturalistic inquiry in which the design was emergent. Data and setting influenced the methodology and grounded theory was constructed throughout data collection (Lincoln & Guba, 1985). The research was based upon an interpretive research model. Data were generated from portfolios, portfolio letters, artifacts, fieldnotes, audiotapes, and videotapes. Strategies for analysis included analytic induction, which involved varying types of coding and the constant-comparison so that data were analyzed throughout the data collection process (Bogden & Biklen, 1991; Oropallo, 1994).

## Participants

The vignettes and descriptions for this research were generated from three undergraduates (prospective teachers) and their course instructor in a multicultural education course at a state university. These participants were part of Phase III of the ongoing examination of reflective portfolios. The following are brief descriptions of each participant:

> *Kara:* The course instructor was a teaching assistant with full responsibility for the course. This was her first experience in constructing a reflective portfolio. She had been an elementary teacher for seven years and was pursuing her Ph.D.
> *Jake:* The only male enrolled in the course, he teaches emotionally handicapped boys in addition to being a full-time minister.
> *Lisa:* A mom returning to college in order to pursue a career as her children began school full time, her first bachelors degree was in business.

*Cassie:* The youngest participant, she worked in an adult community home for developmentally disabled men. All of the residents were African-American males. She originally attended another university to study law, but dropped out .

## Constructing the Reflective Portfolio

One of the main assignments prospective teachers were asked to complete during the multicultural and language arts courses was the construction of a reflective portfolio. The main criteria for the assignment was to create a portrait of themselves as a reader, writer, learner, and teacher. They were asked to examine themselves in relation to roles of the teacher, the learner, the subject matter, and the social milieu. Prospective teachers were asked to write four sequential letters describing both the construction of the portfolio and the purpose in selecting the artifacts which they chose as representatives of the portfolio portrait. The initial letter was a planning letter. The next two letters were descriptive rationales, and the final letter was a reflection of the semester-long process of portfolio construction. The following discussion describes the three main assertions addressing the decisions prospective teachers engaged in throughout the portfolio construction process and the developmental stages that they portrayed throughout the semester.

***Assertion #1: There were five decisions portfolio keepers make in constructing reflective portfolios: design and form, purpose, ownership, congruence with external criteria, and degrees of disclosure.***

During portfolio construction, prospective teachers made decisions in five areas: *design and form, purpose, ownership, congruence with external criteria, and degrees of disclosure.* The first decision that prospective teachers grappled with was *design and form. Design and form* refers to the physical form of representation portfolio keepers sought to best match their determined purpose. This was often experimented with early in the process by collecting artifacts (items to be placed in the portfolio) without housing them in anything more than a folder. Later, the portfolio keeper decided whether to place them in a three-ring binder, scrapbook form or any other self-selected container.

Decisions regarding *purpose* were often explicated in the first portfolio planning letter. These decisions, however, were extremely difficult for some. Lisa, for example, struggled with her purpose well into the third portfolio letter. Determining a purpose was directly related to two of the other decisions influencing portfolio construction: *congruence with external factors* and *ownership.* Lisa could not make the transition from what the instructor wanted (the *external criteria* of creating a portrait of herself as reader, writer, learner, teacher), and her use of the portfolio as a tool to explore her own learning *(ownership)*. All three of these decisions were influenced by the instructor's efforts to remain purposefully ambiguous so that participants would have to resolve these questions independent of a power authority.

The final decision to be considered was *degree of disclosure*, the amount of personal or intimate details prospective teachers were willing to disclose, and the relevancy of such disclosures to their purpose. All participants reported on having difficulty in determining degree of disclosure. During the initial sharing of the portfolios, one class member revealed to the class that she had first-hand knowledge of issues regarding abuse and did not know if she wanted to share these kinds of personal experiences in her portfolio. This was an emotional moment in class. Jake responded with a comment about his feelings regarding the degree of disclosure and his decisions about it:

> As I was going through some photographs trying to decide what to put in my portfolio, I decided that I would reserve some of those for just my family. They were intimate moments for my family's eyes, not that they were naked pictures or anything like that, they were just private moments that I didn't want to share with strangers. Then there were others I thought, well this is OK. You have to share what you feel comfortable sharing.

Lisa reiterated what Jake had said by commenting, "Don't feel you *have* to share anything you're not comfortable with." At times participants had difficulty deciding which types of artifacts to share. Once prospective teachers felt they owned their purposes, they then *wanted* to share some personal insights and experiences, while also recognizing they walked a fine line in degree of disclosure.

Decisions made at various stages of the portfolio construction process were often revisited each time prospective teachers constructed and reconstructed their portfolios. Assertion #2 describes three developmental stages of portfolio construction. How the participants moved in unique ways through these stages will be discussed and examples of the decisions discussed above will be provided.

### Assertion #2: There were three developmental stages present during reflective portfolio construction: ambiguity, discovery and ownership, and process reflection.

The three identifiable stages listed above represent transitional periods in the developmental process of portfolio construction. The process of portfolio construction was found to be similar to the characteristics associated with developmentalist theories. The portfolio process and student movement throughout the developmental process was as Wadsworth (1978) suggests:

> *Both* continuous and discontinuous. Continuous means that each sub-

sequent development builds on and incorporates and transforms previous developments. Discontinuous in this case means that qualitative changes take place from stage to stage. Thus, the periods of development are functionally related and part of a continuous process. (p. 12)

Participants varied in their length of stay at each stage, and traveled to the next stage only after they had accommodated and reflectively resolved the conflict presented by the portfolio assignment.

Each participant began with unique understandings of what portfolios were, and some range of experience with the term itself. The process of change began when the prospective teachers' existing frame of reference for the portfolios did not fit pre-existing experiential references in which they could assimilate the process of portfolio construction. In order to accommodate this, qualitative changes and new schema had to be developed to operationalize the external criteria and construct a portfolio. The experiences of portfolio keepers were not all the same because each was affected by his or her unique life circumstances. In all cases, however, participants moved through each of the developmental stages at some point during portfolio construction. The length of time they rested at each stage and in level of understanding within each stage differed greatly.

**Ambiguity: "What do you want??"** Each participant began in the stage of ambiguity, as illustrated in the following part of this conversation from a class discussion about the portfolio assignment:

Kara: If you have your portfolio letters, you can . . .

Lisa: I don't and I'll tell you why. I'm having a hard time formulating what . . .

Kara: One looks like?

Lisa: Anything, so I could put it together. I'm just not doing it, I'm sorry . . .

Kara: No, you're not at all [reassuringly].

Sue: I've thought what in the world do they want?

Lisa: I've never done one before. It sounds wonderful and I'm looking forward to doing it, it's just I just can't quite get a handle on it . . . What I want to do so far is, I would like to do remedial reading and after, get a specialist degree in reading. See I'm still so much behind having a bachelors in business that I can't really, its hard for me to really think that far ahead. But I have a goal, but it's just going to be years down the line.

Kara: So how do you want the portfolio to contribute to that goal?

Lisa: I don't know.

Kara: And see, maybe you can think of a goal that's closer to you.

Lisa: OK, I can do that.

Lisa's uncertainty about the assignment was not unique. Both Jake and Cassie supported Lisa's feelings of ambiguity in discussions. Jake commented, ". . . at first it was very confusing, very thought provoking. I liked it because it was reflective and I think that's what teaching is all about." Cassie reflected back on the beginning, "It wasn't very black and white. What do they want? What does she [Kara] want?".

Lisa and Cassie, who had no prior knowledge of portfolios, had the most reservations about what the instructor wanted. Since Jake was teaching a class and had some experience working with another portfolio model, the term was not totally unfamiliar to him. These feelings paralleled Kara's purposeful ambiguity and caution in guiding her students too much. While Kara attempted to clarify some of the ambiguity, she purposefully left much of the assignment's criteria open for students to define. Kara believed the ambiguity functioned as a problem solving activity which became a catalyst for reflective thought. This ambiguity is represented in the following responses to a questionnaire given at the end of the semester asking, "When you were first introduced to the portfolio what were your thoughts?"

> Lisa:    I did not know what you wanted us to do-it was so confusing in the beginning . . .
>
> Chris:   At first I was excited about the portfolio, but as I began putting it together I became hesitant and confused about what to put in there.
>
> Jane:    My first thoughts were: What do I put in the portfolio? What is required to be in the portfolio? . . .
>
> Sue:     I felt unsure about what was actually wanted in the portfolio.

There are other tacit characteristics of the reflective portfolio and the academic context that may have also contributed to the initial ambiguity. Although the reflective portfolio was not a graded assignment, it was a project introduced as part of the fulfillment of course requirements, therefore lending itself to the power structures present within the academic community. Thus some ambiguity discussed here may have been related to the prospective teachers' tacit concerns regarding this power structure. Nevertheless, each student needed to resolve this dilemma in order to construct a portfolio that satisfied their personal agendas and their concern for the possible agendas of their instructor.

By the time the students wrote their first letter, Jake and Cassie had resolved their conflict with ambiguity, but Lisa was still uncertain as to what to do. She labored over her focus well into the third portfolio letter (due six weeks into the course), as is evidenced in her first letter about portfolio planning:

> I might want to expand or delete some of these topics. . . . To be per-

fectly honest, I am not quite sure about this assignment. It is thought provoking and I will continue to dig deeper and figure it out as I go.

In their first letters, Jake and Cassie had clearly defined agendas. Although agendas were subject to change, nowhere in their letters did they use language that revealed uncertainty in the direction they were taking.

**Discovery and Ownership**. In order to begin constructing their portfolios, prospective teachers needed to discover a purpose that enabled them to focus on what they wanted to include or discard. Once prospective teachers gained trust in the instructor, they began to expand their purposes and develop personal ownership. At the ownership stage, prospective teachers realized that one of the portfolio's purposes was for them to reflect on their intrapersonal contexts (how they perceived themselves), and not for the instructor to grade and evaluate them. This stage was important for both instructor and students. For the instructor, it meant her goals of establishing trust and initiating reflective learning had been accomplished. For the prospective teachers it meant that they were truly free to explore and construct a portfolio in a way that best suited them. This provided a framework in which they could define their portfolios as they were constructing them, and continue to redefine them each time they interacted with classmates and the instructor throughout the semester.

One way in which students began to explore their purpose was by using the portfolio to answer questions they asked of themselves. For example, Jake asked himself, "Who am I?" and "Why must I feel so accepted?". Lisa explored, "Why am I like I am?"; "Where does all this emotion come from?" "Why does a person turn out like they do? How much of their success and failure can they attribute to their family upbringing?"; "How can a child's self-esteem be elevated within a family unit?"; and "How much influence has your Mother had in your life?" Cassie wondered about her clients and ". . . why they breathe so much life into my very being . . ." These questions helped the prospective teachers establish ownership over the portfolio by making it a tool to address pressing issues they felt were important to themselves.

**Process Reflection**. Process reflection occurred often, and was critical in the construction of the portfolio. Evidence of process reflection occurred in each letter in varying degrees, but the final portfolio letter contained the final reflection of the semester long process and was most revealing. This was a result of the letter's intent (students were asked to write a reflective letter) and the length of time portfolio keepers had been participating in the process. The following are examples of the reflections in the final letters:

Jake: I have concluded the gathering of data and other materials to place in my portfolio. I have been fairly successful in acquiring the things I felt I needed and wanted to include. My concentration now will be to bring together the meanings and importances of the items I felt important to the portfolio. I will spend some time looking over the portfolio, reading, thinking and finally composing my thoughts in some concise way to express what I have learned from this project.

Lisa: What an experience this portfolio production has been! . . . I have thought a great deal this semester about wanting to become a teacher. I feel as if my wanting to be a teacher stems from wanting to make a difference in the lives of some children . . . I have benefited from the portfolio assignment. I have dug a little deeper into the 'why's' of what I am doing in school and the important priorities in my life. I think you benefit personally anytime you take the time to look back and to look ahead. Looking back to see what has and has not worked for you is part of being a reflective teacher. Assessing where you have been and where you are headed is part of the flexibility that you need as an instructor at any level.

As a result of these final reflections it became apparent that the relationship between the portfolio keepers (the prospective teachers) and the portfolio manager (the course instructor) was a collaborative and dialogic process. This led to a closer examination of the quality of this relationship and how it directly affected the level of reflection a portfolio process may allow.

Building upon Seger's (1992) representation of the stances in portfolio models, the relationship between portfolio keepers and the portfolio manager in this study added a new dynamic to the central stance, which helped to create a relational portfolio continuum (See Figure 2). As the level of portfolio discourse increased between keeper and manager, the portfolio

**Figure 2. Relational Portfolio Continuum (Author, 1994)**

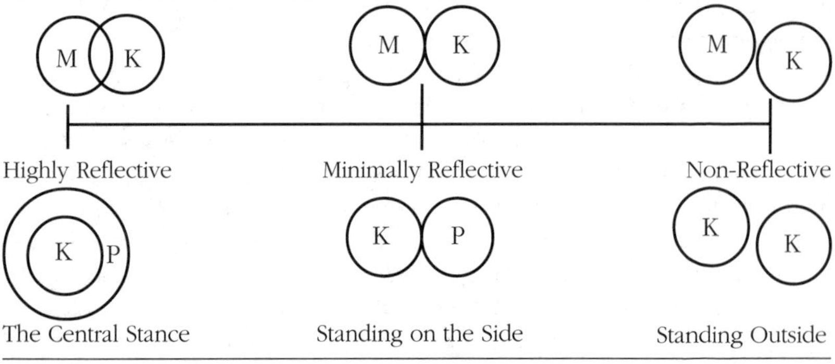

Highly Reflective     Minimally Reflective     Non-Reflective

The Central Stance     Standing on the Side     Standing Outside

*Note: M=Portfolio Manager*
*K=Portfolio Keeper*
*P=Portfolio & Contents*

keeper became more involved in decisions regarding the contents of the portfolio, thereby placing the portfolio keeper closer to the center of the process. The closer the keeper came to being the primary agent of the decision making process, the more "central" a stance the keeper assumed so that the portfolio became truly reflective.

The relationship of portfolio keeper and manager to stance demonstrated how managing and implementing the portfolio directly affected the portfolio keeper's stance and level of reflection. As the level of reflectivity for the portfolio keepers increased, they faced more key decisions and problematic questions in deciding purpose, content, and design. The more responsibility the portfolio keepers were given, and the more transactions they were allowed to make with the portfolio and the portfolio manager (in this case the course instructor), the higher the degree of reflectivity. As the level of reflectivity for portfolio keepers decreased, they assumed a role of mere producer of externally defined products. Absence of a direct role in the problem solving position of the portfolio process shifted the purpose of the portfolio from a reflective learning tool to an assessment tool that was used to diagnose student products.

When instructors (portfolio managers) actively involve portfolio keepers in determining a purpose for their portfolio and making decisions regarding its contents, the portfolio is more likely to be highly reflective, and the keeper is more likely to assume a central stance. In this study, reflective portfolios clearly occupied a central stance on the relational continuum. This continuum is characterized by a new reflective dynamic which adds to Seger's (1992) description of stance and helps one understand Kara's role as portfolio manager.

Instructors will naturally choose a portfolio model congruent with their pedagogical beliefs and interpretations (Oropallo, 1994). Consequently, the portfolio keepers' involvement is predetermined by the pedagogical beliefs and interpretations of the instructor acting as portfolio manager. Kara believed that prospective teachers should determine their portfolio's purpose and contents, and use the portfolio to examine reflectively their personal experiences in relation to course curriculum. As a result, the prospective teachers in this study occupied the central stance.

### Assertion #3: A conduit emerges throughout portfolio construction.

Reflective portfolios represent a portrait of the portfolio keepers collective experiences (Sheridan,1993). One of the tensions which emerged in the construction process was the development of some type of organizational schema. The schema portfolio keepers (prospective teachers) used to explore their purposes and reflect, was a *conduit* through which portfolio keepers could accommodate and adapt the development of the portfolio to their needs and purposes. Another way of looking at the conduit would be as a theme or focus through which participants filtered their questions, purposes, and reflections. The conduit influenced the organizational structure as well as the design and the medium of the portfolio container itself. For some, this conduit appeared to be a conscious part of the process. For others, the conduit remained tacit and emerged holistically when the portfolio process was reflected upon. Through this conduit, participants filtered and expressed the meanings synthesized from re-examining their personal experiences. These meanings were products of the merger of both old and new beliefs and values.

In this study the conduit operated differently for each of the participant's efforts in the portfolio construction process (Figure 3). For Cassie, Jake, and Lisa, the conduit represented a conscious guide for making decisions about what to contain in their self-portraits. For Kara, the conduit emerged as she

**Figure 3. The Portfolio Conduit (The Portfolio Keepers).**

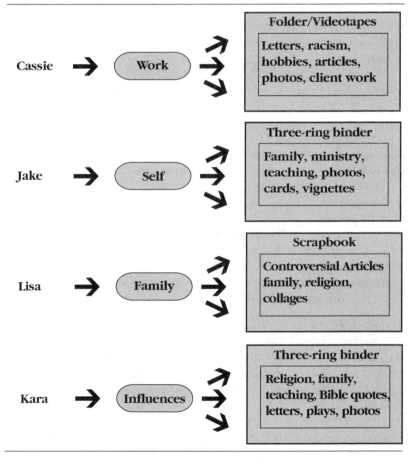

constructed her portfolio. Only after viewing the portfolio holistically did the influences in her life become a filter and guide for Kara's selection of artifacts.

## Conclusion

Results of this study demonstrate that reflective portfolios are a powerful tool that facilitates the development of prospective teachers in several important ways. Portfolios guide prospective teachers to examine themselves as readers, writers, learners, and teachers by providing a forum for discussion of pedagogy, curriculum, and literacy development.

Findings also provide a greater understanding of the construction and management processes associated with reflective portfolios. Particularly significant is the emergence of a strong relationship between the level of reflection and portfolio stance. The existence of this relationship, illustrated by the relational continuum (Figure 2), reinforces the utility of reflective portfolios in teacher development. Further, a clearer understanding of the functions and types of portfolios can guide instructors in selecting the type of portfolio model which best suits their pedagogical purpose.

Based upon these results, it can be inferred that reflective portfolios in reading and language arts methods courses can improve the quality of literacy instruction by enhancing prospective teachers' understanding of their own literacy development. However, results also indicate that the nature of the reflective portfolio and its use are dependent upon the stance, construction, and management processes used by the instructor. Therefore, the implementation of reflective portfolios in any teacher education course will be greatly influenced by the instructor's decisions. Investigation of the varieties of management and implementation strategies used by instructors in other types of teacher education courses is a logical next step in this vein of research. Another issue to be examined is the question of how reflective portfolios might be used in graduate education courses with students having greater amounts of teaching experience and professional development.

---

## References

Belanoff, P., & Dickson, M. (1991). *Portfolios: Product and process.* Portsmouth: Heinemann.

Bogden, R.C., & Biklen, S.K. (1991). *Qualitative research for education: An introduction to theory and methods.* Boston, MA: Allyn and Bacon.

Butt, R., Raymond, D., & Yamagishi, L. (1988, April). *Autobiographic praxis: Studying the formation of teacher's knowledge.* Paper presented at the American Educational Research Association annual meeting, New Orleans.

Carter, K. (1993, January/February). The place of story in the study of teaching and learning. *Educational Researcher, 22,* (1), 5-12.

Collins, A. (1991). Portfolios in biology teacher assessment. *Journal of Personnel Evaluation, 5*(2), 147-168.

Graves, D., & Sunstein, B. (1992). *Portfolio portraits.* Portsmouth, NH: Heinemann.

Grimmet, P., & Erickson, G. L. (Eds.). (1988). *Reflection in teacher education.* New York: Teachers College Press.

Hansen, J. (1992). Literacy portfolios emerge. *The Reading Teacher, 45,* 604-607.

Howey, K. R., & Zimpher, N.L. (1989). *Profiles of preservice teacher education: Inquiry into the nature of programs.* Albany, NY: SUNY Press.

Lincoln, Y.S. & Guba, E.G. (1985). *Desiging qualitative research.* Newbury Park, CA: Sage.

Oropallo, K. (1994). Opening Doors: Portfolios and pedagogy. (Doctoral dissertation, Florida State University, 1994). *Dissertation Abstract International, 55,* A2798.

Seger, D. (1992). Portfolio definitions: Toward a shared notion. In D. Graves and B. Sunstein (Eds.), *Portfolio portraits* (pp. 114-124). Portsmouth, NH: Heinemann.

Sheridan, D. (1993). Writing to the archive: Mass observation as autobiography. *Sociology, 27* (1).

Wadsworth, B.J. (1978). *Piaget for the classroom teacher.* New York: Longman.

# THE ANNOTATION EXCHANGE SYSTEM: A WAY FOR SCHOOLS AND UNIVERSITIES TO CONNECT USING CHILDREN'S LITERATURE

## Susan L. Strode

Jefferson City Public Schools

## Abstract

*The Annotation Exchange System (AES) is an organized means for readers to share their responses to a variety of literature. Using AES, university students share annotations of children's literature with one another and with children in schools. The exchange encourages universities to meet their major mission while acting as both agent and catalyst for the clarification and distribution of fresh ideas and perspectives.*

One of the goals of reading educators at the university level is to provide teachers and future teachers with expertise in a variety of learning strategies (Fry, 1977) and to communicate with teachers and children in the public schools where children are using those strategies. The educational research community also has addressed these needs as more and more university researchers are collaborating with teacher researchers (Moll, Amanti, Neff, and Gonzales, 1992; Nicholls & Hazzard, 1993).

This paper describes the Annotation Exchange System (AES), in which university students and elementary school students communicate with one another so that both groups read a variety of children's literature, produce written annotations, and share ideas (Manzo, 1973; 1986). Also presented are descriptions of the instruction in annotation writing that is necessary for the operation of this system.

## The Annotation Exchange System

The Annotation Exchange System (Manzo, 1973, 1986) contains three major components: reading, writing and sharing. First, the AES is an exciting and innovative method for promoting reading interest and enjoyment. Second, it creates an organized collection of reader's responses to literature that has been read and later recorded in the form of written annotations. Finally, the AES encourages students, ranging from elementary to graduate school, to share perspectives and ideas with one another.

### *The University*

The Annotation Exchange can be set into operation in the teacher education department at any university or college. For example, students in children's literature courses may participate.

The AES requires students (teachers and future teachers) to produce personal view annotations rather than summaries. This type of annotation combines a summary, which requires critical thinking (Spires, Johnston, & Huffman, 1993), with a personal reaction, another type of higher level thinking. A rationale for including summarizing can be found in Kintch and Van Dijk's (1978) model of reading comprehension, which maintains that readers construct a mental summary of text as they read and remember that summary. A rationale for including personal reactions also is theoretically grounded. Rosenblatt's (1978) transactional theory of response holds that as readers try to understand text they explore how the text affects them personally by moving back and forth between the text, personal experiences, and other knowledge. Since readers' personal experiences will vary, their interpretations of text also vary. Other research speaks directly about college students' improved summary writing as a result of annotation training (Eanet, 1977; Strode, 1990). Annotation writing also has been found to have positive effects on college students' reading comprehension because it helps students organize their thoughts (Eanet & Manzo, 1976).

In the AES, the annotations college students produce are kept in a "Children's Literature Notebook" and are combined with those produced by children. This combination results in summarized ideas and opinions expressed by both children and adults and provides a unique opportunity to view children's literature from both a child's eye and from the perspective of an adult. It also can establish a dialogue among readers from elementary to graduate school.

Annotations can be recorded and saved on computer disks. This method, used at the University of Missouri-Kansas City, simplifies the process of adding annotations. Copies of all annotations should be kept for the college students' "Children's Literature Notebook," which can be kept in a media center, a library, or even brought to class. The annotations also should be sent to any other teacher (university or classroom) whose students are participating in the AES via postal mail or electronic mail (e-mail).

Children in nearby elementary schools also participate in the Annotation Exchange System, and their involvement is similar to that of the college students. Classroom teachers have their students read stories from various tradebooks and write annotations. The annotations are sent to the university where they are combined with those from college students in the children's literature classes. The classroom teacher also can keep a collection of annotations in a "Children's Literature Notebook" that contains annotations from students from different grades, schools, and universities.

The method of sending and receiving annotations can vary and most likely will depend on the availability of computers in the schools. Children's annotations can be sent to universities on paper in their own print, on computer disks, or by e-mail. These annotations can be typed into computers by the teachers or by the children themselves. At this point, the person sending the annotations should include the grade level of the children who produced them.

There are many benefits of having the elementary schools participate in the Exchange. First, benefits result when children are allowed to choose the tradebooks that they will read. Research has shown strong correlations between high interest and positive reading attitudes (Lipson & Wixson, 1991; Mason & Au, 1990), and also between reading attitude and reading achievement (Casteel, 1989; Morrow, 1987). Furthermore, children who have experienced instruction with tradebooks have shown superior reading comprehension and vocabulary acquisition (Holdaway, 1982; Reutzel & Fawson, 1989), and reading or listening to stories can increase the vocabulary of young children (Elley, 1989).

Second, annotation writing benefits children's learning, specifically comprehension and retention. Most research on the effects of annotation writing has been limited to college students, however, annotations are similar to both summaries and precis and there is much support for this type of writing (Bromely, 1985; Cunningham, 1982; Hayes, 1987; Taylor 1986). The annotations, with their personal reactions, move the communication from author and reader to a "general median of communication" (Rosenblatt, 1978). This type of communication encourages children to connect and compare a given text with personal experience and other texts as well (Cox & Many, 1992).

Finally, benefits include children's delight in seeing their work in print and their use of the annotations of others when chosing books to read. Here, the enjoyment of reading is demonstrated and a social dialogue can develop in a dynamic learning environment.

## Instruction

University instructors should help students understand differences between annotations and other forms of writing. First, an anotation is brief. There is no need for phrases like "This story was about. . . ." Instead it should begin immediately with "A little boy and his dog. . . ." Second, the annotation should focus on key ideas or the gist. It also should focus on what the reader thinks is important. In brief, anotations do not include trivia, redundancies, descriptors, or conversations. They should, however, reflect the annotator's point of view.

### Younger Elementary Children

One way teachers might begin teaching annotation writing to beginning writers is by talking about how different stories can make people feel. Children can be asked to tell how stories have made them feel in the past and also can discuss the kinds of stories they enjoy. Next, the class can take a trip to the library where children can select a book to read. Time should be set aside to either read a story aloud to the children, or to let them read their own stories individually or in small groups.

After the children have read or heard their stories, they should be asked to give words describing how they feel (i.e., bored, happy, sad, scared). These words then should be written in a column on the chalk board. Next, the class can talk about words that can be used to describe different stories (i.e., funny, scary, awful) and they should be written in a second column on the chalkboard. Finally, the class can discuss words that can be used to describe various characters in a story (i.e., tall, nice, old, sweet) and they should be written in a third column on the chalkboard.

Next, the children should begin writing annotations. They can begin with:

This story made me feel _____

because _____

The above phrase should be printed where it can be seen by all the children.

Another way that annotation writing can be taught to young children is to give them the opportunity to orally convince others to read books they have read. After the children have practiced annotating orally, they may annotate in writing.

### Older Elementary Children

Teachers of older children can use short stories for practice. These stories should be easy reading and fairly short, as children tend to have more difficulty identifying key ideas in longer text (Coffman, 1994; Taylor, 1986). In addition, the teacher should have examples of good annotations, as well as the key ideas that need to be included. After the students have read the story, the teacher can model an annotation procedure in which different colors of crayons are used for summarization (Brown & Day, 1983). For example: green (to delete trivia & redundancy); purple (to delete details); yellow (to delete conversations); blue (to cross out lists and write a subordinate above the lists); and red (to underline key ideas).

After the teacher models the above procedure, children should practice with the teacher working on an overhead. Much discussion can result from this practice with respect to what information to delete. This type of discussion should be encouraged with the teacher asking "why ?" Children also should be encouraged to include any thoughts or feelings they have about the characters in their stories. Here, teachers guide children as they practice deleting with the use of colored markings. Children's written annotations are the final result of this instruction.

## Conclusion

Anthony Manzo first introduced the Annotation Exchange System in 1979. At that time, technology had not advanced enough to make the AES as practical as it is today. Electronic mail, for example, has recently created a successful avenue for the AES. While the Annotation Exchange System shows a great deal of promise, research is necessary in order to demonstrate its potential effectiveness.

---

## References

Bromely, K. D. (1985). *Writing in the secondary school.* Urbana, IL: National Council of Teachers of English.

Brown, A., & Day, J. D. (1983). Macrorules for summarizing texts: The development of expertise. *Journal of Verbal Learning and Verbal Behavior, 22,* 1-14.

Casteel, C. A. (1989). Motivating reluctant readers to become mature readers. *Reading Improvement, 26*(2), 98-101.

Coffman, G. A. (1994). The influence of question and story variations on sixth grader's summarization behaviors. *Reading Research and Instruction, 34*(1), 19-38.

Cox, C., & Many, J. (1992). Toward an understanding of the aesthetic response to literature. *Language Arts, 69*(1), 28-33.

Cunningham, J. W. (1982). Generating interactions between schemata and text. In J. A. Niles and L. A. Harris (Eds.). *New inquiries in reading research and instruction.* Thirty-first yearbook of the National Reading Conference.

Eanet, M. G. (1977). An investigation of the REAP reading/study procedure: Its rationale and efficiency. (Doctoral Dissertation, University of Missouri-Kansas City, 1976). *Dissertation Abstracts International, 37,* 3471A.

Eanet, M. G. & Manzo, A. V. (1976). REAP: A strategy for improving reading/writing study skills. *Journal of Reading, 19,* 647-652.

Elley, W. B. (1989). Vocabulary acquisition from listening to stories. *Reading Research Quarterly, 24*(2), 174-187.

Fry, E. S. (1977). *Elementary Reading Instruction.* New York: McGraw-Hill Book Company.

Hayes, D. A. (1987). The potential for directing study in combined reading and writing activity. *Journal of Reading Behavior, 19*(4), 333-352.

Holdaway, D. (1982). Shared books experience: Teaching reading using favorite books. *Theory into practice, 21*(4), 293-300.

Kintch, W., & Van Dijk, T. A. (1978). Toward a model of text comprehension and production. *Psychological Review, 85,* 363-394.

Lipson, M. Y., & Wixson, K. K. (1991). *Assessment and instruction of reading disability: An interactive approach.* New York: Harper Collins.

Manzo, A. V. (1973). Compass: English -a demonstration project. *Journal of Reading,* 539-545.

Manzo, A. V. (1986). Letter to the editor. *Reading Today, 3*(3).

Mason, J. M., & Au, K. H. (1990). *Reading instruction for today* (2nd ed.). Glenview, IL: Scott, Foresman/little Brown.

Moll, L., Amanti, C., Neff, D., & Gonzales, N. (1992). Funds of knowledge for teaching: Using a qualitative approach to connect homes and classrooms. *Theory into Practice, 31*(2), 132-141.

Morrow, L. M. (1987). Promoting voluntary reading: Activities represented in basal reader manuals. *Reading Research and Instruction, 26*(3), 189-202.

Nicholls, J., & Hazzard, S. (1993). *Education as adventure: Lessons from the second grade.* New York: Teachers College Press.

Reutzel, D. R., & Fawson, P. (1989). Using a literature webbing strategy lesson with predictable books. *The Reading Teacher, 43*(3), 208-215.

Rosenblatt, L. (1978). *The reader, the text, and the poem: The transactional theory of the literary work.* Carbondale, IL: Southern Illinois University Press.

Spires, H. A., Johnson, L. H., & Huffman, L. E. (1993). Developing a critical stance toward text through reading, writing, and speaking. *Journal of Reading, 37*(2), 114-122.

Strode, S. L. (1990). Re-evaluation of the effects of annotation training on comprehension and summary writing abilities of college students. (Doctoral Dissertation, University of Missouri-Kansas City, 1989). *Dissertation Abstracts International, 50,* 3196A.

Taylor, K. (1986). Summary writing by young children. *Reading Research Quarterly, 21,* 193-208.

# THE BIBLIOTHERAPEUTIC EFFECTS
# OF LUDIC READING

**Mary A. Duchein**
**Deidra W. Frazier**

Louisiana State University

**Elizabeth L. Willis**

University of Southwestern Louisiana

## Abstract

*This study, which emerged from a broader examination (Duchein, et al., 1994) of ludic reading in the literacy life histories of preservice teachers, suggests that in addition to its impact on future pedagogical practices, ludic reading often has a bibliotherapeutic effect. A subgroup of the participants in the larger study identified a particularly sensitive period during which reading for pleasure became an obsession and recalled this reading as sustaining and healing. In the reported experience of these preservice teachers, the pleasure of reading arose in conjunction with emotional or physical pain. For these participants, books were solace and salvation. Implications of this bibliotherapeutic effect will be discussed for teacher education.*

Ludic reading is reading for pleasure or play (Nell, 1988). The present paper emerged from a larger study of ludic reading (Duchein, et al., 1994) in which autobiographical writing (e.g., Pinar and Grumet, 1976) was used to create literacy life histories as a part of a reading methods course for teachers. The individual narratives revealed linkages between the participants' personal reading experiences and their visions for future classrooms and teaching. One hundred and twenty education majors were asked to reflect upon and describe in journals the bearing of home, formal schooling, methods courses, and classroom field work on their reading habits. Twenty of a large group reported benefits flowing from reading and included among those benefits therapeutic effects, which they explicitly identified as instrumental in the establishment of their ludic reading habit. This identification, because of the power and poignancy with which it was expressed, compelled further examination of this subgroup's responses.

Characteristically the habit of ludic reading in this group was formed in the context of emotional or physical pain and represented a response to that context. Recognition of literature's therapeutic effect goes back at least to Aristotle, who defined the proper function of tragedy as the arousal of "the emotions of pity and fear in the audience . . . in such a way as to effect that special purging off and relief *(catharsis)* of these two emotions" (Aristotle, trans. 1947). Aristotle's translator, Lane Cooper, comments that "Pity and fear are two from among the general class of disturbing emotions which it is the office of the various arts to relieve" (p.20). Cooper notes that the presence of pity and fear in some people to "a disquieting degree" necessitates "tragic excitement," which "serves as a sort of medicine, producing a *catharsis* to lighten and relieve the soul of the accumulated emotion within it." A "harmless pleasure" attends this "process of relief . . . [or *catharsis* which] is itself a form of pleasure" (p. 22). For Aristotle, pleasure arose from literature: tragedy in a context of pain.

Despite the commitment of teacher educators to foster the joys of literacy in their students, the pedagogical value and usefulness of Aristotle's insight may have been lost. In classrooms where lockstep commercialized packages hold sway, assessment driven, forced-choice instruction may actually hinder the students' enjoyment of and pleasure in reading. We propose that lest the significance of Aristotle's insight be lost on educators, literature's potentially therapeutic effects receive full light in teacher education.

Bibliotherapy, literally, healing through books, has been defined as "the dynamic interaction between a person and a piece of literature, an interaction through which the person satisfies emotional needs or finds solutions to personal problems in stories" (Savage, 1994). Grumet (1992) suggests, further, that by its very tendency to connect readers with meaningful lifeworlds of others, the act of reading is essentially an affective, even "romantic" occupation. Similarly, Duchein (1993) in her study of the lifelong reading practices of women, found that wide reading fostered tolerance, understanding, and compassion, as readers gained insights into lifeworlds of persons with different experiences. It is proposed, therefore, that for some readers ludic reading may be a bibliotherapeutic activity. It admits the reader to an internal terrain wherein connectedness and conversations that occur through the text between reader and other persons provide pleasurable relief from these readers' external context of pain.

Moffett (1984) proposes a model of the psychological mechanism that may be operative in the activity of ludic reading. He describes the literacy practices of reading and writing as phenomena which actually modify inner speech, i.e., "verbal currents of our inner stream" (p. 57). Thus, reading actually modifies how we talk to ourselves. Moffett notes that literacy activities have the power to change our stream of consciousness. While reading, according to Moffett, readers introject the text into their inner lives while simultaneously projecting their inner lives onto the text. Furthermore, the reader may spin off from the text through the use of fantasy, recollection, and reflection. Ludic reading entails the ability to let go of one's self and enter into the text with a receptivity and willingness to allow someone else's inner life temporarily into one's own, in a kind of benign "possession" (Moffett, p. 59) which is reflected in the phrase "getting lost in a book."

Pleasure, the pleasurable play of losing oneself in a text, is a central element in ludic reading. Arguably, play in itself has therapeutic effects. As defined by Huizinga (1950), play is a voluntary activity that possesses the quality of freedom. "It is never a task. It is done at leisure during 'free time'" (p.8). Thus, reading for play differs significantly from reading circumscribed by productive constraints placed on the reader to learn under mandatory conditions. The notion that play behaviors are an integral and important part of the lived experiences of animals and of homo sapiens is developed in studies of the brain, evolution, and ethology. Brown (1994) asserts that play may be as important to life in animals and in humans as sleeping or dreaming. "Play has benefits. It clearly aids in the healthy development of young animals, both physically and mentally, and is probably a boon to animals that continue to play into adulthood. Conversely, if young are prevented from playing or maltreated so that their play is abnormal, their development may also be abnormal" (p. 8). The element of play becomes critical to the formation of the habit of ludic reading within the context of pain. In ludic reading as pleasure emerges from pain, the mind engages in playful cathartic sorties with text. Hence, we propose, ludic reading becomes bibliotherapeutic. It is addictive, and almost hypnotic, or trance-like as it transports the reader into the world of books (Nell, 1988).

A classroom provides an environment for learning and growing in appreciation for diversity, and the teachers' role is to facilitate that environment. The teachers' past experiences as people who have developed a love of reading and who have chosen to read extensively for pleasure are critical to the success of the educational enterprise. Moreover, if the proper object of education is promoting the health and well-being of the intellectual faculty along with the physical and emotional faculties, preservice teachers must have an understanding of the nature and context of the therapeutic function of the study of literature.

Accordingly, this paper will seek to characterize the contexts of pain and the cathartic or therapeutic effects associated by this group of preservice teachers with ludic reading. How do these particular ludic readers characterize the painful circumstances from which their habit of ludic reading emerged? Precisely what therapeutic effects do they attribute to ludic reading? Specifically how do readers who read because they have experienced therapeutic effects characterize the linkage between those effects and the circumstances from which they arose? These questions focus the present investigation.

## Method

The twenty participants who included therapeutic effects among the benefits they perceived to flow from reading were enrolled in reading and language arts methods courses at a major southeastern university. The instructor modeled her beliefs through literature-based instruction, naturalistic assessment, and integration of curriculum. As part of this course, the students wrote autobiographical literacy life histories which described and reflected upon the myriad influences which shaped their beliefs and practices concerning literacy. Data sources included these preservice teachers' literacy life histories and personal interviews. Using constant comparative analysis (Miles and Huberman, 1984), these data were analyzed by four literacy educators for trends and patterns among the autobiographical pieces. The researchers began with broad categories—home, school, and literacy course experiences. Data sources were triangulated to verify occurrences and to control for biases; the final interpretation involved the multiple perspectives of the research team.

## Results

As we have said, the researchers began with the broad categories of home, school, and literacy course experiences. However, as they developed these data categories, a major theme emerged that defined a small but interesting subgroup. Perhaps the most important finding revealed in the literacy life histories of this group is the surprising conjunction of pain and joy in the circumstances antecedent to the formation of their ludic reading habit. They characteristically identified a particularly sensitive period during which reading books for pleasure became an obsession. Their stories suggest that, for them, the pleasures associated with reading arose from the circumstance of emotional or physical pain, which their reading either alleviated or rendered manageable. The conjunction of pain and pleasure overshadowed the particular location—home, school, etc.—in which the ludic reading habit arose. Their narratives were more occupied with the sources of the pain: the generic discomfort associated with maturing and adolescence (changing bodies and accompanying self consciousness); the angst associated with transition from childhood to adulthood; loss of loved ones (usually parents or grandparents); and changes in family circumstances (divorce of parents or geographical relocation). These participants found sustaining and nurturing value in the habit of ludic reading and continued to pursue it as a pleasurable activity. The accompanying self-nurturing, or ameliorative benefits of connection with others' lifeworlds and streams of consciousness were described typically as being a "savior, solace, even a kind of salvation."

The following representative accounts render vividly the particularities of the conjunction of pain and joy in association with the reading experience that we have characterized as bibliotherapeutic. We quote them at some length because these accounts convey the compelling intensity of this significant experience.

"Books were my solace and salvation . . . when my world was falling apart, the books were always there, and I always had a book with me."

"When I was eight, my parents got divorced. I really got into reading books then as a kind of diversion from what was going on at home. I would lock the door to my room and get lost in a book."

"Something really bad happened to me when I was a young girl. Only two people know about it. I am better now, but for a long time I felt different from everyone else, and it was during those times that I sought to escape from the bad feelings through reading books."

"We moved from Venezuela when I was eight. I was forced to learn English and struggled in a school that was not as nurturing as the one I went to in Venezuela. I remember crying in front of the class. My parents tried to help me adjust, but for a long time I went to books to feel better."

"When I entered the fifth grade, I discovered the joys, not only of reading, but of writing . . . I was addicted . . . Miss G. saw this happening and used it to draw me out of the protective shell I had built around myself. I saw myself as a freak, and so I was reluctant to show anyone too much of myself, fearing another rejection. She helped me to see that my love for words was not something to be ashamed of, but part of my whole self, every bit as necessary as my heart."

"Even my earliest memories brought reality that I was different from my peers . . . my mother had died when I was born, and I lived with my grandparents. I always felt different. First grade was a fascination. Books brought me into a world about which I knew nothing. And they opened me up like a budding flower. The books that were read to me were a marvel. I loved them. I really did. Each one brought something new and exciting into my life. The world of school was a growing, learning, and happy experience, different from the unhappy home I lived in. I had many teachers who read from the classics and showed films too. Those were my favorite times, unsurpassed by all other times until I discovered the school library. It was a hole in the wall, no librarian and limited books. But to me it was a storehouse of ecstasy. After my grandmother's death, it was just my grandfather and me. Loneliness lived beside me. Books were my friends."

Several of the participants in this group also noted a time of forced inactivity during which reading for pleasure was a therapeutic response to physical pain:

"During two years of hospitalization, I sought out reading and word games as a way to soothe the pain and forget the unpleasant emotions involved. Reading was my escape into whatever state of mind I wanted to be in. It was my savior . . . I know from experience that reading can be healing."

"When I was eleven, I broke my leg. My mom would read me the King Arthur legends to help pass the time. During that time, I forgot about the heavy plaster cast on my leg and felt normal again. She brought me lots of books from the library, and I devoured them."

A second important finding is that those preservice teachers for whom ludic reading performed this sustaining and healing function intended to create classroom environments that support ludic reading. For example, one participant enthusiastically anticipated her

"future as a teacher filled with books. Reading and writing will be a way of life in my classroom. I hope I can convey the power of the written word to the children through literature. I hope I can encourage them to gain self-confidence and inner strength to allow themselves to express themselves through writing."

Another who intended to "surround" her class in reading activities, looked forward to her children spending some of their day

"immersed in their own world reading books of their choice. . . . Reading in general will be seen as a positive relaxing thing for children to do. It will be something that they will grow up loving."

And yet another:

"I decided that I wanted to be the kind of teacher that would teach children to love to read."

These examples convey the zeal and passion generated by recognition of the healing force of ludic reading. Thus, the roles of independent reading during free reading time, access to books of choice, reading aloud, and the sanctity of their own literacy experiences were perceived as important aspects of their future classrooms.

A third major finding of this study concerned the preservice teachers' appreciation of the autobiographical writing assignment. They felt that this was an opportunity that allowed them to discover and recognize the influences that contributed to their own love of learning, and to realize the full value of their own experience of reading's therapeutic effect in future practices. For example, one preservice teacher reflected on her writing experience in these terms:

> "Why am I the way I am today? What happened in my life to make me grow into the person I have become? These are questions we do not ask ourselves very often, but are pretty interesting and . . . . important."

As she looked back on her life, she "remembered several events and people who" she had "encountered and been influenced by." Others, in class, expressed thanks for the opportunity to make these discoveries afforded by the literacy life history assignment. Ludic reading became for them a way to assist their students in becoming able to nurture themselves by finding their own joys in reading, and ultimately, to use literacy abilities and behaviors to embrace one's world and one's self with largesse and compassion.

## Conclusions and Implications

These particular ludic readers claim to have found in reading a mechanism of response to the stress of emotional or physical pain. As readers they merged their own lifeworlds with the minds and lives of the characters about whom they read. Reading became for them a self-nurturing sortie, pursued because it provided a healing intimacy of heart and mind. Their identification of a particularly sensitive period during which reading books for pleasure became an obsession is an important finding of our study. It suggests that just as cognitive aspects of reading are critical to intellectual health, affective aspects of reading are critical to emotional health. In teacher education a consequence of focusing on cognitive aspects of reading without regard to affective aspects of reading may be the loss of an important opportunity to achieve our educational objectives. Indeed, preservice teachers' recognition and deep appreciation of ludic reading's bibliotherapeutic effect can strengthen their overall pedagogical strategy in their future classrooms. This will require that teacher educators in their reading methods courses explicitly address this potential dimension of the reading experience. Both their own and their students' intellectual and emotional health may, thereby, be enhanced.

Well armed with the personal experience of having been touched by the affective aspects of literacy the preservice teachers in this study are uniquely positioned to pass this benefit on to their students. Their evangelical fervor, so apparent in their literacy life histories, bespeaks a renewed emphasis on the classroom library, the pleasures of reading aloud, and the interpretive study of literature. While literature may be pursued for its own sake, the cathartic pleasure which can arise from ludic reading serves an additional function in the lifeworld of the reader. Another implication for teacher educators flows from our third finding: the seminal importance of encouraging preservice teachers to write literacy life histories. It is through this act of composition that they may realize the conjunction of the pain and pleasure associated with their ludic reading. .

Does Aristotle, then, urge us today as literacy educators to acknowledge the difficulties and pains which may have given birth to our own stories of loving to read? And to offer to our preservice teachers, as others have offered to us, the blessings of discovering in libraries, schools, and bookshelves, the palliatives that will, in the midst of pain, restore joy to our souls and our hearts? In the largest sense, we suggest, this is the mission of teacher education.

---

# References

(Aristotle, trans. 1947) *Aristotle: On the art of poetry* (L. Cooper, Trans.). Ithaca, NY: Cornell University Press.

Brown, S.L. (1994, December). Animals at play. *National Geographic, 186,* 2-35.

Callois, R. (1961). *Man, play, and games.* Glencoe, IL: Free Press.

Duchein, M. (1993). *Women's stories of reading and writing: Three Literacy Life Histories.* Unpublished doctoral dissertation, Louisiana State University, Baton Rouge.

Duchein, M., Frazier, D., Konopak, B., & Palmer, P. (1994). *Who are these people we teach? Exploring literacy life histories during an elementary reading methods course.* Manuscript submitted for publication.

Grumet, M. (1992). Romantic research: Why we love to read. In C. Kinzer & D. Leu (Eds), *Literacy research, theory, and practice: Views from many perspectives.* Forty-first Yearbook of the National Reading Conference (33-49). Chicago: National Reading Conference.

Huizinga, J. (1950). *Homo ludens.* Boston: Beacon.

Miles, M.B., & Huberman, A.M. (1984). *Qualitative data analysis.* Beverly Hills, CA: Sage.

Moffett, J. (1984). Reading and writing as meditation. In J.M. Jensen (Ed.), *Composing and comprehending* (pp. 57-65). Urgana, IL: ERIC Clearinghouse on Reading and Communication Skills and National Conference on Research in English.

Nell, V. (1988). The psychology of reading for pleasure: Needs and gratifications. *Reading Research Quarterly, 23,* 6-48.

Pinar, W.F., & Grumet, M.R. (1976). *Toward a poor curriculum.* New York: Peter Lang.

Savage, J.F. (1994). *Teaching reading using literature.* Madison, WI: Brown & Benchmark.

# LITERACY IN PRESCHOOL, ELEMENTARY, AND SECONDARY SETTINGS

# THE RELATIONSHIP BETWEEN WRITING FORM AND EMERGENT READING BEHAVIOR: PATTERNS ACROSS 3-, 4-, AND 5-YEAR-OLDS

## June E. Barnhart

Northern Illinois University

## Abstract

*This research focused on the relationship between children's emergent reading of storybooks and their own self-composed text by comparing patterns within and between cohorts of 3-, 4-, and 5-year-olds (10 children per age group). Further, in an effort to examine the concurrent development of children's reading and writing behaviors, the relation between the writing systems used by children to produce their own text and their emergent reading of that text was examined. Differential patterns across 3-, 4-, and 5-year-olds and similarities in patterns across age groups are reported. These results suggest that there are aspects of becoming literate that are both developmental and universal. Age-related differences in literacy learning may be most salient to individuals who design and implement instructional programs, while features of literacy behaviors that form common patterns that can be generalized across age levels hold implications that may contribute to our understanding of the mechanism(s) of becoming literate.*

Current descriptions throughout the literature are describing ways in which reading and writing are related to literacy learning among elementary grade children (Heller, 1991; Shanahan, 1990; Tierney & Pearson, 1985). Barr (1985) suggests that while reading and writing processes are different from each other, they are related and mutually reinforce each other in the process of becoming literate throughout the elementary grades. Recent research in emergent literacy suggests that reading and writing are not independent or sequential processes in preschool children's literacy learning prior to formal instruction (Barnhart, 1988, 1991; Ferreiro & Teberosky, 1982; Sulzby, 1985a; Sulzby, Barnhart & Hieshima, 1989), but are mutually supportive processes (Sulzby & Teale, 1985). Based on descriptive research, the emergent literacy perspective considers the young child to be a "writer/reader" (Teale & Sulzby, 1986, p. xviii), and this view is expressed by the term "literacy." Furthermore, the term "emergent" reflects the view that literacy learning in young children is a developmental, continuous process.

While studies to date have yielded rich descriptions of young children's emergent reading and writing behaviors (e.g., Barnhart, 1991; Clay, 1975; Dyson, 1986; Ferreiro & Teberosky, 1982; Read, 1971; Sulzby, 1985b; Teale, 1986), they have tended to focus on either reading or writing. Few studies have examined the concurrent development of young children's reading and writing behaviors prior to entry into formal literacy instruction. Furthermore, little attention appears to have been directed at studying the interactive nature of reading and writing processes in children prior to entry into kindergarten. The present research was built on the work of others who have examined the reciprocal processes of reading and writing behaviors in elementary grade and kindergarten children. The current study sought to extend our knowledge base by sampling emergent literacy behaviors in young children of various ages, and thus focused on the developmental nature of reading and writing as complementary and reciprocal literacy processes. The study focused on the relationship between emergent reading of storybooks and self-composed text, as well as the relationship between the reading of self-composed text and the writing system(s) used by preschool and kindergarten children to produce that text. In order to compare developmental patterns within and among cohorts of 3-, 4-, and 5-year old children, the present study asked the following questions:

(1) What patterns of emergent literacy behavior can be described in children when they are asked to read a conventionally printed storybook and when asked to read their own self-composed text?

(2) Will there be similar patterns in the reading of these two types of text?

(3) What is the relationship between children's reading of their own self-composed text and their use of not-yet-conventional writing systems?

## Method
### Subjects

To address these three questions, 10 subjects in each of three age groups (3, 4, and 5 years old) participated in the study. In the 3-year-old group, there were 5 females and 5 males; in the 4-year-old group there were 6 females and 4 males; and in the 5-year-old group there were 4 females and 6 males. Subjects came from an upper-middle to lower-middle socioeconomic community that was located in a northwestern suburb of Chicago. Subjects represented a range of ethnic backgrounds, including Caucasian, Hispanic, and African American. None of the subjects had attended any formal preschool.

### Materials and Procedure

Each subject was individually involved in two literacy tasks, each presented separately over two interview sessions. All sessions were tape recorded by the examiner, later transcribed, and double-checked for accuracy.

Task 1, *Storybook Reading Re-enactment*, followed the method and analysis scheme of Sulzby (1985b). Subjects were asked to read a familiar storybook to the examiner. This task was designed to elicit an independent emergent reading attempt from each subject. The child was allowed to choose the storybook, and the examiner elicited the reading attempts by saying to each subject, "Read me your book."

Task 2, *Storywriting Production and Reading*, followed the method and analysis scheme used by Sulzby (1985a) and Sulzby, Barnhart and Hieshima (1989). Subjects were individually asked to write a story about something scary or exciting that had happened to them, and then were asked to read their production to the examiner.

### Analysis

Analyses were based on detailed transcriptions of the subjects' reading attempts on both tasks. Transcriptions were scored by two trained raters who independently scored each subject's responses during reading in Task 1 and Task 2. Transcriptions were scored according to the classification scheme for young children's storybook reading attempts devised by Sulzby (1985b) with five-year-olds. This branching categorization scheme is arranged across 11 levels, with Level 1 representing behaviors involving the least mature reading reenactment. Briefly described, this scheme categorizes responses as: (a) Governed by Print; (b) Governed by Pictures and Forming Stories Using Written Language-like Speech; (c) Governed by Pictures and Forming Stories Using Oral Language-like Speech, or; (d) Governed by Pictures but Not Forming Stories (Following the Action or Labeling and Commenting). Subjects' written productions in Task 2 were categorized with regard to writing system(s) used. Writing was scored according to the following classification scheme: drawing, scribble, letter strings, letter-like units, and invented or conventional spelling (Sulzby, Barnhart & Hieshima, 1989). Initial agreement between raters was 92.6%, with consensus reached through discussion.

### Results

**Children's Reading of a Conventional Storybook and Their Own Self-Composed Text**. Table 1 shows the distribution of subjects across age groups in the major categories of the Sulzby (1985b) classification scheme when asked to read either a conventional storybook or their own text.

**Table 1. Percentage of Subjects by Categories\* Across Age**

Task 1: Storybook Reading Re-enactment
Task 2: Storywriting Production and Reading

| Categories of Reading Attempts | 3-year-olds (n=10) | | 4-year-olds (n=10) | | 5-year-olds (n=10) | |
|---|---|---|---|---|---|---|
| | Task 1 | Task 2 | Task 1 | Task 2 | Task 1 | Task 2 |
| Governed by Pictures, Stories Not Formed | 100 | 100 | 20 | 20 | | 30 |
| Governed by Pictures, Oral Language-like Stories | | | 80 | 80 | 30 | 20 |
| Governed by Pictures, Written Language-like Stories | | | | | 50 | 20 |
| Governed by Print | | | | | 20 | 30 |

\*Sulzby (1985). *"Classification Scheme for Emergent Reading of Favorite Storybooks"*

Across age groups, reading reenactment behaviors ranged the entire span of the Sulzby (1985b) classification scheme on both Task 1 and Task 2. However, there also were age-related differences in the patterns of reenactment behaviors. In this regard, on both tasks the distribution of subject's reading reenactment behaviors changed as a function of age. The least mature reading reenactments were produced by subjects in the 3-year-old group, and the higher levels were increasingly represented by subjects in the 5-year-old group.

In addition to these differential patterns across ages there were also overlapping patterns across age groups. For example, when asked to read a conventionally printed storybook or their own self-produced text, all (100%) subjects in the 3-year-old group were classified at the lowest levels of the classification scheme, where they used speech involving Labeling and Commenting or Following the Action. Like subjects in the 3-year-old group, all of the 4-year-old subjects used pictures as the source of the story, including 20% on both tasks who were classified at the lowest levels of the Sulzby (1985b) classification scheme.

Beyond this overlap with the 3-year-olds, however, were differential patterns between children in these two age groups. Table 1 shows that greater variety in language was used by subjects in the 4-year-old group, with most of these subjects (80%) forming a story by using the wording and intonation of oral language to read either the storybook or their own written production.

The greatest variety was seen among subjects in the 5-year-old group. Only a few were classified at the highest level by using the print as the source of the message and were reading independently in both Tasks 1 and 2 (20% and 30%, respectively). Most were classified across the lower levels of the scheme where, like subjects in the 4-year-old group, they used the pictures to form a story using either the wording and intonation of written language (50% on Task 1 and 20% on Task 2) or the wording and oral intonation of a storyteller (30% on Task 1). None of the 5-year-old subjects on Task 1 were classified at the very lowest level (Governed by Pictures, Stories Not Formed). On Task 2, 50% of these subjects were classified at this level, and used Labeling and Commenting or Following the Action.

Beyond these patterns in emergent reading reenactment behaviors, when subjects in the present study were asked to write their own story in Task 2, Table 2 shows that they used a wide range of writing systems. These systems included conventional spelling, invented spelling, letter strings, scribbling, and drawing. Further, Table 2 shows the differential patterns across age groups with regard to writing systems.

More specifically, drawing was used exclusively by all of the subjects in the 3-year-old group, and only drawing and scribbling were used by the 4-year-olds. The widest range of writing systems was used by subjects in the 5-year-old group, and included drawing, scribbling, letter strings, and a combination of conventional and invented spelling.

**Table 2. Percentage of Subjects by Forms of Writing Systems Used to Produdce Text Across Age**

| | Task 2: Storywriting Production and Reading | | |
|---|---|---|---|
| Writing System | 3-year-olds (n=10) | Group 4-year-olds (n=10) | 5-year-olds (n=10) |
| Drawing | 100 | 90 | 10 |
| Scribbling | | 10 | 10 |
| Letter Strings | | | 20 |
| Invented Spelling | | | 30 |
| Conventional Spelling | | | 30 |

Data from Tasks 1 and 2 support previous research by Barnhart (1992) who used the Sulzby (1985a) classification scheme to describe the emergent reading behaviors of 5-year-olds when asked to read two kinds of text. These data also extend previous research by suggesting that this developmental classification scheme can be used to differentially describe emergent reading behaviors of children younger than 5-years old (i.e., 3- and 4-year-olds).

**Patterns Across Ages in Children's Reading of a Conventional Storybook and their own Self-composed Text.** Results reported in this study showed that in all three age groups, there was stability in reading behaviors across the two types of text. Spearman Rank-Order Correlations comparing subjects' emergent reading of a storybook containing conventional orthography and their reading of their own self-composed text (containing a variety of graphic forms) were significant using a critical ratio z-test ($p < 0.05$, two-tailed) for each age group (3-year-olds: r = +0.63; 4-year-olds: r = +0.72; 5-year-olds: r = +0.67).

**The Relationship Between Children's Reading of Self-composed Text and Writing Systems.** Several observations can be made concerning the relation between subjects' reading of their own text and the graphic form of that text. To illustrate the characteristic patterns across age groups in this relationship, Figures 1-5 present photocopy reductions of the writing of several representative subjects of different ages, along with their reading of these productions (pseudonyms have replaced actual names to preserve privacy).

The first pattern is illustrated in Figure 1 by *Patrick* who was in the 3-year-old group. Although this pattern was observed in all three age groups, its greatest frequency occurred among subjects in the 3-year-old group. In general, less mature reading behaviors were observed when subjects were reading from drawing, with readings consisting mainly of labeling and commenting on parts of the drawings.

A second pattern that was observed across all three age groups was also the most frequent pattern among 4-year-olds. As illustrated in Figure 2 by *Maria* (a 4-year-old), many subjects also used drawing to produce their story, reading their production using a mix of written or oral language-like speech.

**Figure 1: Patrick**

Reading: This is me. These are my two presents. There's my birthday cake. Umm. There's my cash register and there's my *Jungle Book.*

### Figure 2: Maria

Reading: Um, once upon a time there was a little girl named _____ and she went to Sam's baseball game. Any Mommy was sittin down watchin the baseball game real nice at Sam's game. And she went down to the playground and was real good and she was very nice. So then Mommy said "Come on _____, it's time to leave." And then, um, sh-- she um took um _____ to the candy store. And then she thinks about what she was gonna say, um, I mean, what she was gonna buy. And then she said, "Why don't you buy those peanut butter things cause they're your favorite." "Oh, no, no, no, no, no, no, no. I just want to pick out my own. I'm gonna find my own that I like. Oh, there's Jurassic Park eggs! I wonder what kind of dinosaur toy will be in here." The end.

A third pattern is shown in Figure 3 by *Trellis,* and can be described for several children in the 4- and 5-year-old groups who read their written production by forming a story using written or oral language-like speech (or a mix) but were reading from their written production that consisted of scribble.

### Figure 3: Trellis

Reading: Jess is my friend. She's at school. And she lives with Barney and she's in love. Then she has to come back to my house because then she needs to go to bed. And then when she wakes up she goes to the mall. Sometimes bears come in her room. Then she climbs out of bed. And then she goes under the rocks. Then she goes under the bridge. Then she goes up the wall. Well, then she goes under the lake and then she goes up the hill and sees owl and he says whoo whoo (child makes hooting noises). And then they run down the hill. Then they come back to my house. And go to bed. That's the end.

## Figure 4: John

Reading: I wrote when I fell of my bike. It all started one warm sunny day, a long time ago. I was on top of the hill. I then decided to drive down from the top of the hill and I was riding on the concrete. I slipped and fell and my lip got all swollen up and I put on new shorts on and new clothes and then I got all better.

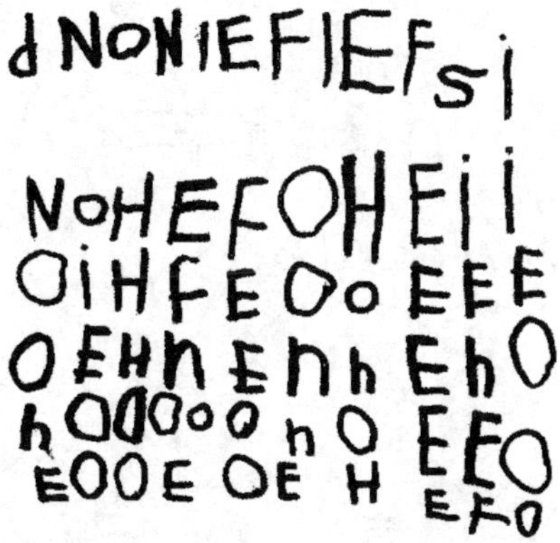

A fourth pattern, illustrated in Figure 4 by *John,* was observed among other 4- and 5-year-old subjects who read their own text using written or oral language-like speech (or a mix) to form a story but who used strings of patterned or random letters to produce their story.

Finally, as illustrated in Figure 5 by *Mateo* several 5-year-olds who showed the most mature reading behaviors were reading independently from self-composed text that they themselves had written using a combination of invented and conventional spelling.

## Discussion

Results of children's storybook reading attempts in the present study support the presence of and lend validation to the categories proposed in 1985 and used by Sulzby in cross-sectional research with 2-, 3-, 4-, and 5-year-olds to demonstrate developmental literacy trends in independent storybook reenactments. Further, in the present study when the scale was used to analyze children's reading of their own self-composed text, the scale maintained its sensitivity to differentially describe emergent reading behaviors across 3-, 4-, and 5-year-old children.

This research also examined the developmental link between reading and writing, lending support to the position that there is an overlap in children's hypotheses about the rules of the written language system of their culture. Considerable attention has been devoted to the reading-writing connection in older children (Tierney & Pearson, 1985). The present study documents this complementary process in younger children. Results from the present work underscore the suggestion that the forms of writing and their relationship to reading also play a prominent role in our understanding of

**Figure 5: Mateo**

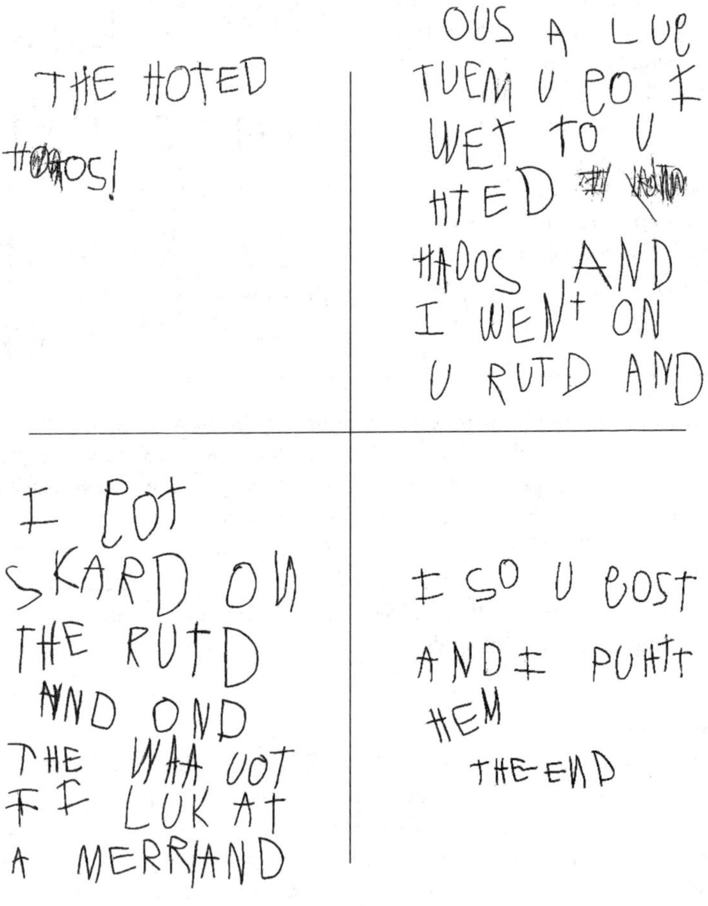

THE HOTED

H@OS!

OUS A LUP
TUEM U PO I
WET TO U
HTED ~ ~~
HADOS AND
I WENt ON
U RUTD AND

I POT
SKARD OV
THE RUTD
NND OND
THE WHA UOT
F I LUK At
A MERRAND

I SO U POST
AND I PUHTt
HEM

THE END

Reading: The haunted house. That's the title. Here's the story. Once, once, a a, once a long time ago. A long time ago. Ago. A long time ago I went to a haunted house, and I went on a ride and I got scared on the ride and on the way out I looked at a mirror. Mirror (child points to MERR/AND). These two words are going to be separate. I'm going to put a line down to separate them (child draws line in). A mirror. And I saw a ghost. An I punched him. The end. Do you know what this is? (child points to !) It's an excited mark.

young children's literacy development. Through a comprehensive study of the various aspects of reading and writing and an acknowledgement of their mutual interdependence, the value of each process in becoming literate can be realized in our efforts to help the learner.

Finally, it is likely that developmental differences may account for much of the variance, or heterogeneity, in literacy behaviors observed across children of different ages in the present study. However, the homogeneity, or similarities, in patterns reported here suggests that we need to take note of what is shared across ages in the process of forming an understanding of reading and writing so that we may perhaps move forward in our efforts to elucidate the mechanism(s) of becoming literate.

---

# References

Barnhart, J. E. (1988). The relationship between graphic forms and the child's underlying conceptualization of writing. In J. E. Readence & R. S. Baldwin (Eds.), *Dialogs in literacy research. Thirty-seventh yearbook of the National Reading Conference* (pp. 297-306). Chicago: National Reading Conference.

Barnhart, J. E. (1991). Criterion-related validity of interpretations of children's performance on emergent literacy tasks. *Journal of Reading Behavior, 24*(4), 425- 444.

Barnhart, J. E. (1992). Children's emergent reading behaviors across different kinds of text and the relation to writing systems. In N. Padak & T. Tasinski (Eds.), *Literacy research and practice: Foundations for the year 2000. College Reading Association Yearbook* (pp. 193-201). Kent, OH: Kent State University.

Barr, J. E. (1985). Writing and reading: A marriage between equals. In M. M. Clark (Ed.), *New directions in the study of reading* (pp. 103-111). London: Falmer Press.

Clay, M. M. (1975). *What did I write?* London: Heinemann.

Dyson, A. (1986). Children's early interpretations of writing: Expanding research perspectives. In D. B. Yaden & S. Templeton (Eds.), *Metalinguistic awareness and beginning literacy* (pp. 201-218). Portsmouth, NJ: Heinemann.

Ferreiro, E., & Teberosky, A. (1982). *Literacy before schooling.* Exeter, NH: Heinemann.

Heller, M. F. (1991). *Reading-writing connections: From theory to practice.* White Pines, NY: Longmann.

Read, C. (1971). Preschool children's knowledge of English phonology. *Harvard Educational Review, 41*(1), 1-34.

Shanahan, T. (Ed.) (1990). *Reading and writing together: New perspectives for the classroom.* Norwood, MA: Christopher Gordon.

Sulzby, E. (1985a). Kindergartners as writers and readers. In M. Farr (Ed.), *Advances in writing research, Vol. 1: Children's early writing development* (pp. 127-199). Norwood, NJ: Ablex.

Sulzby, E. (1985b). Children's emergent reading of favorite storybooks: A developmental study. *Reading Research Quarterly, 20,* 458-481.

Sulzby, E., Barnhart, J. E., & Hieshima, J. (1989). Forms of writing and rereading from writing: A preliminary report. In J. Mason (Ed.), *Reading/writing connections* (pp. 31-63). Newark, DE: International Reading Association.

Sulzby, E., & Teale, W. (1985). Writing development in early childhood. *Educational Horizons, 6,* 8-12.

Teale, W. H. (1986). Home background and young children's literacy development. In W. H. Teale & E. Sulzby (Eds.), *Emergent literacy: Writing and reading* (pp. 173-206). Norwood, NJ: Ablex.

Teale, W. H. & Sulzby, E. (Eds.) (1986). *Emergent literacy: Writing and reading*. Norwood, NJ: Ablex.

Tierney, R. J., & Pearson, P. D. (1985). Toward a composing model of reading. In C. Hedley & A. Baratta (Eds.), *Contexts of reading* (pp. 63-78). Norwood, NJ: Ablex.

# READING WORKSHOP: AN EARLY READING INTERVENTION APPROACH FOR AT-RISK STUDENTS

**Belinda Zimmerman**
**Tracy Foreman**
Kent City Schools, Ohio

**Timothy V. Rasinski**
Kent State University

## Abstract

*This pilot study examined an approach to early compensatory intervention in reading that was developed and implemented by classroom teachers. The intervention, called Reading Workshop, involved 45-minute instructional periods before school three days per week. Six of the most at-risk students in reading from two first-grade classrooms received systematic and engaging instruction from October through May of the school year. This instruction included theory-based instructional strategies and high levels of authentic reading. Achievement in reading was compared with that of similar at-risk first graders who received a more traditional form of compensatory instruction (Chapter I). In all posttreatment analyses of reading achievement, the Reading Workshop students outperformed the control group. The study suggests that successful compensatory instruction is possible for young at-risk readers and that it can be designed, implemented, and owned by informed and motivated teachers.*

We now know enough to guarantee that virtually every child will learn to be a good reader and writer during the first two years of school. To us, as educators, that means that there are no excuses for having a large number of children who cannot read or can read little. (Lyons, Pinnell, & DeFord, 1993, p. xv)

The development of high degrees of literacy among all elementary students remains a major concern of educators. According to the 1994 National Assessment of Educational Progress (NAEP), fully 42% of fourth grade students assessed nationwide performed below the most basic level of achievement in reading (Williams, Reese, Campbell, Mazzeo, & Phillips, 1995). Moreover, the results of the 1994 NAEP in reading represent a retreat from the levels of achievement found in the 1992 assessment.

Obviously, a significant number of students at the elementary level are at risk in reading. However, compensatory education efforts for elementary students have not had the desired results. For example, many scholars believe that Title I (identified as Chapter I prior to 1995), the federally funded compensatory education program for students in reading, has not accomplished expected results (Allington, Steutzel, Shake, & Lamarche, 1986; Cooley, 1981). Indeed, remedial efforts have demonstrated markedly small effects on student achievement, as measured by standardized tests of reading (Johnston & Allington, 1991).

Problems that have been associated with compensatory education reading programs include few opportunities for students to engage in higher-order thinking skills (Birman, et al., 1987); continual emphasis on lower-level drill and repetition of basic skills rather than high level tasks (Calfee, 1986); emphasis on the completion of skills sheets and other skill-related activities rather than on authentic contextual reading (Johnston & Allington, 1991); and little attempt to coordinate the compensatory program instruction students receive with the instruction they are provided in their regular classrooms (Allington, et al., 1986; McGill-Franzen & Allington, 1990). Allington and his colleagues also have found that significant amounts of time given for compensatory literacy education are lost in transition from the regular classroom. Moreover, although compensatory programs are intended as supplemental to the reading instruction students receive in their regular classrooms, in some cases this instruction is the main or only literacy instruction that at-risk students receive. It is, therefore, clear that alternative models are needed for students who experience considerable difficulty in becoming literate.

## Program Models for the Early Grades

The early grades are particularly critical for reading development. Difficulty in attaining proficiency in the early grades can lead to severe academic difficulties throughout students' school careers. Longitudinal studies have found that third-grade students who are reading below grade level and have failed at least one grade are unlikely to complete 12th grade (Kelly, Veldman, & McGuire, 1964; Lloyd, 1978). Moreover, efforts aimed at alleviating reading difficulties for students above third grade are seldom successful (Kennedy,

Birman, & Demaline, 1986). Thus, it is critical that primary grade students be given strong instructional support to develop early proficiency in reading. As Stanovich (1986) suggests, paraphrasing Walberg and Tsai (1983), ". . . individuals who have advantageous early educational experiences are able to utilize new educational experiences more efficiently." Intervention programs for younger students, therefore, hold the greatest promise for lasting success (Slavin, Karweit, & Madden, 1992).

One alternative to the traditional model that aims specifically to intervene with children in reading at a young age is Reading Recovery (Pinnell, DeFord, & Lyons, 1988). Based upon the work of Marie Clay (1985), Reading Recovery seeks to identify children at risk in literacy during their first-grade year and provide intensive remedial treatment and "recovery" before the reading difficulties become permanently embedded in the individual. Although Reading Recovery has been shown to be successful in remediating young students' difficulties in reading (Pinnell, Lyons, DeFord, Bryk, & Seltzer, 1994), the program can be exceedingly expensive, and therefore may impact only a few of the many students who require tutorial assistance (Rasinski, 1995).

The Reading Workshop program reported here was developed by the first two authors, in consultation with the third, in order to address the instructional needs of groups of first grade students experiencing significant difficulty in attaining proficiency in reading. Belinda and Tracy are first grade classroom teachers who sought to develop a compensatory and accelerative reading program that would meet the needs of children in their own classrooms. This paper describes the Reading Workshop program and provides some preliminary evaluative data on its pilot implementation over the course of a year.

## Reading Workshop

Reading Workshop is based on the assumption that all children can successfully learn to read, because we concur with Slavin and his associates that:

> the first goal of reform should be to ensure that every child, regardless of home background, home language, or learning style, achieves the success that he or she so confidently expected in kindergarten, that all children maintain their motivation, enthusiasm, and optimism because they are objectively succeeding at the school's tasks. Any reform that does less that this is hollow and self-defeating (Slavin et al., 1995).

In developing the program, we explored models and principles verified through research with young learners, including but not limited to the Reading Recovery model (Clay, 1985; Pinnell, DeFord, & Lyons, 1988), Rasinski's

(1989) guiding principles for fluency instruction, Cunningham and Cunningham's (1992) word recognition instruction, and Richek and McTague's (1988) ideas related to intertextual links in children's reading. In addition to developing an intervention program based upon the work of others, we also felt that the intervention instruction must be supplemental to, but coordinated with, the regular first grade curriculum. Thus, we designed Reading Workshop to be implemented with students outside of the regular instructional day.

The Reading Workshop was implemented by the first two authors with four selected first grade students from each of their classes from October through June of the school year. The workshop occurred during the 45-50 minutes preceding the beginning of school on Tuesdays, Wednesdays, and Thursdays. Students were selected for the workshop based upon observations and assessments by their classroom teachers that they were most at risk for failing at reading. These observations were corroborated by assessments by the school reading specialist.

Students' parents were notified that their children were selected for participation in the workshop and agreed to bring their children to school at the arranged time on workshop days. In one case a teacher regularly picked up a child at her home and brought her to school.

The workshop followed a regular weekly routine that focused on the development of word recognition strategies and fluent and meaningful reading of connected text. The three-day workshop routine is outlined in Figure 1. During each workshop, eight students sat at a table where, from October through November, instruction was provided by one teacher with the second teacher observing and providing individual encouragement and support as needed. Since the workshop was a collaboratively planned and implemented venture between the two first grade teachers, the teachers switched roles routinely throughout the duration of the workshop. Beginning in December, the teachers divided the group of eight children into two groups of four in order to better meet the individual needs of the students. The stronger of the two groups was able to move along at a slightly faster pace. The teachers felt strongly that their primary goal should be to accept the child at his or her current level of achievement and then accelerate learning as much as possible.

The third author of this paper consulted with the teachers, regularly observed the workshop in action, completed individual assessments of students in the workshop as well as a group of students having similar reading characteristics from a control first grade classroom not participating in the project, and evaluated the overall effects of the program. Observations revealed several key characteristics that seemed to permeate the workshop. These are described below.

**Figure 1. Reading Workshop Schedule**

***Day 1***

| | |
|---|---|
| 8:00-8:10 | Introduce new book and read aloud by teacher |
| 8:10-8:15 | Choral reading of the book by teacher and students |
| 8:15-8:20 | Students make word cards from words selected from the book for their word banks (Words taken home by students to practice) |
| 8:20-8:30 | Students read a phonogram text (text that reinforces a particular word family) |
| 8:30-8:40 | Word card practice and games and words in boxes (Elkonin boxes with words from phonogram text or book) |
| 8:40-8:45 | Action phonics—Large letter cards associated with student actions (e.g. M=march, J=jump) |

***Day 2***

| | |
|---|---|
| 8:00-8:10 | Reread and discuss book from Day 1. Can be reread more than once. |
| 8:10-8:20 | Reread and discuss phonogram text from Day 1 |
| 8:20-8:25 | Practice and discuss word cards from Day 1 book and phonogram text |
| 8:25-8:35 | Working with cut-up sentence written/dictated by students (students read sentence, cut it up into words, and reassemble words into sentence) |
| 8:35-8:45 | Word sort activities from students' word banks. Words are usually sorted by letter features (consonant vs vowels) or phonetic characteristics of words. |
| 8:45-8:50 | Action phonics (see Day 1) |

***Day 3***

| | |
|---|---|
| 8:00-8:15 | Reread, chorally and individually, story and phonogram text from Day 1 |
| 8:15-8:20 | Students make a journal entry about their work in the workshop or about their day |
| 8:20-8:30 | Work with new cut-up sentence (see Day 2) |
| 8:30-8:40 | Word games from word bank (e.g. word war, word bingo, go fish) |
| 8:40-8:50 | Individual students begin to write and make their own storybooks. (The activity is continued during the regular day with all the students. Workshop students have a head start and can help other students later. Finished storybooks are read by the authoring students as well as classmates throughout the school year) |

**High levels of engagement.** Teachers worked to focus students' attention on the instructional tasks at hand. Students were expected and reminded to attend to the teacher's instruction and the tasks the students were asked to do. The small groups as well as the second observing and assisting teacher helped to keep students focused. In addition, the percentage of time actually spent on authentic contextual reading was high.

**Effective instructional strategies.** Teachers engaged students in reading tasks that were based on effective instruction as described in the professional literature. Adaptations were made to meet the needs of the students or the instructional styles of the teachers. The "Making Words" activity (Cunningham & Cunningham, 1992) is one example of a research-based instructional technique that was used.

**Authentic reading.** In each workshop lesson, students were asked to read literature. Narratives, poems, and short expository texts made up the bulk of this reading. Many of the instructional strategies were selected to help students successfully read the literature they encountered in the workshop.

**Systematic instruction.** The instructional strategies and authentic reading activities were implemented in systematic ways that were highly predictable for students. Instruction followed a regular routine between and within days. Each week, instruction centered around a book children wanted to learn to read. The instructional sequence within each individual lesson tended to go from whole text reading to various levels of decontextualization of the reading (i.e. examining progressively smaller units of text, from sentences, to phrases, to words, to word families, etc.) and returning to whole text reading.

**Coordination with the regular reading curriculum.** Because the teachers teaching the workshop were also the students' regular classroom teachers, it was easy for them to ensure the activities and reading during the workshop were coordinated with and reinforced the reading instruction students received during regular classroom reading instruction. For example, during the Thursday workshop students usually created a story and made books based on the week's reading theme. This activity also occurred in the regular classroom. The earlier involvement by the workshop students gave them a head start on the activity and put them in the position of guiding other students in making their own books. This was a new position of responsibility and expertise for many of the workshop students.

**Ownership and investment.** The workshop program described in this paper was designed, planned, and implemented by the first two authors. Because Belinda and Tracy had ownership of their own program, they were fully knowledgeable about their work and felt committed to the success of the program. The teachers believed that their sense of ownership would have been less if the program had been mandated by the school administration or if an existing and external model of instruction had been required.

**Additional instructional time.** The Reading Workshop program was consciously designed to extend the amount of instructional time available to students most in need of instruction. In effect, students received over two hours of small group, highly motivating instruction per week in addition to the instruction afforded through the regular classroom.

## Workshop Effects

At the beginning and end of the study, the third author assessed the reading achievement of six Reading Workshop students and a control group of five children from another first grade classroom. The assessment of the Workshop students was limited to six since one student moved away during the year and a second student was absent on the day of post-testing. All students were considered by their teachers to be at risk in reading and at a similar level of reading development at the beginning of the study.

The control group students did not participate in the Reading Workshop. However, this group did receive Chapter I compensatory reading instruction by a trained reading specialist five times a week for at least 30 minutes per session (the Reading Workshop students did not receive Chapter I assistance). Thus, both groups of students received approximately 150 minutes of reading instruction per week in addition to their regular classroom instruction. The Chapter I instruction consisted largely of reading skill reinforcement activities and additional help with classroom reading assignments.

All students were tested prior to the implementation of the reading workshop in October of the school year and at the conclusion of the workshop in June. In this reading assessment students were asked to read graded word lists and graded passages from an informal reading inventory (Johns, 1991). Each child read lists and passages of increasing difficulty until he or she reached a frustration level in word recognition. Based upon these data each child's overall instructional reading level was estimated

The results of the reading assessments are shown in Tables 1 and 2. In the October pretreatment assessment, none of the students could read any of the words on the preprimer word lists or passages. By the June post-treatment assessment, the mean instructional reading level of the workshop students was between primer and grade 1, while the mean instructional level of the control group was slightly above the preprimer level. On the word lists, workshop students made mean gains of 13.4 and 15.0 words on the preprimer and primer word lists from the pre- to the post-treatment assessment; control group students, on the other hand, had mean gains of 9.8 and 8.8 words on the same lists. The workshop students' gains on the preprimer and primer word lists exceeded the gains of the control students by 36.7% and 70.5% respectively. Differences in mean gains on the grades 1 and 2 word lists also favored the workshop students by substantial margins. The workshop students' gains exceeded the gains of the control group students by 102.8% and 192.9% on the grades 1 and 2 word lists.

Four of the six workshop students were able to successfully read the primer level passage while only two of the five control group students were able to do so. Two of the control students were still below the preprimer level at the June assessment while the lowest achieving workshop students read instructionally at the preprimer level.

**Table 1. Mean Gains on Word List Reading***

|  | Preprimer | Primer | Grade 1 | Grade 2 |
|---|---|---|---|---|
| Control Group (n=5) | 9.8 | 8.8 | 7.2 | 4.2 |
| Workshop Group (n=6) | 13.4 | 15.0 | 14.6 | 12.3 |

*Words from the Basic Reading Inventory (Johns, 1991).*
*Twenty words per graded list.*
*Testing occurred in October and June.*

**Table 2. Mean Gains on Passage Reading and Mean Instructional Levels in June.**

|  | Preprimer # Words Correct | Preprimer* Rate | Primer # Words Correct | Primer Rate | June Instructional Level (Mean) |
|---|---|---|---|---|---|
| Control Group | 29.2 | 26.2 wpm | 36.6 | 49.2 wpm | Preprimer |
| Workshop Group | 39.7 | 52.9 wpm | 65.2 | 66.7 wpm | Primer/ Grade 1 |

*Notes: Overall instructional level based upon performance on word list and passage reading.*
*\*Top three reading students from each group.*

As shown on Table 2, mean gains in student word recognition accuracy and fluency (as measured by reading rate) on two passages substantially favored the workshop group in every comparison. The workshop students' performance gains exceeded that of the control students by 35.6% to 101.9%.

## Discussion

Several limitations to the present study and its findings need to be noted at the outset of this discussion. The study was based on a small sample of students, limited by the number of students experiencing difficulty in Belinda and Tracy's own classrooms. The study should be replicated in various other settings, perhaps with larger samples, in order to substantiate the initial findings reported in this paper. The current study also does not include measures of student comprehension or attitude toward reading and reading instruction. Future research may want to include a more comprehensive set of reading measures. Moreover, the present study is not able to determine those characteristics of the Reading Workshop that were most responsible for student gains in reading. Again, future research may wish to examine the differential effects of the various components of this and other similar programs.

The analyses suggest that students in the Reading Workshop group clearly outperformed students in the control group, who received more traditional compensatory reading instruction. Students in the Reading Workshop also seemed more prepared to make continued progress in reading. The third author noted in his observations that Workshop students retained a high level of enthusiasm for reading while control students appeared to have developed a passive and frustrated stance toward reading.

Based upon the results of this study we feel that several tentative conclusions are warranted and worthy of further consideration. First, students who are early at-risk readers can benefit from early compensatory intervention that adds to the instruction they receive in the regular classroom. Additional instructional time appears to benefit students' growth in literacy. Second, not all compensatory literacy instruction has the same effects. Compensatory instruction must be systematic and coordinated with the regular classroom curriculum. It also should include high levels of authentic reading as well as theory-based instructional strategies. Moreover, such instruction needs to engage students at a high level of involvement. These characteristics tend not to be descriptive of traditional compensatory instructional models, which often are characterized by low levels of engagement and authentic reading, unsystematically presented reading skill activities that come from a commercial source, and lack of connection to other areas of the school curriculum (McGill-Franzen & Allington, 1990).

Finally, and perhaps most importantly, this study demonstrates that informed and motivated teachers can successfully design and implement compensatory reading programs that both meet the needs of their students and match their own teaching styles. It is not necessary for teachers to slavishly follow the prescriptions of a prepared program that is not sensitive to the individual teacher and students or classroom and community contexts. Indeed, Lyons, Pinnell, and DeFord (1993) point out that telling teachers what to do in a prescriptive manner may lead to rigid and ineffective ways of teaching. Teachers *can* design and implement effective instruction. A more appropriate role, perhaps, for literacy scholars and curriculum designers is to provide support and consultation for teachers as they develop their own curricula, rather than prescriptions over which teachers have little control, ownership, and investment.

---

## References

Allington, R., Stuetzel, H., Shake, M.C. & Lamarche, S. (1986). What is remedial reading? A descriptive study. *Reading Research and Instruction, 26*, 15-30.

Birman, B. F., Orland, M. E., Jung, R. K., Anson, R. J., Garcia, G. N., Moore, M. T., Funkhouser, J. E., Morrison, D. R., Turnbull, B. J., & Reisner, E. R. (1987). *The current operation of the Chapter I program: Final report from the National Assessment of Chapter I.* Washington, DC: U. S. Government Printing Office.

Calfee, R. (1986, May). *Compensatory reading.* Paper presented at the OERI Conference on Effects of Alternative Designs in Compensatory Education, Washington, DC.

Clay, M. M. (1985). *The early detection of reading difficulties.* Exeter, NH: Heinemann.

Cooley, W. W. (1981). Effectiveness in compensatory education. *Educational Leadership, 38,* 298-301.

Cunningham, P. M. & Cunningham, J. W. (1992). Making words: Enhancing the invented spelling-decoding connection. *The Reading Teacher, 46,* 106-115.

Johns, J. L. (1991). *Basic Reading Inventory* (5th edition). Dubuque, IA: Kendall Hunt.

Johnston, P. & Allington, R. (1991). Remediation. In R. Barr, M. L. Kamil, P. Mosenthal, & P. D. Pearson (Eds.), *Handbook of Reading Research: Volume II* (pp. 984-1012). New York: Longman.

Kelly, F. J., Veldman, D. J., & McGuire, C. (1964). Multiple discriminant prediction of delinquency and school dropouts. *Educational and Psychological Measurement, 24,* 535-544.

Kennedy, M. M., Birman, B. F., & Demaline, R. (1986). *The effectiveness of Chapter 1 services.* Washington, DC: US Department of Education, Office of Educational Research and Improvement.

Lloyd, D. N. (1978). Prediction of school failure from third-grade data. *Educational and Psychological Measurement, 38,* 1193-1200.

Lyons, C. A., Pinnell, G. S., & DeFord, D. E. (1993). *Partners in learning.* New York: Teachers College Press.

McGill-Franzen, A. & Allington, R. L. (1990). Comprehension and coherence: Neglected elements of literacy instruction in remedial and resource room services. *Journal of Reading, Writing, and Learning Disabilities, 6,* 149-180.

Pinnell, G. S., DeFord, D.E., & Lyons, C. A. (1988). *Reading Recovery: Early intervention for at risk first graders.* Arlington, VA: Educational Research Services.

Pinnell, G. S., Lyons, C. A., DeFord, D. E., Bryk, A., & Seltzer, M. (1994). Comparing instructional models for the literacy education of high-risk first graders. *Reading Research Quarterly, 29,* 8-39.

Rasinski, T. V. (1989). Fluency for everyone: Incorporating fluency instruction in the classroom. *The Reading Teacher, 42,* 690-693.

Rasinski, T. V. (1995). On the effects of Reading Recovery: A response to Pinnell, Lyons, DeFord, Bryk, and Seltzer. *Reading Research Quarterly, 30,* 264-270.

Richek, M. A. & McTague, B. (1988). The "Curious George" strategy for students with reading problems. *The Reading Teacher, 42,* 220-225.

Slavin, R. E., Madden, N. A., Dolan, L. J., Wasik, B. A., Ross, S., Smith, L., & Dianda, M. (1995, April). *Success for all: A summary of research.* Paper presented at the annual meeting of the American Educational Research Association, San Francisco.

Slavin, R. E., Karweit, N. L., & Madden, N. A. (1992). Effective programs for students at risk. Boston: Allynand Bacon.

Stanovich, K. E. (1986). Matthew effects in reading: Some consequences of individual differences in the acquisition of literacy. *Reading Research Quarterly, 21,* 360-407.

Walberg, H. J. & Tsai, S. (1983). Matthew effects in education. *American Educational Research Journal, 20,* 359-373.

Williams, P. L., Reese, C. M., Campbell, J. R., Mazzeo, J., & Phillips, G. W. (1995). *1994 NAEP reading: A first look.* Washington, DC: US Department of Education, Office of Educational Research and Improvement.

# Writing Changes and Young Children: A Study of Self-Assessment

## Jill C. Miels

Ball State University

## Abstract

*This research report focuses on results obtained at the end of the first year of a two-year ethnographic study which was implemented to gather data on how young children (K-2) view their own writing. The focus of this paper is on responses given by 78 kindergarten and first-grade students. Results indicated that even young children were capable of noting and explaining changes found in their writing samples. Self-assessment abilities appeared to be consistent across both developmental and grade levels.*

Early writing behaviors have been well documented (Chomsky, 1979; Clay, 1975; Newman, 1985; Temple, Nathan, Burris and Temple, 1988). Writing grows developmentally from random, non-specific marks toward conventional forms used by adults. Young children come to school with large amounts of information about writing, yet early writing behaviors fluctuate back and forth between stages.

Graves (1983) supplied important generalizations about young writers' perceptions. For example, written messages are planned primarily through drawing. Even when the child has differentiated text from illustration, the former is usually dependent on the latter. Early writing efforts also focus on the encoding process rather than the content of any given piece of work. In addition, children often want to write before they want to read (Graves, 1978). Given this information, writing seems to be a very personal endeavor for the young child. Therefore, classroom teachers must begin to investigate and understand the personal ways in which writing is approached by each child. One way to identify children's personal perceptions is through the use of self-assessment.

Many scholars support the value of student self-assessment (Costa, 1989; Paulson, 1991; Tierney, Carter, & Desai, 1991; Valencia & Paris 1991); however, few report results of self-assessment in kindergarten or first grade. In case studies of kindergarten writers, Dyson (1987) found major differences in the ways that individual children approached the orchestration of their writing and suggested that "not only are our portraits of young writers too uniform, our conception of writing development needs to be expanded out from its current narrow shape" (p. 1). Dyson's contention was that even within a developmental framework, there are variations in how each child approaches the process of writing and those variations must be accommodated (1987).

In an effort to learn more about how young children self-assess writing growth, 78 kindergarten and first-grade children in a large suburban school district were interviewed. These data were drawn from a larger two-year study (Miels, 1996).

# Method

The question guiding this investigation was: What do children think about the changes that take place in their writing over time? A qualitative approach to applied research was used (Patton,1990), and data were gathered within the context of the ongoing classroom.

### *Data Collection*

At the beginning of the 1992-1993 school year, participants were chosen from three kindergarten and four first grade classrooms in a large suburban school district in Texas. Parent permission was requested for all children in these two grade levels. A total of 78 permission slips were returned. Participants were not identified to the teachers in an effort to avoid any special attention given to assessment of writing growth. Of the 78 participants, 22 were from three kindergarten classrooms and 56 were from four first grade classrooms. Writing samples were copied and saved in portfolios during the school year. During the first week of May, 1993, participants were interviewed while they reviewed the writing samples in their portfolios.

The researcher was known to all the children because she also was a classroom teacher in the K-1 unit. Interviews were recorded on both audio and videotape. The researcher transcribed tapes for each participant and then examined the data for response patterns. Data analysis was conducted solely by the researcher. The questions asked here included:

1. Is there anything you would like to tell me about your writing?
2. Has your writing changed?
3. How? (Explain the changes)

### *Participants and Setting*

While cultural diversity was evident in all classes, the socioeconomic status of the neighborhood where the children lived was middle to upper middle class. Most of the children started school with some type of pre-K experience and the parents from this community were highly involved in their children's education.

As a teacher and team leader in one of the first-grade classes, the researcher was well acquainted with the literacy programs emphasized in each room. An integrated, thematic approach to language arts instruction was documented in each class using an observation guide developed by Vogt (1991). Although implementation varied from room to room, all seven classrooms encouraged an emergent literacy approach to early reading and writing as described by Teale and Sulzby (1986). This approach views children as literate individuals upon arrival at school, each with a repertoire of reading and writing skills along a developmental continuum. Instruction in these emergent literacy classrooms supported each child's development along that continuum.

The classrooms included in this investigation provided a variety of reading, writing, speaking, and listening opportunities throughout the school day. The adopted first-grade reading curriculum was literature based, while the kindergartens relied on a language experience approach. Children in all rooms were given multiple opportunities to choose learning activities, communicate with classmates, and exhibit literacy skills at a variety of levels.

Teachers from two of the first grades and all three kindergartens chose the writing samples to be saved for each child. Teachers from the other two first grades also allowed child self-selection. The bulk of the writing samples were obtained from writing journals that were used on a regular basis in each classroom. In addition to allowing children to make independent choices about literacy activities, the teachers modeled literacy behaviors. The teachers felt it was important to provide both the opportunity to write and an environment that supported experimentation.

There were some differences in the amount of choice given to the children, but these differences did not appear to affect the interviews reported here. For example, in one first grade classroom, children chose writing topics, chose samples to be saved, and had free access to the samples over the course of the project. In another first grade room, the children had access to the samples, but the samples were chosen and saved by the teacher. The kindergarten teachers used weekly writing journals that were passed out at the beginning of each week and collected at the end of each week to be sent home. Copies were made and saved once a month during the study. In the kindergartens, the children had no access to saved samples until they were seen during the interview at the end of the project.

### Data Analysis

Data analysis was largely inductive. Analysis was guided by data reduction methodology (Miles & Huberman, 1984), a process of focusing and simplifying the raw data found in interview transcripts. The purpose of this analysis was to identify recurring regularities among the student responses. Categories were developed and a simple tally system was used to record response frequency within each category.

## Results

A summary of results appears in the table. Details in relation to each research question are provided below.

### Question 1: Is there anything you would like to tell me about your writing?

Forty-six percent of the children either gave no response to the first question or indicated that they had nothing to say about the samples in their folders. There were no evident patterns in the two groups that did not respond based on developmental level or grade placement. The interviewer was known to all participants so that should not be a related factor. Also, although two of the first grade groups had been given in-class opportunities to talk about their writing and had free access to their writing samples, there was no indication that this opportunity translated into talking about writing samples during the interview. An equal number from these classes made no response when asked to tell the interviewer about the work.

A smaller number (23%) engaged in a discussion of the topics found in the writing samples. For example:

V.P.: On this day we were talking about quilts so I wrote, 'Quilts are fun to look at.' We had our own classroom quilt.

R.R.: This was when my mommy came home. She was gone on a visit.

J.W.: I really like this one because I like Cobra a lot.

J.W.: This is the one—The Little Red Ladybug. We mixed it up from the Little Red Hen.

Thirty-two percent of the children responded using references to the quality of the handwriting when asked to tell about their writing. They were concerned with what the writing looked like rather than what it said:

E.P.: They used to be sloppy. They were sorta messy.

A.H.: They, they've changed a lot. I was writing sloppy but now it's neater.

Most student responses referred to a single area, either handwriting quality or topic. Only a small number addressed both. Also, when these kindergarten and first-grade students were asked to tell about changes in their writing over time, they either had nothing to say, discussed the topics they chose to write about, or made comments about changes in the quality of the handwriting. Knowing what concerns are relevant to a particular student would certainly have implications for curriculum planning. For example, a teacher

## Table. Response summary for questions 1, 2 and 3

### 1. *Is there anything you would like to tell me about your writing?*

| Response | % |
|---|---|
| No/no response | 46 |
| Topic discussion | 23 |
| Handwriting or neatness related | 31 |

### 2. *Has your writing changed ?*

| Response | % |
|---|---|
| No/not very much | 4 |
| Yes | 96 |

### 3. *How? Explain the changes.*

| Response | %* |
|---|---|
| Write "better" | 22 |
| Speed/slowed down | 6 |
| Letter formation/handwriting | 59 |
| Length | 5 |
| More/better ideas | 5 |
| Punctuation/capitalization | 14 |
| Spacing | 6 |
| Spelling improved | 28 |
| Better reader | 2 |
| Improved drawing | 6 |
| Color change (photo copy) | 4 |
| Different media | 2 |

*Note: *68% (n=53) gave multiple responses to question 3.*

who overemphasizes quality of handwriting might send the message that content is unimportant.

### *Question 2: Has your writing changed?*

The overwhelming response to the second question was "yes." Ninety-six percent of the children saw changes in their writing, one saw no change and two saw "not very much." The two children who saw very little change did eventually go on to talk about changes that they saw as evidenced by the following comments:

"I'm writing the harder words."

"I know how to write more."

"I know how to read."

### *Question 3: Explain the changes.*

The most interesting results came from the responses to question 3. The four most prevalent answers (letter formation/handwriting, improved spelling, write "better," and punctuation/capitalization) seemed related to the concrete perspective of young children. In addition to noting concrete changes in their writing, 68% (n=53) gave multiple explanations for the change. This suggests that the children were able to assess growth on a variety of criteria.

## Discussion

Because children must experience writing to understand it, it seems logical that the physical characteristics actually being manipulated will be of interest to them. R. D. Walshe (1984) labeled these surface features of writing "conventions of print" (p 78). These conventions were often referred to by the children in the self-assessment process. The results also were supported by the work of Tierney, Carter, and Desai (1991) who found that students don't evaluate pieces using the same overall standards as adults. Adults strive to look at the whole piece of writing and its purpose, while children "see things from a more personalized perspective . . . focusing on what is important to them" (p. 17).

Exceptions to the tendency to use concrete changes in self-assessment came from the children who judged writing changes based on having "more/better ideas" or who saw themselves as becoming "better readers." These children, whose responses seemed to represent more abstract thought, were all first graders, but not all were from the same classroom. It appeared that previous opportunity to self-assess was not a vital factor influencing responses.

Five kindergarten children mentioned changes for the better in their drawing without mentioning their improvement in print awareness. Strickland and Morrow (1989) believe that drawing is a legitimate part of the early literacy process as "many different writing forms are seen: scribbling, drawing, non-phonetic letter strings, phonetic (invented) spelling, and conventional orthography" (p. 67). R. D. Walshe (1984) found that when asked to write, some children did not differentiate writing from drawing but saw both as a part of the same process.

The children in this study showed the ability to self-assess and had a clear knowledge of criteria they used for self-assessment. A large number saw growth in their writing and articulated the basis on which they assessed that growth.

## Limitations

Several limitations should be noted. Children were asked to self-assess writing samples as an end product. There was no attempt to judge self-assessment abilities over the course of the study. In addition, there was no documentation as to what self-assessment behaviors, if any, were modeled for the children. The amount of time spent on writing "instruction" also was not documented. Finally, most of the children were not involved in the writing sample selection process which, in itself, is a form of self-assessment. Results represent responses given by this particular group of children, given certain conditions and educational experiences. Additional data is needed from a variety of settings before any generalizations can be made.

## Implications

This study reveals that even in the earliest grades, children are capable of assessing their own performance. By examining the results presented here, teachers can expect self-assessment behaviors based on writing concepts which are important to the child. Knowledge of what is important to an individual child can be used to enhance and enrich the learning environment for that child.

## Conclusion

The children who participated in this investigation have provided insights into some of the self-assessment abilities of young children. They have shown that children can set standards on which to assess their own growth, although the standards differ from child to child. For the classroom teacher, this data confirms the contention that writing is a personal act. Children can tell us what is important to them at given points in their development; this information can then provide a focus for instruction. By providing the opportunity to self-assess, teachers allow children to be more actively involved in their own learning. Information gained from children involved in self-assessment can open up new directions for curriculum development and can help classroom teachers establish environments that enhance rather than inhibit early literacy growth.

---

## References

Chomsky, C. (1979). Approaching reading through invented spelling. In. L. Resnick & P.A. Weaver (Eds.), *Theory and practice of early reading,* Vol. 2 (pp. 43-65). Hillsdale, NJ: Lawrence Erlbaum Associates.

Clay, M. M. (1975). *What did I write?* Portsmouth, NH: Heinemann.

Costa, A. L. (1989). Re-assessing assessment. *Educational Leadership, 46,*(7), 2.

Dyson, A. H. (1987). *Individual differences in beginning composing: An orchestral vision of learning to write.* Berkeley, CA.: Center for the Study of Writing.

Graves, D. (1983). *Writing: Teachers and children at work.* Exeter, NH.: Heineman.

Graves, D. H. (1978). *Balance the basics: Let them write.* New York: Ford Foundation.

Klein, M. L. (1985). *The development of writing in children.* Englewood Cliffs, NJ: Prentice-Hall, Inc.

Miels, J. C. (1996). *Self-assessment of writing growth in young children.* Manuscript submitted for publication.

Miles, M. B., & Huberman, A. M. (1984). *Qualitative data analysis: A sourcebook of new methods.* Newbury Park, CA: Sage Publications, Inc.

Newman, J. (1985). *The craft of children's writing.* Portsmouth, NH: Heineman.

Patton, M. Q. (1990). *Qualitative evaluation and research methods.* Newbury Park, CA: Sage Publications, Inc.

Paulson, L. (1991). *[Thinking about thinking in the classroom].* Unpublished data.

Strickland, D. S., & Morrow, L. (1989). *Emerging literacy: Young children learn to read and write.* Newark, DE.: International Reading Association.

Teale, W. H., & Sulzby, E. (1986). *Emergent literacy: Writing and reading.* Norwood, NJ: Ablex Publishing Company.

Temple, C., Nathan, R., Burris, N., & Temple, F. (1988). *The beginnings of writing* (2nd ed.). Boston, MA: Allyn and Bacon.

Tierney, R. J., Carter, M. A., & Desai, L. E. (1991). *Portfolio assessment in the reading-writing classroom.* Norwood, MA: Christopher Gordon.

Valencia, S. W., & Paris, S. G. (1991). Portfolio assessment for young readers. *The Reading Teacher, 44,* 590-91.

Vogt, M. E. (1991). An observation guide for supervisors and administrators: Moving toward integrated reading/language arts instruction. *The Reading Teacher, 45,* 206-211.

Walshe, R. D. (1984). Attend to "skills" as part of "process." In W. McVitty (Ed.), *Children and learning: Some aspects and issues,* (pp. 78-83). Rosebery, Australia: Primary English Teaching Association.

# REPLAYING THEIR OWN LIVES: CHILDREN'S CHOICES FOR DRAMATIC PLAY IN ONE HEAD START CLASSROOM

## Carolyn Ann Walker

West Virginia University

## Abstract

*This paper describes the ways in which children in one Head Start class-room selected and dramatized familiar topics relating to home, school, and media experiences. These general categories were often related. The children understood the role of language and literacy in relation to their topic choices, and they recreated classroom discourse patterns during dramatic play. These results indicate a need for further research into relationships between children's prior experiences, including instructional contexts, and children's literacy-related dramatic play.*

Young children learn about literacy through contact with a variety of reading and writing materials and through literacy-related communication with others (McGee & Richgels, 1995; Strickland & Morrow, 1989; Teale & Sulzby, 1986). In a manner similar to oral language development, children's literacy development is functionally oriented (Halliday, 1978; Rogoff, 1990; Teale & Sulzby, 1986). Young children can use written language in a multifunctional and sophisticated manner long before they enter kindergarten (Halliday, 1978, McGee & Richgels, 1995). More able others, who usually are adults but some-times are other children (Rogoff, 1990; Vygotsky, 1978; Wertsch, 1985), fur-ther literacy understanding by interacting with children as literacy is used.

Young children also exert at least partial control over the nature and duration of their literacy experiences. If a child does not want to continue sharing a book, she or he usually stops participating. This control extends to the multiple functions of literacy. For example, young children may co-con-struct the nature of a child/parent book sharing in order to establish a bond between the caregiver and the child and to gain information from the text.

Child-initiated dramatic play that includes the use of reading and writing materials provides another opportunity for children to exert control over and mediate their literacy experiences and development. Within these contexts, researchers have found that children select topics, literacy materials, and play partners and have opportunities to examine the multiple forms and functions of reading and writing (Allgeier, 1991; Walker, 1992). However, research of literacy events within dramatic play in preschool and elementary school settings has not yet fully explored relationships between children's dramatic play topic choices and their experiences outside of play (Allgeier, 1991; Pelligrini & Galda, 1993; Walker, 1992). More information is needed about how or upon what basis children make literacy-related topic choices during dramatic play, including whether or not they draw upon familiar contexts.

This paper, which reports a part of a larger study (Walker, 1994), describes children's literacy-related topic choices for dramatic play in one Head Start classroom. In particular, the focus was upon the nature of the dramatic play during free play periods and the contexts the dramatic play in this classroom provided for literacy development..

## Context and Participants

This non-intervention observational study was conducted during the free play period of one Head Start class. Located in a small midwestern city, this class was part of a program that served children of low-income families. Children attended class Monday through Thursday for approximately three–and–one–half hours per session. Seventeen children, ages 4 and 5, were enrolled. Six of the seventeen children were male. Sixteen children were white and one was African American. The teacher was African American and the assistant teacher was white.

Free play period occurred daily and lasted from approximately 8:30–9:30 A.M. During free play the children engaged in dramatic play, defined as play in which the children pretended and took on roles by themselves and with others. Children also played with blocks, the sand table, paint, writing materials, and puzzles. Play occurred in four centers: blocks and manipulatives, writing, books and computer, and housekeeping. Play also occurred in temporary centers such as the sand table. The teacher occasionally participated in dramatic play by weaving together topics through talk, and on rare occasions she suggested play topics that assisted in classroom management including straightening up the housekeeping center. The assistant teacher participated less frequently, although she sometimes asked children to stop a particular activity such as crawling or yelling (Walker, 1994).

## Methodology

Data collection was structured by a unit of analysis that was developed after a pilot study was conducted. The unit combined Hymes' (1964) description of an overarching communicative event and Halliday's description of contexts for language use. Pilot data (Walker, 1992) indicated that incidents of dramatic play were comprised of topic, participants, and various modes of communication including literacy. These elements are described by Halliday (1978) as contexts of language use. Pilot data also indicated that similar forms and functions of language occurred as children engaged in contexts related by topics and participants. Hymes' (1964) description of the communicative represents the qualities of the relationships between these contexts; it was, therefore, incorporated into a framework for describing related incidents of play.

Data collection occurred for six weeks during the months of April and May. A one-week break occurred after the third week of data collection. In all, data were collected for 24 hours of free play. One researcher collected and analyzed data.

Non–intervention ethnographic methods of data collection were used because the purpose of the study was to understand the nature of the play. Data collection included observations, field notes, video, audio, literacy artifacts, and interviews with the teacher, assistant teacher, and children. These interviews provided information about children's background experiences, including those relating to literacy, and they also clarified behaviors during play. Previously developed questions were asked during structured interviews and questions were generated for semi-structured interviews as play behaviors were observed. The use of multiple forms of data collection allowed for triangulation of data.

Dramatic play was identified by talk, gestures, topics, and actions with primary attention paid to the children's talk and conversations. Attention was given to several talk indicators, including: "pretend I am . . . ," "I am . . . ," "pretend you are . . . ," and "play with me . . ." Copious notes were taken after these indicators were observed. Notes were taken about topic selection; gestures and actions (such as going to the doctor) were also recorded.

Observation included videotaping, audiotaping, and note taking. A second audio recorder was placed in centers that were not observed to provide information about dramatic play throughout the classroom. The housekeeping center was observed first, and the books and computer and writing center observed next. Pilot data indicated that these three areas, in particular the housekeeping center, were places where dramatic play could occur. Observations of other areas did occur after initial data collection when focal children moved into other centers and second source audio data indicated dramatic play was occurring.

The limitations of data collection in this study made it impossible to gather comprehensive data for all children in the classroom. Therefore, it was determined that six focal children would be identified early in the data collection. This identification of a smaller group of children has similarities to that of Dyson (1989), who focused on a smaller group of children within a larger classroom setting in order to understand imaginative writing.

The focal children selected in this study represented the genders, leadership qualities, and personalities of the seventeen children. Interestingly, focus on these children resulted in data collection in all of the centers and included many non-focal children as they participated in play with the focal children. Therefore, while it is true that comprehensive identification of all dramatic play did not occur, a sampling of the types of play that occurred was made.

Constant comparative data collection procedures were used (Strauss, 1987). Data analysis began during data collection and continued until final assertions were made in the study. For example, a central question in the greater study regarded the nature of the play. Early examination of data appeared to yield preliminary categories of structure in the play, and these findings focused observations and collection of subsequent data, as well as analysis of that data.

Over 100 individual contexts of dramatic play were observed during data collection. Examination of a comprehensive log of dramatic play including topic, participants, and modes of communication was undertaken in order to reduce the amount of data analyzed to a representative number (48) of the 100 total dramatic play contexts. All 14 of the literacy-related play contexts (14% of total) were included for further analysis. Play contexts were defined as contexts that included the use of literacy materials and/or the creation of literacy artifacts. Other contexts of play were also included because they represented topics chosen, locations, and actions of the focal children.

## Results

### Topics of Children's Play

The children selected and dramatized topics relating to home activities, school activities, and television and movies. Observations of the children's dramatic play, their instructional activities, and interviews with the children and the teachers provided evidence that children understood the role of the language and literacy in relation to the topics they chose. Topics were familiar to the children. The teacher and the assistant teacher emphasized the children's familiarity with the topics of play during an interview. Beverly (the teacher) stated: "They are replaying their lives. Re-playing-their -own-lives." (Interview, April 16, 1993).

Further, the topics of dramatic play were based on school, home, and media experiences, but these topics did not fall into discreet categories. They were often related. For example, several children dramatized a homework assignment which combined the areas of home and school. One child dramatized a movie that he had seen on video at his home.

A low number of literacy-related play contexts were observed in relation to the total number of play contexts (14 were observed out of 100). However, it was interesting that when the children used reading and writing materials, they used literacy in their play in a variety of ways, such as letter writing, book sharing, calendar time, homework, library, and environmental print. So, while the children did not select a great many literacy-related topics, they did show a developing understanding of the multiple forms and functions of literacy when they chose to include it.

The dramatic play vignettes presented below provide evidence of the children's familiarity of topics, their ability to recreate literacy events, and their understanding of the forms and functions of literacy.

### *Vignette 1: Shared Reading*

Kress (1990) pointed out that teachers engage in an educational discourse with particular features such as questioning strategies. These discourse features affect the nature and uses of literacy in instructional contexts. And while teachers (and in this case assistant teachers) may or may not be aware of their discourse features, the following example indicates that children may be more aware of what teachers do than we realize.

Several children gathered in the blocks and manipulative center one day as free play time was coming to a close. The initiator of this activity was Brandy T., who was also beginning to read the book *The Very Hungry Caterpillar* by Eric Carle. The children had heard this book on several other non-play occasions.

| Participants | Verbal | Nonverbal |
|---|---|---|
| 1. Brandy T: | 1, 2, 3 plums and he ate four. | (She looks down at the pictures and then she points to them with her fingers.) |

As Brandy T. emergent read the text, she focused on print and pictures and moved between oral-like storytelling and labeling of pictures (Sulzby, 1985). This movement between levels of emergent reading supports Elster's (1994) assertion that children do not always remain at one level of emergent reading while reading a text.

While Brandy encouraged one other child named JR to participate, she was not enthusiastic about the participation of other children. Richard received a great deal of criticism from Brandy during the play. Although he did not move very much at all and remained mostly quiet he was told several times by Brandy to be quiet. Interestingly, Richard also was often corrected by teachers for misbehaving.

| Participants | Verbal | Nonverbal |
|---|---|---|
| 5. Brandy T: | No, No, No Richard. | (Again she looks indignant, being corrective.) |

And later,

| | | |
|---|---|---|
| 12. Brandy T: | He ate through . . . | |
| 13. | BE QUIET RICHARD! | (Points finger at Richard and looks at him.) |

And again,

| | | |
|---|---|---|
| 16. Brandy T: | SHHH!! | (She appears really aggravated at this point and she directs herself to Richard, whom she is correcting.) |

Brandy and the other children showed their familiarity with book sharing, and their play indicated a developing understanding of the forms and functions of print. The children sat facing the book and watched while it was displayed. They listened as the text was read. They sometimes attempted to verbally participate, although it was not always easy to do so.

This play context illustrates Kress' (1990) point that teachers' discourse extends beyond their classroom lessons. Language functioned in this context in a similar manner to circle time ( a time when the teacher or assistant teacher shared a lesson or activity). In both contexts language (including print) was used to establish and maintain control. During play, Brandy told children to be quiet and tightly held on to the book as she announced that she was the teacher. During circle time the assistant teacher often instructed the children not to move and to remain quiet. Brandy T. viewed herself as having more opportunities to use language in the leadership role. She also reflected the common circle time practice of correcting Richard even though he was not disruptive during this play context.

### Vignette 2: Calendar Time

Some children recreated familiar social contexts while playing alone. Their inclusion of imaginary others in play, and their use of language, gestures, and literacy provided evidence that they were familiar with multiple roles and forms of communication regardless of how many children were present.

Calendar time was a classroom activity that included instruction in months, days, and numbers. Danny demonstrated his understanding of calendar time when he recreated this daily event during one free play period. He was in the block center sitting on the teacher and assistant teacher's chair when I first observed him. I began audio and video taping after he began, and I was not able to capture much of the talk. But Danny's gestures, in relation to the small amount of verbal language data revealed what he was doing and his familiarity with the process. Danny's physical movements mimicked calendar time very closely. The following field note excerpt shows this.

| Participant | Verbal and Nonverbal Action |
|---|---|
| 1. Danny: | He is sitting in the teacher's chair in a direction that typically faces the children and is positioning himself like the teacher. |
| 2. | He is pointing to the numbers and gesturing in the direction that the calendar progresses. (It is April and there are umbrellas on the calendar.) |
| 3. | The gestures he makes are recognizable as the teacher's gestures. |
| 4. | He is talking as if to children and I hear him say "you kids" even though there is no one participating with him. |
| 5. | He follows the directionality of the calendar and the follows square by square left to right—first row down—the poster next to it. |

Danny actually did the same things during play that the teacher did during calendar time. He identified his activity as calendar time by his physical proximity to the calendar and by his talk and gestures throughout. Danny also demonstrated an ability to reinvent the activity and go through the literacy-related aspects step by step in the role of the teacher. He sequentially moved from square to square in a left to right motion (line 5). He understood that the teacher led the group, and he defined this aspect when he said "you kids" (line 4). He used movements and some of the comments that had occurred during the actual event.

While there were no children present except for Danny, he viewed the activity as including participants in a regular calendar time. In addition to his comments, "you kids" (line 4) his turns toward the direction of the children indicated he viewed them as present in the scene. Danny did not need to have the other children present in order to recreate the experience. This was typical for Danny, who often played alone and was considered a "loner" by the teacher and assistant teacher (interview, April 16, 1993).

### Vignette 3: A Trip to the Library
The children in this classroom took a trip to the public library. The following field note vignette makes evident two children's understanding of

concepts related to trips to the library and book handling. In this excerpt, Julieanna and Chelsey act out a library trip while they are playing in the books and computer center.

| Participant | Verbal and Nonverbal Action |
|---|---|
| 12. Chelsey | Chelsey says she's going to the library alone. |
| 13. Julieanna | Julieanna says, "no," and she joins her. |
| 14. Kindra | Kindra comes along too. |
| 15. Julieanna & Chelsey | Julieanna pretends like she is walking and then she and Chelsey get a number of books from the book-shelf. |
| 16. Julieanna | Says "The Three Little Pigs" while looking at the books. |
| 17. Julieanna | Says, "We have to set them right here cause this is the library." |
| 18. Julieanna | Asks me to move my tape from the area where she is putting the books. |
| 19. Julieanna | Lines up all the books on top of a bookshelf. |
| 20. Julieanna | Leaves for a short while to talk to some adults and then comes back. |
| 21. Julieanna & Chelsey | They look through the books and page through from left to right. |

During this literacy-related dramatic play, Julieanna and Chelsey recreated a library context by stating they were going to the library, picking out a stack of books, naming stories, and paging through the books. They used verbal and nonverbal language as well as the books to indicate that they understood that you can select books at the library, organize books, and look through books.

## Conclusions

While this study cannot be generalized to a larger population because it focused on only one group of children in one setting and lasted only a short period of time, it does show how this group of children's literacy-related choices for dramatic play reflected their prior experiences. Previous investigations of child-initiated literacy-related play have not focused on children's prior experiences in relation to their dramatic play topic choices.

The children in this study chose to further explore the familiar and in this process brought out many of the nuances of prior experiences. The children's communication surrounding the use literacy materials also provided further opportunities for them to explore both the forms of the literacy and their past experiences.

These findings also raise questions and have implications for practice and research. Specifically, more research is necessary that explores children's literacy learning through the recreation of lived experiences in play. In addition, further investigation of the types of literacy-related choices children make during dramatic play would provide information about how these choices relate to children's literacy development.

Futhermore, if children select prior experiences as topics for play then teachers should carefully consider the ways in which they structure experiences that children might later recreate. This study reveals that children may listen to subtle messages as well as planned instructional messages. As Kress (1990) pointed out, instructional discourse may be repeated in other circumstances such as play. Future study could provide insight into the relationship between instructional discourse and children's literacy-related play behaviors.

It seems likely that if teachers value the participation of certain children, or value certain kinds of participation (such as remaining quiet and orderly), children may carry those values into play as they recreate and further explore literacy. Such practices could impact both children's interactions with one another and their opportunities to increase their understanding of literacy. Further investigation also could increase our understanding of relationships between prior experiences and dramatic play and answer questions about children's use of literacy materials.

---

# References

Allgeier, I. L. (1991, February). *Naturalistic study of the literate behavior of four-year-old children occurring during spontaneous play in the hollow block area of a preschool classroom.* Paper presented at the Annual Conference of the Eastern Educational Research Association, Boston, MA.

Dyson, A. H. (1989). *Multiple worlds of child writers: Friends learning to write.* New York: Teachers College Press.

Elster, C. (1994) "I guess they do listen": Young children's emergent readings after adult read-alouds. *Young Children, 49,* 2-31.

Halliday M. A. K. (1979). *Learning how to mean: Explorations in the development of language.* London: Edward Arnold.

Halliday, M. A. K. (1978). *Language as social semiotic.* London: University Park Press.

Hymes, D. (1964). Toward ethnography of communication: The analysis of communicative events. In P. Giglioli (Ed.), *Language and social context.* (pp.21-44). Middlesex: Penguin.

Kress, G. (1990). *Linguistic processes in sociocultural practice.* Oxford: Oxford University Press.

McGee, L. M. & Richgels, D. L. (1995). *Literacy's beginnings.* (2nd Ed.) Needham heights, MA: Allyn & Bacon.

Pelligrini, A. D., & Galda, L. (1993). Ten years after: A reexamination of symbolic play and literacy research. *Reading Research Quarterly, 28* (2), 165-175.

Rogoff, B. (1990). *Apprenticeship in thinking: Conceiving development in social context.* New York: Oxford University Press.

Strauss, A. (1987). *Qualitative analysis for social scientists.* Cambridge: Cambridge University Press.

Strickland, D., & Morrow, L. (Eds.). (1989). *Emerging literacy: Young children learn to read and write.* Newark, Delaware: IRA.

Sulzby, E. (1985). Emergent reading of favorite storybooks: A developmental study. *Reading Research Quarterly, 20* (4), 458-481.   .

Teale, W., & Sulzby, E. (Eds.). (1986). *Emergent literacy: Writing and reading.* Norwood NJ.: Ablex.

Vygotsky, L. S. (1978). *Mind in society.* Cambridge, MA: M.I.T. Press.

Walker, C. A. (December, 1992). *Dramatic Play and Literacy in a Head Start Classroom.* Paper presented at the National Reading Conference, San Antonio, TX.

Walker, C. A. (1994). *Contexts For Literacy Development: A Study of Literacy Practices During Dramatic Play in One Head Start Classroom.* Unpublished doctoral dissertation, Purdue University.

Wertsch, J. V (1985). *Vygotsky and the social formation of Mind.* Cambridge, M.A.: Harvard University Press.

# PRELIMINARY VALIDATION OF THE WRITER SELF-PERCEPTION SCALE

**William A. Henk**
**Diane M Bottomley**
**Steven A. Melnick**

Penn State University at Harrisburg

## Abstract

*This study sought to empirically validate the* Writer Self-Perception Scale (WSPS), *an affective instrument based largely upon Bandura's (1977, 1982) model of self-efficacy. Formal instrument development guidelines were followed, including a judgmental review of items, pilot testing with 304 intermediate level children, and corresponding analyses for reliability, factor integrity, and the relationship of the scale to children's writing achievement. The* WSPS *exhibited strong reliability characteristics for each scale as well as an overall six-factor structure that included Observational Comparison and Physiological States and two scales each for Progress (General and Specific) and Social Feedback (Family and Classmates/Teacher). Correlational analyses revealed significant, albeit modest interrelationships existing between the WSPS (and its scales) and children's writing sample performance. Overall, the WSPS possesses desirable psychometric properties that bode well for its use in the classroom and in research contexts.*

A recurring problem in both the assessment of individual students and the evaluation of literacy programs has been the glaring lack of viable affective instrumentation. In recent years, some significant headway has been made in this regard, most notably in the emergence of the *Elementary Reading Attitude Survey* or *ERAS* (McKenna & Kear, 1990) and the *Reader Self-Perception Scale* or *RSPS* (Henk & Melnick, 1995). These instruments not only allow for a richer and more complete individual appraisal to be made of a child's literacy motivation, but also permit various group instructional initiatives to be compared along important affective dimensions.

In this spirit, the present study attempted to validate a new affective instrument that focuses on the writing process, and in effect, logically parallels the *RSPS*.

To our minds, the attempted development of the Writer *Self-Perception Scale (WSPS)* made natural sense on at least two counts. From an instructional standpoint, writing and reading proficiencies clearly represent the primary literacy outcomes sought by schools, and therefore, warrant equal treatment. Secondly, the respective cognitive operations of reading and writing mirror one another sufficiently well that exploring the parallel construct of "perception of self as **writer**" seemed to be clearly justifiable.

## Theoretical Background

Like the *RSPS,* the *Writer Self-Perception Scale* or *WSPS* is essentially grounded in Bandura's (1977; 1982) theory of self-efficacy. In the same way that the theory would predict an individual's self-perception of reading ability impacting upon subsequent reading growth, personal judgments of writing proficiency likewise figure to motivate or inhibit writing acquisition. That is, an individual's perception of self as a writer might determine whether opportunitites to write would be sought or avoided, the amount of effort that would be expended during specific writing engagements, and the general degree of persistence exhibited in pursuing writing competence.

Basically, Bandura's self-efficacy model posits four major factors related to personal ability appraisals. The conceptual definitions of these factors are as follows: Performance (an extremely broad category that includes past success, necessary effort, task difficulty, task persistence, need for assistance, and patterns of progress); Observational Comparison (how one's performance compares with peers); Social Feedback (direct or indirect cues derived from teachers, classmates, and family); and Physiological States (bodily feedback in the form of relative comfort/discomfort, calmness/nervousness, etc.). While research with the *Reader Self-Perception Scale* (Henk & Melnick, 1992, 1993) largely supported this four factor model, the inclusiveness of the Performance category ultimately precluded a meaningful factor analysis. However, by conceptually redefining the category more narrowly as a Progress scale (i.e., how one's perception of present reading performance compares with past performance) and focusing the items accordingly, the researchers found that all four scales partitioned as desired. For this reason, the "Progress" redefinition was used in the present study to develop writing-related items.

## Need for the Instrument

Given the overall scarcity of assessment-related work in the affective domain, it is not altogether surprising that the construct of writer self-perception has received limited attention. This oversight is unfortunate because an instrument that taps the writer self-perception construct would naturally complement other affective scales as well as numerous reading and writing achievement measures. For individual children, such an instrument would almost certainly be a valuable addition to a literacy portfolio by virtue of its explanatory value. At the same time, the instrument could provide valuable insights into the general literacy climate of a classroom as a whole.

From a research standpoint, a valid scale that addresses children's perceptions of themselves as writers could serve several functions. It could be used as a dependent variable, covariate, or blocking variable in experimental research that compares literacy approaches. Moreover, across a wide range of descriptive studies, the instrument could serve as an important trait indicator.

Another compelling argument for the *WSPS* is simply that at present there are very few scales specifically designed to evaluate writer self-efficacy. Most existing scales are marked by relatively few items, limited norming, or a tendency to measure the negative, albeit related dimension of writing apprehension. In addition, while extant scales may address writing self-perceptions in general, they tend not to incorporate specific aspects of writing including focus, content, organization, style, and conventions within their item pools. Perhaps most importantly, none of the scales appear to be grounded in an overarching theory of motivation in the same way that self-efficacy undergirds the *Writer Self-Perception Scale.*

## Method

The construction of the *WSPS* adhered to affective instrument development guidelines as described by Gable and Wolf (1993). The steps included: (a) developing conceptual definitions as well as operational definitions in the form of corresponding items, (b) selecting a scaling technique, (c) conducting a judgmental review of items, (d) selecting a response format, (e) preparing drafts of the instrument and gathering pilot data, (f) analyzing the data using factor and item analyses as well as techniques of reliability estimation, and (g) collecting ongoing validity and reliability data.

### Item Development

After conceptual and operational definitions had been established for the four writer self-efficacy categories (Progress, Observational Comparison, Social Feedback, and Physiological States), a preliminary pool of 44 items was developed. One item was included simply to tap a general perception ("I think I am a good writer"). Each of the remaining 43 items corresponded to one of the four proposed writer self-efficacy scales. The items were generated by two literacy professionals and an expert in affective instrument development. While most of the items dealt with overall writing ability, others touched upon specific aspects of writing including focus, content, clarity, organization, and coherence. To prevent children from focusing on the writing process at a mechanistic level, no items dealing with grammar or conventions were included. Care was taken to word the items in a straightforward and positive manner to foster accurate and easy responding and to prevent any deficits in reading ability from confounding the assessment.

## *Judgmental Review*

Twenty-five graduate students enrolled in a reading specialist certificate program served as respondents for the judgmental review phase. The respondents received the pool of randomly-arranged pilot items as well as conceptual definitions for each of the four self-efficacy categories. They were asked to place each item into the category in which it seemed to fit best or into an "Other" category if they were either undecided or simply did not see a definite match. In addition, the respondents were asked to indicate how strongly they felt an item belonged to a category using a 3-point scale (1=not very sure; 2=strongly; 3=no question about it).

Modifications were made to the item pool based upon feedback received in this judgmental review process. Following data collection, each item was analyzed for fit within the intended category. A 90% agreement across raters and a mean strength rating of 2.5 was required for an item to be retained. Items failing to meet these criteria were revised or eliminated accordingly.

## Figure 1. Writer Self-Perception Scale Sample Items by Category.

### Progress:
Writing is easier for me than it used to be.
I am getting better at writing.
The words I use in my writing are better than the ones I used before.
The order of my sentences makes better sense now.

### Observational Comparison:
I write better than other kids in my class.
When I write, my organization is better than the other kids in my class.
My sentences and paragraphs fit together as well as my classmates.
My writing seems to be more clear than my classmates.

### Social Feedback:
People in my family think I am a good writer.
My teacher thinks my writing is fine.
My classmates would say I write well.

### Physiological States:
I like how writing makes me feel inside.
When I write, I feel calm.
I feel comfortable when I write.
Writing makes me feel good.

This process resulted in a preliminary instrument that consisted of 38 items designated in the following manner: 15 Progress, 9 Observational Comparison, 7 Social Feedback, 6 Physiological States, and 1 general. Sample *WSPS* items are presented in Figure 1.

### Pilot Validation

Following judgmental review, three components were added to the instrument: a 5-point Likert response format, directions to the children, and a sample item. The response format included the options Strongly Agree, Agree, Undecided, Disagree, and Strongly Disagree. The written directions instructed the children to read each statement carefully and to circle the letters (i.e., SA, A, U, D, SD) that showed how much they agreed or disagreed with the statement. The sample item was stated, and then five qualifying sentences appeared below it. The qualifiers talked children through the process of making their answer selections by using the form "If you think that . . ., then circle ___).

As an assurance that the children knew what they should do, the classroom teachers were given written instructions for administration of the instrument and asked to go over the sample item orally with the group, providing additional examples if necessary. The set of instructions also provided explicit guidance on how the writing samples were to be obtained and scored.

The pilot *Writer Self-Perception Scale* was administered to 304 students (170 males and 134 females) in grades four (n=99), five (n=85), and six (n=120). The children were drawn from 14 classrooms in eight schools located in both urban and suburban school districts in southcentral Pennsylvania. All of the students in these classrooms, regardless of reading and writing ability levels, participated in the data collection. Full participation allowed for the most inclusive range possible in the pilot norming group.

Prior to the administration of the WSPS, the children were told that they would be completing a questionnaire about writing. The teacher emphasized that it was not a test and that there were no "right" answers. The children were encouraged to be as honest and thoughtful as possible, and they were allowed as much time as necessary to complete all items.

### Writing Assessment

When children had finished the *WSPS*, their teachers began the process of obtaining writing samples. To prepare them for the task, the teachers read aloud the instructions that had been included in the children's response packets while they followed along. The children were asked to think about an unforgettable event that had happened to them. They were further prompted to picture the time, the place, the people involved, and what had taken place so that they could write about it. The children were encouraged to write and revise their papers, to give specific details, to present ideas clearly, and to correct any mistakes in spelling, punctuation, and capitalization. The teachers fielded any questions, then started the children on the task. Ample time was provided to generate complete writing samples.

Scoring was done both by the classroom teachers (prior to returning the packets) and by a group of senior undergraduate students enrolled in advanced reading and language arts courses. Prior to the actual scoring, these research assistants underwent an extensive training session conducted by one of the investigators. During training, numerous anchor papers were evaluated using the rubric recommended by the state department of education. Since the rubric had also been covered in class, the research assistants had considerable familiarity and facility with it. After the practice scoring, the research assistants and the faculty trainer discussed the appraisals of the sample papers. The discussions focused on both the holistic scoring approach as well as on analytically rating focus, content, organization, style, and conventions.

When the trainer felt sufficient rater congruence existed, the actual scoring of the collected writing samples began. On a rotating basis, three research assistants scored each child's writing. To determine final scores for use in the data analyses, it was necessary to implement a resolution procedure because some variation still existed among raters. Whenever any disagreement existed, a final holistic or analytic score was determined either by selecting the rating that had two-thirds agreement, or by selecting the middle rating of the three. Overall, the average inter-rater reliabilities (i.e., rater 1 with rater 2, rater 2 with rater 3, and rater 1 with rater 3) measured as follows: .76 (Holistic), .72 (Focus), .74 (Content), .69 (Organization), .74 (Style), and .70 (Conventions). While these reliabilities were not especially high, they were deemed to be acceptable given the number of raters and the subjective task of evaluating writing.

The classroom teachers received no formal training in the use of the rubric. Their guidance was restricted to the instructions they had been sent, although they were familiar with the rubric due to its recommendation by the state. Because the researchers sought the perspective of naturalistic, field-based applications of the rubric, the lack of formal training was actually desirable. Intercorrelations between the ratings of the teachers and the research assistants ranged from .58 (Content and Organization) to .69 (Holistic). All correlations were significant beyond the .001 level.

## Analyses and Results
### *Reliability*
As a measure of scale reliability, Cronbach Alphas were computed on the four originally conceptualized individual scales. All of the coefficients exceeded .80. More specifically, the reliability estimates were Progress (.92),

Observational Comparison (.88), Social Feedback (.82), and Physiological States (.87). Reliability estimates in this range are most acceptable for affective constructs (Gable & Wolf, 1993). Interestingly, the analysis revealed that all items seemed to fit well with the rest of the respective scales.

### Factor Analysis

A principal components analysis was conducted for 37 of the *WSPS* items. Only the general item (#15) was excluded from the analysis. As Table 1 indicates, each of the items generated factor loadings of .40 or higher within an identifiable scale.

The analysis indicated the existence of six factors. Clearly identifiable scales were evident for both Observational Comparison (9 items) and Physiological States (6 items). Two other scales appeared to be measuring related dimensions of the Progress category, a General dimension (8 items) and a Specific one (7 items). The Social Feedback scale also seemed to take on

**Table 1. Rank Ordered Factor Loadings for Each WSPS Item by Scale**

| Scale/Item | Factor Loading |
|---|---|
| **Progress** | |
| *General* | |
| 17. My writing has improved. | .77 |
| 18. My writing is better than before. | .74 |
| 6. I am getting better at writing. | .69 |
| 19. It is easier to write better now than it used to be. | .69 |
| 14. I write better now than I could before. | .67 |
| 3. Writing is easier for me than it used to be. | .64 |
| 12. I need less help to write well than I used to. | .58 |
| 20. The organization of my writing has really improved. | .41 |
| *Specific* | |
| 31. When I write, the sentences and paragraphs fit together better than they used to. | .69 |
| 36. My writing is more clear than it used to be. | .66 |
| 22. The words I use in my writing are better than the ones I used before. | .65 |
| 25. My descriptions are more interesting than before. | .65 |
| 34. The order of my sentences makes better sense now. | .65 |
| 38. I choose the words I use in my writing more carefully now. | .57 |
| 29. My sentences stick to the topic better now. | .51 |

*Table 1 continued on next page.*

**Table 1. (Continued)**

| Scale/Item | Factor Loading |
|---|---|
| **Observational Comparison** | |
| 16.   I put my sentences in a better order than the other kids. | .75 |
| 26.   The words I use in my writing are better than the ones other kids use. | .73 |
| 8.   My writing is more interesting than my classmates. | .69 |
| 21.   The sentences I use in my writing stick to the topic more than the ones other kids use. | .69 |
| 1.   I write better than other kids in my class. | .68 |
| 4.   When I write, my organization is better than the other kids in my class. | .66 |
| 30.   My writing seems to be more clear than my classmates. | .64 |
| 11.   My sentences and paragraphs fit together as well as my classmates. | .56 |
| 23.   I write more often than other kids. | .45 |
| **Social Feedback** | |
| *Family* | |
| 5.   People in my family think I am a good writer. | .77 |
| 13.   People in my family think I write pretty well. | .71 |
| *Others* | |
| 28.   My teacher thinks I am a good writer. | .85 |
| 9.   My teacher thinks my writing is fine. | .81 |
| 33.   I can tell that my teacher thinks my writing is fine. | .70 |
| 37.   My classmates would say I write well. | .48 |
| 10.   Other kids think I am a good writer. | .43 |
| **Physiological States** | |
| 35.   I enjoy writing. | .81 |
| 32.   Writing makes me feel good. | .79 |
| 24.   I am relaxed when I write. | .71 |
| 2.   I like how writing makes me feel inside. | .68 |
| 27.   I feel comfortable when I write. | .68 |
| 7.   When I write, I feel calm. | .57 |

*Note 1. Copyright 1996 for the* Writer Self-Perception Scale *held by William A. Henk, Steven A. Melnick, and Diane M. Bottomley.*

*Note 2. General item #15 ("I think I am a good writer") was not included in the principal components analysis.*

two dimensions. One dimension was related to feedback from Family (2 items), while the other centered on feedback from Teachers and Classmates (5 items). Our suspicion is that these Social Feedback scales might merge as additional data are collected. By contrast, we suspect that the two dimensions of Progress (General and Specific) will likely maintain their distinctiveness, although item #20 ("The organization of my writing has really improved") could potentially drop out of the general dimension into the specific dimension. From a perceptual standpoint, the possible confusion with this item is understandable. It is not difficult to imagine how broad the notion of organization in writing could be viewed globally by some children, yet viewed specifically by others, because by definition this item is more akin to the items dealing with specific writing aspects.

### Correlational Analyses

With regard to validity in the present study, samples of the children's writing were taken as a related comparative benchmark. The accompanying holistic and analytic indices of performance (i.e., focus, content, organization, style, and conventions) were scored by the children's classroom teachers and by trained research assistants. Both sets of data were used in correlational analyses that cross-referenced the writing measures with children's total *Writer Self-Perception Scale* score as well as their four individual *WSPS* scale scores. Pearson Product-Moment correlation coefficients were computed among the Progress, Observational Comparison, Social Feedback, Physiological States, and Total scores of the *WSPS* and both the teacher and research assistant ratings of the children's writing. The intent here was to demonstrate the existence of significant, albeit modest relationships between how children perceived themselves as writers and how well they actually wrote.

Table 2 presents the intercorrelations between the *Writer Self-Perception Scale* and the *teacher ratings* of children's writing. As the table indicates, 27 of the 30 correlations were significant beyond the .05 level, ranging from .12 to .27. The three non-significant correlations (i.e., focus, organization, and style) occurred within the Physiological States scale column.

Intercorrelations between the *WSPS* and the *research assistant ratings* appear in Table 3. These results very much resembled those associated with the teacher ratings (in Table 2). The 24 significant correlations that were observed ranged from .13 to .28 with actual corresponding $p$ levels from .03 to beyond .001. None of the correlations between the Physiological States scale and the children's writing scores, as rated by the research assistants, were significant.

Overall, the correlational analyses indicated that modest interrelationships exist between the *WSPS* and the various indicators of writing. However, as desired, the limited amount of shared variance between measured

**Table 2. Intercorrelations Between the WSPS and Teacher Ratings of Children's Writing**

|  | Progress | Observational Comparison | Social Feedback | Physiological States | Total |
|---|---|---|---|---|---|
| Holistic | .22*** | .18*** | .27*** | .13* | .25*** |
| Focus | .15** | .12* | .23*** | .09NS | .20*** |
| Content | .23*** | .22*** | .26*** | .12* | .27*** |
| Organization | .24*** | .18*** | .23*** | .10NS | .26*** |
| Style | .21*** | .18*** | .23*** | .11NS | .23*** |
| Conventions | .19*** | .11*** | .22*** | .15* | .21*** |

*Note. All correlations are significant except where indicated by the NS (Non-Significant) label.*

*$p < .05$. **$p < .01$. ***$p < .001$.*

**Table 3. Intercorrelations Between the WSPS and Researcher Ratings of Children's Writing**

|  | Progress | Observational Comparison | Social Feedback | Physiological States | Total |
|---|---|---|---|---|---|
| Holistic | .23*** | .14* | .21*** | .08NS | .22*** |
| Focus | .21*** | .13* | .21*** | .09NS | .20*** |
| Content | .21*** | .13* | .18** | .07NS | .18** |
| Organization | .28*** | .15* | .22*** | .12NS | .25*** |
| Style | .23*** | .13* | .19** | .05NS | .19** |
| Conventions | .28*** | .18** | .25*** | .09NS | .26*** |

*Note. All correlations are significant except where indicated by the NS (Non-Significant) label.*

*$p < .05$. **$p < .01$. ***$p < .001$.*

writer self-perceptions and actual writing ability is sufficiently small to indicate that they are not measuring the same construct.

Additional intercorrelations were computed among the four *WSPS* scales and between these scales and the total score. These coefficients measured from .47 to .55 among the scales, as well as from .72 to .87 between the scales and the total *WSPS* score. In particular, the inter-scale correlations fell into the desired range, so far as the limited shared variances demonstrated scale distinctiveness. Correlations between the four scales and the general item (i.e., "I think I am a good writer") ranged from .47 to .61. The total score correlated .65 with this general item. All of these additional intercorrelations were significant beyond the .01 level, and collectively, they bode well for the instrument's viability.

## Discussion

In the present study, the *Writer Self-Perception Scale* demonstrated highly desirable psychometric properties, and as a result, clearly warrants additional attention. Of major import, scale reliability estimates for the Progress, Observational Comparison, Social Feedback, and Physiological States categories were well within acceptable ranges for affective measures. Likewise, the corresponding factor structure revealed that the partitioning of items by scales was indeed meaningful. Moreover, the modest correlations observed between children's *WSPS* scores and their writing sample performance provide further evidence that the instrument possesses definite measurement integrity. For that matter, the series of additional correlations involving the *WSPS* total and scale scores argue for the promise of the instrument. In fact, the quantitative analyses as a whole strongly suggest that it is both valid and reliable.

As the data collection process progresses, it will be interesting to note whether or not the Social Feedback scale continues to exhibit two dimensions (Family versus Classmates/Teacher) or whether they will eventually merge. Similarly, the twofold nature of the Progress scale (General versus Specific) bears continued examination, although this latter distinction is likely to remain stable. The eventual factor structure is important because it will determine the items that "belong" to each scale. In turn, item composition will influence the reliability estimates of the scales as well as their interrelationship properties.

In sum, the *WSPS* appears to possess considerable promise as a measurement tool. Should the instrument withstand the scrutiny that will accompany future data collections, it might rightly be considered as a legitimate counterpart to the *Reader Self-Perception Scale*. On the assumption that such a level is attained, the *Writer Self-Perception Scale* should qualify for widespread usage in a broad range of both classroom and research contexts.

## References

Bandura, A. (1982). Self-efficacy mechanism and human agency. *American Psychologist, 37,* 122-147.

Bandura, A. (1977). Self-efficacy: Toward a unifying theory of behavioral change. *Psychological Review, 84,* 191-215.

Gable, R. K., & Wolf, M. B. (1993). *Instrument development in the affective domain* (2nd ed.). Boston, MA: Kluwer-Nijhoff Publishing.

Henk, W. A., & Melnick, S. A. (1993, December). *Quantitative and qualitative validation of the Reader Self-Perception Scale,* Paper presented at the Annual Meeting of the National Reading Conference, Charleston, SC.

Henk, W. A., & Melnick, S. A. (1992). The initial development of a scale to measure "perception of self as reader." In C. K. Kinzer & D. J. Leu (Eds.), *Literacy research, theory, and practice: Views from many perspectives,* Forty-first Yearbook of the National Reading Conference. Chicago, IL: National Reading Conference, 111-117.

Henk, W. A., & Melnick, S. A. (1995). The Reader Self-Perception Scale (RSPS): A new tool for measuring how children feel about themselves as readers. *The Reading Teacher, 48,* 470-482.

McKenna, M. C., & Kear, D. J. (1990). Measuring attitude toward reading: A new tool for teachers. *The Reading Teacher, 9,* 626-639.

# Adult and College Learners and Literacy

# Finding Books
# for Adult New Readers

Patricia L. Bloem
Nancy D. Padak

Kent State University

## Abstract

*This article describes an ongoing research project carried out by the Ohio Literacy Resource Center. The project is designed to identify appropriate picture books and young adult novels for adult basic education (ABE) learners and to propose changes in conventional literacy instruction in ABE classrooms.*

How appropriate that at a conference with a theme of "The Joy of Reading" we consider a population for whom reading generally brings little joy: adult new readers. Not only is learning to read as an adult often a Herculean task, but we believe that the methods and materials used in most adult basic education (ABE) classrooms do little to promote love of reading. In this article we describe an ongoing research project carried out by the Reading Group at the Ohio Literacy Resource Center, which is designed to identify appropriate picture books and young adult novels for ABE learners and to propose changes in conventional literacy instruction in ABE classrooms. Below we describe the rationale for the project, the methods we have used, and the results of our work thus far.

## Why Picture Books in ABE Classrooms?

Why are we recommending picture books and young adult books—books not marketed for adults—to adult new readers? Why are we recommending radical changes in both curriculum and instruction in ABE classes? Our reasons are many. First, we believe that all people, no matter what age, need stories. Stories engage our imaginations, invite us to another reality, and encourage us to consider another perspective on the world. Stories are what we live by (Hickman, 1995), and books are a primary source for stories. Although ABE students' lives may be rich with oral stories or religious stories, books and literature offer another important resource to fill the need for story.

Similarly, we want students to value print as a source of practical information and to recognize the role that nonfiction can play in enriching their lives. Informational books can connect with learners' lives, whether they have a personal interest in learning about slavery, wish to help a child learn about animals' habitats, or want a sense of what life is like in Jamaica. But many ABE programs use reading instruction as a time for learners to work on isolated skills, do worksheets, read short selections, and answer questions about them without real-life application. In contrast, when learners work with authentic literature, they often find real reasons for reading and learn to view books as a source of information and pleasure.

Teachers who use authentic literature in their ABE classes are demonstrating the belief that education is no quick fix. Of course we want students to pass their GEDs as quickly as they can, but is the GED the end goal or are we educating for a larger purpose? Kazemek (1985) decries the assumptions behind many ABE programs—that working hard for 6 months will ensure the acquisition of literacy and that literacy is a skill that students can "get" from their tutors. By recommending dozens of books and encouraging teachers to work from a new instructional philosophy, our Reading Group has adopted the opposite of the "quick fix" approach.

When we take time to read, we grow as readers. For example, we learn what reading skills really are for when we take time for a book such as MacLachlan's picture book *What You Know First* (1995). This book presents an account of leaving the family farm during the Depression. It is simple in vocabulary, sentence structure, and cast of characters. The simplicity, however, is deceptive. This reminiscence, full of complex emotions, offers the kind of rich story that adult students can appreciate and learn from.

Even though picture books and young adult novels are marketed narrowly, many are meant for a wide range of readers. Cynthia Rylant, an author who has many books on our list, says "I write picture books that speak to any person, any age." She adds, "I like picture books because that medium gives me a chance to capture in a brief space what I consider life's profound experiences" (Commire, 1988, p. 186). Many books for children and young adults demand maturity, so a book like *What You Know First* can be read on several levels. For example, a child can think about saying goodbye to a familiar place. But adults can grieve for the child who is so young to be saying goodbye to a way of life, can feel for her sad father, can respect her wise mother, and can wish that the world didn't include bankrupt farms and painful goodbyes. Carefully chosen picture books resonate in our minds long after the first reading.

Picture books and young adult literature have the same range of quality found in adult fiction. We recommend books that offer compelling reading, that may delight or inspire readers, and that may ultimately help students become life-long readers. Books such as Paulsen's powerful and haunting *Nightjohn* (1993), the account of a runaway slave who returns to the South to teach others how to read, deserve a wider audience than the few young adults who pick them off library shelves or read them as part of social studies units on slavery.

The fact that some of our recommended books are beautifully illustrated provides additional intrinsic appeal for readers of all ages (Neal & Moore, 1992; Rief, 1992). In our visual age, most people are drawn to colorful or visually appealing books, such as Thomas Locker's *Catskill Eagle* (1991), which blur the line between picture books and coffee table books. The text of *Catskill Eagle* is a few lines from Melville's *Moby Dick*. Although not leisure reading material for most of us, the illustrations draw readers in.

Another important reason for using picture books and young adult literature for ABE instruction is that they're available in public libraries and thus inexpensive and convenient for teachers to collect and distribute. Almost every title our Reading Group has reviewed was easily obtained through one member's town library or its interlibrary loan program. Publishing companies that sell easy-to-read and content-appropriate books for adult new readers, such as New Readers Press, are doubtless making an important contribution, but our recommended trade books have the advantage of easy accessibility and a minimal price tag.

There are as many ways to use trade books instructionally as there are creative teachers. The books can be used to teach the same skills and strategies addressed in ABE workbooks, but with the advantage of carefully crafted texts used in their entirety. Consider, for example, this exercise from an often-used ABE workbook from a reading and writing skills series. The page is labeled "making decisions" and begins, "The same event can be judged in several different ways, depending on who is doing the judging and what the criteria are" (Barnes, Burgdorf, & Wenck, 1987, p. 73). Four short sentences about a storm follow, such as "The storm has taken a most unusual course," and adult students must decide who uttered the statement (a child, an artist, a homeowner, or a meteorologist) and the criteria used. Included on the page is a small photograph of palm trees being whipped by a wind storm.

An alternative text to address similar issues is Robert McCloskey's *Time of Wonder* (1977), a picture book about a hurricane that threatens the coast of Maine. Teachers could easily adapt the lesson on perspective and judgment by asking students to rewrite portions of the text to reflect various points of view. Discussion could follow, in which students read what they have written and talk about the changes they made in the original text. Students would have a rich context from which to draw, because they could read about the storm from beginning to end; inspect the illustrations for visual details about the storm; and read rich, descriptive language. For example:

Suddenly the wind whips the water
into sharp, choppy waves.
It tears off the sharp tops and slashes them
into ribbons of smoky spray.
And the rain comes slamming down.
The wind comes in stronger and stronger gusts.
A branch snaps from a tree.
A gull flies over, flying backward,
hoping for a chance to drop into the lee of the island.
(McCloskey, 1977, p. 44)

In the above quote, both kinds of imagery, visual and verbal, not only aid comprehension but make aesthetic reading possible. This invitation to focus on images, ideas, feelings, and personal connections (Rosenblatt, 1978) is something the workbook text cannot do. We contend that almost everything ABE teachers can do with a workbook, they can do better with authentic literature. And why not, if an underlying instructional purpose is to bring adult new readers to the joy of reading?

## How the Reading Group Operates

The Reading Group at the Ohio Literacy Resource Center was organized not quite two years ago when several educators agreed to read and evaluate picture books and young adult novels. Our immediate purposes were to identify materials we thought appropriate for adult new readers and to encourage adult literacy teachers to use these materials in their classrooms; our long-term hope is to create change in ABE reading instruction throughout the state of Ohio.

A core group of 6 people and 6 additional advisors includes former and current ABE teachers, family literacy educators, ABE administrators, a volunteer tutor, and a librarian. The group is made up of both men and women, and the perspectives of African-American, Latino, and white readers are represented. We view the diversity of roles and perspectives among members of our Reading Group to be a strength. Our reactions to books have not been uniform, and since we operate by consensus, when someone voices serious objections to a book, we generally delete it from our list of recommended books.

Each book is read by at least three people, who rate it (wholehearted approval, use with guidance, don't recommend), describe teaching ideas, and note possible GED connections. Although we began with three populations in mind, ABE, ESL, and family literacy, our heaviest focus is on making

ABE recommendations. Information about recommended books is maintained in a database (see Figure). Pages from the database are duplicated, three-hole punched, and distributed to ABE programs throughout the state.

Developing criteria for book selection has been a critical part of our work. We worked at selecting books for over a year before individuals attempted to articulate the criteria they were using to recommend books. The following guidelines, which represent consensus among Reading Group members, can help other educators select books for use in adult literacy programs:

- The book should (or could) have an adult message. It should affect the reader as a person, not just as a teacher. That is, the content should be interesting or emotionally satisfying from an adult perspective. Many appropriate books have a timeless quality. Others seem authentic or realistic.
- The point of view should be appropriate. If the book is written from a child's point of view, it should not seem childish. Reminiscences often provide an appropriate point of view.
- The book should provide an opportunity for discussion and/or instruction. For example, it might fit into content area study or become a part of a thematic unit. Or it might stimulate memories, serve as a prompt for writing, or raise issues for discussion that adults would find interesting.
- Book length should be appropriate for adult learners.
- Sentence structure should seem natural, neither too difficult nor too "babyish."
- Presentation and format should be appropriate. For example, the illustrations should not be childish, and the visual layout should not be too "busy."

Other educators have begun to stress the benefits of using literature with adults in family literacy programs (Doneson, 1991; Handel & Goldsmith, 1989; Johnson, Pflaum, Sherman, Taylor, & Poole, 1996; Sharp, 1991), in Read Aloud Parent Clubs (Locke, 1988; Segel, 1994), as part of library discussion programs (Morgenthaler, 1993; Stanek, 1993), or for adult new readers (Wadlington & Hicks, 1995; Weibel, 1994). We have found our criteria to be more stringent than others', in that we reject many suggestions as being too child-centered or childish. We do not wish to send an unspoken message that equates reading level with maturity level. For this reason, many beautifully illustrated, delightful books that are clearly written from a child's perspective do not appear on our list of recommended books. We seek books that are easy to read yet appealing to adults.

## Figure. Database Page Sample

February 1995

| | | | |
|---|---|---|---|
| Author: | Rylant, C. | Illustrator: | |
| Title: | Missing May | Date: | 1992 |
| Publisher: | Yearling | City: | New York |
| ISBN# (Paperback): | 0-440-40865-2 | ISBN# (Hardback): | |

| | |
|---|---|
| Type: | Fiction |
| Rating: | |
| Young Adult: | Y |
| Picture: | |
| Asian: | |
| African American: | |
| Latino/a: | |
| ESL: | |
| Family: | Y |
| ABE: | Y |
| Rural: | Y |
| Urban: | |
| GED Descriptors: | |
| Themes: | Dealing with grief, death, friendship, rural life, nontraditional families, Appalachia, journeys |
| Summary: | A twelve-year-old girl named Summer and her uncle are grieving and trying to carry on after the death of Aunt May (his wife). They decide, with the help of an unusual boy from Summer's school, to try to contact May's spirit, and in the process learn how to let go. |
| Teaching Ideas: | It might be fun to do a whole unit on the books of C. Rylant. Certainly this would pair well with *Appalachia: Voices of Sleeping Birds* or with her book of poems, *Something Permanent*. Teachers should be sure to talk about geography with this book, since the setting is very important. The characters' seemingly strange ways and the issue of how we see ourselves and how others see us may provoke reflection and journal entries. Students may also want to discuss the special dynamics of nontraditional families or their own attempts to deal with loss or think through their own creativity (in terms of Ob's creation of whirligigs). |

## Results to Date

We have read and reviewed 200 books, and database pages for the first 93 recommended titles are available in notebook form (Bloem & Padak, 1995). Notebooks have been distributed to ABE programs in the state through the Ohio Literacy Resource Center and to all public libraries by the State Libraries of Ohio.

In addition, we have written two articles for Ohio adult literacy teachers (Bloem, 1995; Bloem & Padak, 1996), in which we urge teachers to use authentic literature in their classrooms and suggest ways in which they might do so. These have been distributed to teachers in Ohio; each is also available electronically on the Center's World Wide Web site (search for Ohio Literacy Resource Center). We are currently developing a list of recommended books that groups titles thematically. Members of the Reading Group have led several conference presentations, both within Ohio and nationally; we have also sponsored three day-long workshops for Ohio ABE teachers. We continue to look for ways to influence curriculum and teaching methods.

Another Reading Group project has been to develop and field test teaching ideas for young adult novels. Thus far we have written teaching suggestions for three books by Patricia MacLachlan (*Baby,* 1993; *Journey,* 1991; and *Sarah, Plain and Tall,* 1985), two by Cynthia Rylant (*Every Living Thing,* 1984 and *Missing May,* 1992) and George Ella Lyon's book of short stories, *Choices* (1989). We work with volunteer ABE teachers and tutors throughout the state to field test these ideas with adult learners. We provide multiple copies of the books along with the teaching ideas, and teachers and tutors report on students' reactions to the books and provide their perceptions about the value of the activities. We use teachers' feedback, which we have found invaluable, to refine the teaching ideas before distributing them to all ABE teachers throughout the state.

## Conclusion

We have realized during the past two years that we are addressing several of the broad, pressing issues in education, especially in the education of adults: appropriate selection and use of multicultural literature, the difficulties of promoting educational reform, supporting teachers and learners as they change their instructional practices, and the potential benefits of integrated curricula. Grappling with these important educational issues has given our work a sharp edge that has been stimulating.

However, our "proudest" outcome is that Ohio ABE teachers are bringing picture books and young adult novels into their classrooms, piloting our materials, using our booklists, and telling us how their students are beginning to love to read. We conclude with the story of Katie (pseudonym) and her tutor, who piloted our teaching ideas for *Baby*. Katie was in her mid-30s and attended an urban literacy program. Prior to the pilot test, Katie's previous work with her tutor had involved use of Orton Gillingham techniques for dyslexic students. What follows are excerpts from a letter that Katie's tutor sent to us:

"Katie became engrossed in *Baby* immediately during the session in which I read chapters one and two to her. She took the book home to guide her as she completed [the first] assignment and ended up reading ahead because she enjoyed the book so much. Reading *Baby* was thrilling for Katie. It's hard to describe how much she enjoyed it, but maybe these two examples will help you see the impact the story had on her.

"First, Katie was so enthused about the story that she continually kept her family and her best friends updated on what was happening in the story thus far. Reading the book was so exciting for her that she couldn't help talking about it! This gave her a good chance to talk with others about her reading. . . .

"Second, reading this book and doing the assignments that you suggested helped Katie see that she wanted a change in lesson format. Katie would like to set aside the basal reader and focus strictly on . . . [reading] novels, [writing] about them, . . . and [doing] activities similar to the ones you suggested. Katie explained that she knew she hadn't been particularly happy with her previous curriculum, but she didn't know that reading 'lessons' could be like this.

". . . [T]he book really gave her a new, stronger enthusiasm for reading. I think that Katie's other tutor and I would not even have considered a short novel at this point in [her] studies without your pilot project. I hope that other teachers and students will benefit from your suggested materials and lesson plans the way that Katie and I did."

*The research reported in this article was supported by grants from the Governor's Office, State of Ohio, and the Ohio Department of Education to the Ohio Literacy Resource Center.*

---

# References

Barnes, D., Burgdorf, A., & Wenck, L. (1987). *Critical thinking for adults*. Austin, TX: Steck-Vaughn.

Bloem, P. (1995). *Bringing books to adult literacy classrooms*. Kent, OH: Ohio Literacy Resource Center. (ERIC Document Reproduction Service No. ED 385 748)

Bloem, P., & Padak, N. (1996). Picture books, young adult books, and adult literacy learners. *Journal of Adolescent and Adult Literacy, 40,* 48-53.

Bloem, P., & Padak, N. (1995). *Recommended trade books for adult literacy programs: Annotated bibliography with teaching suggestions*. Kent, OH: Ohio Literacy Resource Center. (ERIC Document Reproduction Service No. ED 381 672)

Commire, A. (Ed.). (1988). *Something about the author* (vol. 50). Detroit: Gale.

Doneson, S. (1991). Reading as a second chance: Teen mothers and children's books. *Journal of Reading, 35,* 220-223.

Handel, R., & Goldsmith, E. (1989). Children's literature and adult literacy: Empowerment through intergenerational learning. *Lifelong Learning, 12,* 24-27.

Hickman, J. (1995). Not by chance: Creating classrooms that invite response to literature. In N. Roser & M. Martinez (Eds.), *Book talk and beyond* (pp. 3-9). Newark, DE: International Reading Association.

Johnson. H., Pflaum, S., Sherman, E., Taylor, P., & Poole, P. (1996). Focus on teenage parents: Using children's literature to strengthen teenage literacy. *Journal of Adolescent and Adult Literacy, 39,* 290-296.

Kazemek, F. (1985). Functional literacy is not enough. *Journal of Reading, 28,* 332-335.

Locke, J. (1988). Pittsburgh's Beginning with Books project. *School Library Journal, 34,* 22-24.

Lyon, G.E. (1989). *Choices.* Lexington, KY: University Press of Kentucky.

MacLachlan, P. (1985). *Sarah, plain and tall.* New York: Harper and Row.

MacLachlan, P. (1991). *Journey.* New York: Delacorte.

MacLachlan, P. (1993). *Baby.* New York: Delacorte.

MacLachlan, P. (1995). *What you know first.* New York: HarperCollins.

McCloskey, R. (1977). *Time of wonder.* New York: Puffin.

Melville, H./ Locker, T. (1991). *Catskill eagle.* New York: Philomel.

Morgenthaler, S. (1993). Adult new readers get "a feel for books." *Journal of Reading, 36,* 570-571.

Paulsen, G. (1993). *Nightjohn.* New York: Bantam.

Neal, J., & Moore, K. (1992). The *very hungry caterpillar* meets *Beowulf* in secondary classrooms. *Journal of Reading, 35,* 290-296.

Rief, L. (1992). Good children's literature is for everyone, especially adolescents. In S. Benedict & L. Carlisle (Eds.), *Beyond words: Picture books for older readers and writers* (pp. 69-82). Portsmouth, NH: Heinemann.

Rosenblatt, L. (1978). *The reader, the text, the poem.* Carbondale, IL: Southern Illinois University Press.

Rylant, C. (1984). *Every living thing.* New York: Bradbury.

Rylant, C. (1991). *Appalachia: The voices of sleeping birds.* San Diego: Harcourt, Brace, Jovanovich.

Rylant, C. (1992). *Missing May.* New York: Orchard.

Rylant, C. (1994). *Something permanent.* San Diego: Harcourt, Brace, Jovanovich.

Segel, E. (1994). "I got to get him started out right": Promoting literacy by beginning with books. In D. Dickinson (Ed.), *Bridges to literacy* (pp. 66-79). Cambridge, MA: Basil Blackwell.

Sharp, P. (1991). Picture books in the adult literacy curriculum. *Journal of Reading, 35,* 216-219.

Stanek, L. (1993). *Whole language: Literature, learning, and literacy.* Bronx, NY: H.W. Wilson.

Wadlington, E., & Hicks, K. (1995). Using the big book experience with adult literacy students. *Adult Learning, 6,* 14-16.

Weibel, M. (1994). Literature, whole language, and adult literacy instruction. *Adult Learning, 6,* 9-12.

# A Case Study in Reading Using Holistic Intervention With an Undergraduate University Student

## Karen E. Mayo

East Texas Baptist University

## Abstract

*This paper presents a descriptive case study of holistic intervention in reading with an undergraduate university student who voluntarily sought instructional support in reading. During a three-month period of dialogue, intensive tutorial assistance, and academic support, the instructor documented and described the intervention process while investigating reasons the student was experiencing difficulty. Explanations for this student's lack of academic success included lack of motivation to read, lack of study skills, fear of failing, and perception of self as a poor reader. Through holistic intervention, the student explored a variety of strategies to strengthen her metacognitive skills, develop effective study habits, and promote self-esteem. This student successfully completed the semester and remained in school.*

## Introduction

I'll never forget the day that I first met Donni (pseudonym). Donni was a transfer student at a small private liberal arts university in East Texas who had been admitted conditionally due to failing grades at a community college. Donni transferred to the university in the fall and approached me for assistance with her classes in early spring. Donni particularly wanted help in reading. As the Assistant Director of the Learning Assistance Center on our campus, I was accustomed to working with students in developmental writing, ESL courses, and tutorials. However, it was rare to encounter a college student seeking help voluntarily.

Over a three month period, I worked closely with Donni on strategies to improve study skills, metacognitive abilities, and writing. I involved professors from her other courses in a holistic approach to tutorials and learning assistance. Furthermore, I sought to help Donni identify and understand reasons why she had difficulty in reading. The following case study describes this process of holistic intervention in reading with an adult learner, which is a nontraditional form of learning assistance in the college setting. The study also provides an opportunity to examine the role of the affective domain, particularly motivation and self-confidence, in relation to adult literacy.

## Background

Although historically ignored in most reading models (Athey, 1971), the role of the affective domain in reading was explored as early as 1938 by Louise Rosenblatt. In *Literature as Exploration,* Rosenblatt (1938) introduced the role of reader response in meaning acquisition through the use of an efferent/aesthetic continuum in which different levels of meaning are transacted according to the reader's purpose(s). Moreover, Rosenblatt developed a model to help teachers understand that the reader's purposes always contain both cognitive and affective aspects (Rosenblatt, 1978).

However, it wasn't until the mid-1970s that models of reading began to include the affective component of attitude and its relationship to reading (Cothern & Collins, 1992). In 1976, Mathewson developed the first reading model that articulated the role of attitude in initiating and sustaining reading (Mathewson, 1992). Nearly a decade later, Ruddell and Speaker (1985) incorporated the affective stance into an interactive reading process model.

Although the earlier models lacked elaboration, recent research into the nature and influence of affective factors, particularly in whole language classrooms, has placed the role of affect in literacy acquisition and reading instruction in the spotlight (Frager, 1993; Mathewson, 1992; Oldfather, 1993; Ruddell and Speaker, 1985). Spurred by the realization that skills-based instruction, ability grouping, and tightly controlled basal reading series have failed to produce a generation of readers better than the previous one, research into the affective domain has initiated exploration into the influence of factors such as attitude, motivation, interest, values, and belief on reading (Smith, 1986).

Currently, the relationship between attitude and learning is a topic uniting several research circles. Numerous studies support the belief that affect is paramount to cognition in learning to read (Estes, 1987; Hochschild, 1979; Mathewson, 1992; Oldfather, 1993; Smith, 1986). Moreover, self-esteem, positive self-perception, and the development of one's inner voice are perceived as essential ingredients for learning (Bandura, 1989; Belenky, Clinchy, Goldberger, & Tarule,1986; Fishbein & Ajzen, 1975; Frager,1993). However, research that explores the role of the affective domain in relation to learning assistance with adults and in developmental reading courses is scarce. Likewise, few studies exist that describe the types and nature of intervention programs at the post-secondary and undergraduate levels and that inquire into the attitudes of students who are placed in learning assistance programs.

## Purpose

This paper presents a descriptive case study of holistic intervention with a transfer undergraduate university student who was admitted conditionally and placed in a college study skills course because of a low G.P.A. While the university did not offer courses in developmental reading, this student voluntarily sought instructional support in reading. This case study describes a three-month period of dialogue, intensive tutorial assistance, and academic support designed to improve the student's reading ability and promote her academic success through direct instruction and tutorials.

## Research Design

A qualitative case study design was chosen to allow the instructor to serve as both teacher and researcher (Merriam,1988; Shumacher and McMillan, 1993). It also enabled the subject of the study to actively engage in participant review during the data collection and ongoing analysis, a method which strengthens internal validity (Marshall & Rossman, 1995). Likewise, internal validity was strengthened by multiple sources of data. The research was guided by the following questions:
1. What specific reading difficulties did Donni have?
2. What were Donni's perceptions of the causes of her reading problems?
3. How did Donni's perceptions of her reading ability change during the semester?

## Data Collection and Analysis

The first meeting was set for mid-February. Over the next twelve weeks, Donni and I had ten one-hour meetings. The data collection consisted of taped in-depth interviews, Donni's work samples and assignments, my reflective comments written after the sessions, and feedback from Donni's professors. Also, a colleague in the local public school district administered and interpreted a Reading Styles Inventory (Carbo, 1984) which was used in the study.

On-going data analysis was conducted throughout the semester to determine Donni's specific difficulties related to reading and to examine the success of the strategies that were introduced. Participant review occurred as Donni participated in this weekly analysis (Marshall & Rossman, 1995). Feedback from Donni's professors also served to inform emerging hypotheses.

Following the period of data collection, the researcher conducted an intensive analysis using the constant comparative method (Glaser & Strauss, 1967) to examine the outcomes of the intervention process and to reveal insight into Donni's perceptions of the causes of her reading problems and explore how those perceptions changed during the semester. The steps in this analysis of data included transcribing the audiotapes and reading to locate major points and recurring patterns of behavior (Goetz and Le Compte, 1984). From these patterns, categories or themes were derived by comparing one incidence to another (Merriam, 1988).

In this report, the intervention process is described chronologically followed by a discussion of the findings.

## Case Report: Working with Donni
### First Meeting

I met Donni by accident. I was temporarily occupying a classroom because my office had just been painted. About ten minutes before the next class, the door opened and in walked a college freshman with the usual armload of textbooks. The only striking feature which distinguished her from a hundred others was the sling holding her left arm. She sat down quietly as I looked up.

"I'll be out of your way in a few minutes," I replied.

"That's okay. I'm a few minutes early."

"I'm using this as an office because they're painting mine," I answered.

"Oh, do you teach here?"

"Yes."

"What do you teach?" she asked.

"ESL, mainly, and I supervise student teachers and teach reading courses," I replied.

"Oh," she broke in, "do you teach reading?"

"Well," I hedged. I had taught reading for years in public elementary schools, but no one here had ever asked me whether I simply taught reading. I guessed that it was generally assumed that college students knew how to read or they wouldn't be here.

"Actually," I continued, "I now teach 'how to teach reading' to education majors, but I've taught reading for years. Why?"

"Because I need help in reading," she replied.

That got me. I don't know if it was her sheer candor or the need itself, but I resolved then that I would do anything that I could to answer Donni's plea for help.

I promised that I'd call her to set up an appointment. She scrawled her name and added, "I need help with reading, spelling, and oh yea, grammar."

## Initial Interview

During our first interview, I asked Donni to describe her background and interests in reading. Specifically, I wanted to explore her previous experiences with reading, her feelings toward reading, and her perceptions of herself as a reader.

Donni began by telling me that in third grade she had been placed in a remedial class for reading. She remembered being taken out of her regular class and having twice as much homework because she had to complete the assignments for the resource teacher as well as her homeroom teacher. She recalled her parents making her stay in after school to finish her homework and also said that it had taken her a long time to learn to read.

Donni further recounted being placed in a seventh grade level reading class during eighth grade, and said that when her teachers approached her parents with the possibility of holding her back a year, her parents would not consider it.

When asked how she felt about reading today, Donni replied, "I like reading, it's just making myself sit down and do it [that causes a problem]." She also said it helped her to highlight, but noted having difficulty in remembering what she had read. "I learn better by hearing," she added. Donni clearly felt very strongly about needing help in reading and wished the university offered a reading course. She added that she felt she also needed help in spelling.

Donni further expressed a desire to read fluently: "I can read, but I read slowly. I want to be able to read aloud to my niece. She's five. I don't feel that I'm that interesting of a reader."

Donni then shared a writing assignment, a descriptive paper, and asked for assistance. She described her writing as "choppy." We conferenced on the language of the paper, which I noted in the researcher's log was written in "a stream of consciousness" style.

During the initial interview, we also discussed implementing several strategies, including listening to taped texts to increase comprehension, reading together aloud to boost oral expression and fluency, and writing in a dialogue journal to promote written self-expression. At the close of the first interview, I asked Donni about her goals in college and she expressed an interest in becoming a teacher. Donni felt that as a teacher she would be able to understand students like herself, but also noted a fear of not being able to make grades high enough to get into a teacher education program.

## The First Month of Intervention

Following the initial interview, I resolved to find out additional information regarding Donni's case, including information on her academic background.

I requested Donni's high-school and college transcripts and test data from the registrar. Donni graduated from high school in the spring of 1991 with a cumulative G.P.A. of 2.140. Her ACT composite was 15 with a 12 in reading and a 17 in English. In the 10th grade, on the California Achievement Test, Donni had scored in the 19th percentile in reading with a grade equivalence of 8.1. Her spelling grade equivalence was 6.9 and study skills ranked at 6.5. Similarly, the language grade equivalence totaled 6.8.

Following high school, Donni had entered a local community college where she completed twenty-two credit hours and six non-credit hours of developmental math and developmental writing in two years. Two courses had been dropped. Her transcript reflected a D in English. Donni later explained that during this time she suffered a near fatal car accident and had several successive surgeries on both an arm and leg. This explained the sling she wore on her left arm.

Donni's cumulative G.P.A. was 2.36 when she transferred to the university in the spring of 1994. She was admitted conditionally, placed on academic probation, and required to enroll in a college study skills course. At the time the tutorial began, Donni was enrolled in four courses: speech, sociology, Old Testament, and English (writing).

### *The Second Session*

I opened the second session by asking Donni to describe her weak spots in reading. She replied, "Reading is not the problem, sitting down to read is the problem." Donni indicated no time for pleasure reading, "I know that if I would take the time, I could do it."

I shared a method for chunking longer reading assignments into shorter pieces and then moved to a writing assignment that she brought. I began the writing conference by asking Donni to read her essay aloud. Before reading the paper, Donni recapped the instructor's comments that the paper lacked focus and shifted back and forth from narrative to descriptive. The essay was based on a descriptive prompt.

As she read orally, Donni paused often, making editorial comments about areas that she felt needed reworking. One thing I noted in my log was that she "read fluently." Together we looked for places where the writing veered off the topic. Using both the first and second drafts, Donni worked on meshing vocabulary and ideas into a cohesive five-paragraph theme.

After the writing tutorial, I attempted to move back into reading. I began, "Last week you mentioned reading aloud." I asked her if she would like to read a children's book just for fun.

She answered, "I don't want to read."

"I brought this book—a children's book—it's one of my favorites," I continued.

"Do you want me to read it to you?" Donni asked.

"I thought we might read it together," I replied. How about if we take turns? Or we could do a shadow reading."

Finally, Donni agreed to take turns reading aloud. At the beginning of the reading, Donni was self-conscious of the tape recorder and asked me to turn it off (which I did during the reading). As I listened to her read , immediately I knew that her problems were not in decoding or fluency. She read, "cautiously and hesitantly," but overall, I recorded, ". . . there was feeling and expression even though she had never seen the book before."

After the reading, I commented, "I think a lot of this is how you see yourself. See, you read fine, absolutely fine."

Donni interrupted,

> But . . . I mess up the first time I read anything . . . this is what it stems from. First of all, it took me a long time to learn to read. Then when I learned how, I get (sic) so nervous when people are around. That's why I didn't like reading in school, until my junior year. My body inside, my heart starts to pound if I have to read in front of people. I can get up in front of people and do better verbally than having to read something.

I listened to Donni describe her reaction to reading aloud in school. I asked if she wanted to continue practicing reading aloud and she answered, "Yes, but I think I'll do better without the tape recorder." However, she declined taking material to rehearse in advance, explaining that she needed unrehearsed oral practice.

We then discussed the possibility of listening to soft classical music while reading, and I gave her one of my tapes of baroque music. I also loaned her a set of colored overlays to try with textbook reading. Then I obtained her permission to conduct a case study with the data collected during the semester.

After the visit, I recorded in my reflection log that she "seemed hesitant and self-critical. The problem seems to be really an image thing not actual impairment."

### The Third Session

Donni opened the third session expressing concern about her grades, "But like when it comes to studying . . . I've never been an 'A' student . . . but, I've also been, like, scared of it. It's like I don't study 'cause I still don't do good . . . I mean if I did study, then I'll feel worse. But if I didn't study, I have an excuse."

Reflecting back to the past week, I asked if any of the colored overlays made a difference in studying from her textbooks. She indicated "no," and added, "I really don't have a problem reading, it's just making myself sit down to read."

Then I asked about reading with the classical music. She hadn't tried the tape yet, but explained:

When I do read, I like to be alone and in silence. And I've been trying to work on it because it just seems like I can't get it anywhere. I can't get it in the library, it's just so frustrating.

When I asked Donni what she was reading, she couldn't remember the name of the book but added, "It was a book for young adults. I didn't mind reading it, I just got distracted." I noted that "she seemed apologetic of the reading level" of the book.

Donni pulled out a piece of writing that she was working on in English class. She described her writing as rambling. Then she asked, "How do *you* write a paragraph?"

I replied, "First, I decide what kind of paragraph I need to write." I drew diagrams and explained the various types of paragraph structures. Then we completed a close analysis of her paper. By taking the topic sentence and keying into important words, I showed her how to flesh out the key words into three separate points. We also examined problems in parallelism.

Following the writing tutorial, I asked Donni for additional input on classes, her likes and dislikes. We talked about assignments and the general workload in her classes. She noted that there had never been a class that had been easy for her, but identified English as her favorite class this semester. However, she continued to express her fear of not being able to read well:

I want to learn . . . that's what I'm really kind of afraid of. Even like in Comp II, when it comes to Old English, you know like Shakespeare . . . those books, how well do you read? Or how well can you teach someone to read those books? . . . See I want to be able to read. I want to make a good grade in Lit. II. I was really scared those first few days of class.

In addition, Donni expressed anxiety about sociology, saying that if she didn't get an "A" on the next test, she would have to drop the course. Although most of the discussion dealt with negatives, one positive note emerged when she told me that she had auditioned and been selected for the campus thespian troupe.

She also expressed preference for a "teacher who writes nearly everything on the board that she wants me to have." I drew the session to a close with some pointers on notetaking. I showed her how I study using notes from the teacher's lecture. I modeled my own abbreviated shorthand and demonstrated how to show relationships between points by indenting.

### The Second Month of Intervention

During the second month of intervention, I focused increasingly on helping Donni develop better study habits, raising her self-confidence as a reader, and exploring strategies to combat her fear of failing. Also, I sought increased instructional support in her other classes by conferencing with the professors. Two of the three offered additional assistance with notetaking, taped lectures, and makeup tests.

### The Fourth Session

At this session, Donni expressed fear of failing several of her classes. After studying a combined five hours, she had failed exams in both sociology and Old Testament. She also failed a speech test for which she hadn't studied. She didn't know her grades in English. Donni reiterated her fear of not being able to make the grades to get into teacher education.

> I've got to make good grades. I don't want to just barely make it . . . I foresee me doing it, but it's just, there's something. And I don't know what it is. I don't think it's my reading ability, and I don't know if I would say I know how to be a learner on my own, and that's what I'm trying to be. I'm really getting stressed out over this.

On a more positive note, Donni shared the outcome of a visit with another instructor who seemed to really care and understand her feelings of frustration. This professor offered her the opportunity to retake an earlier failed test. Briefly elaborating, Donni offered an explanation as to why she thought that she failed tests even after studying several hours,

> I don't think reading is the problem. Studying is the problem. Maybe I don't study enough, or maybe I don't study the right way . . . I need to read more, I don't read enough.

To boost her study skills, we practiced dissecting a chapter from a textbook to get the main points from it. I showed her how to read the summaries first, form questions out of the main points, and then go back to the chapter to read and uncover the answers. I also advised her to jot down the key points as she read new material.

In this session, Donni also described not being able to attend to what is spoken after 15 or 20 minutes and getting bored with reading material in a short period of time. I wondered whether there was a possible interference from inattentiveness and discussed with Donni the nature of attention deficient disorder.

We concluded the fourth session by reviewing outlines she had made for Old Testament and developing a game plan for retaking the test. Together we worked on a schedule which allotted time for preparing for assignments, homework, and tests.

### The Fifth Session

The fifth session coincided with the midpoint of the semester and marked a turning point in the intervention process. Donni entered the fifth session jubilantly, saying, "I finally got Old Testament under control." She showed a study outline similar to the one from the previous session. She had scored a "B" on the test.

She was enthusiastic and asked for assistance in arranging an interview for her speech course with a local public school teacher. She also asked for help with the questions for the interview. Her speech teacher had reviewed questions Donni had written and said they were too general and lacked focus. I made a note that this was similar to problems in her writing.

I then asked Donni about her English course. She admitted postponing a paper that was due later in the week because she knew that she was coming to our tutorial session. The paper was a persuasive prompt, and since she didn't like the choices, she needed to come up with an alternative. She explained, "I don't even have a clue where to start."

### *Session Six and Seven*

Much of the second month continued to deal with writing, notetaking, reading independently, and practicing time management. During the sixth and seventh sessions, Donni and I worked primarily on study outlines, spreading out assignments by chunking them into smaller assignments for easier study. During this time, Donni dropped sociology and threw herself into the remaining three courses with vigor.

At this time, I also asked a colleague in the public schools to administer a Reading Styles Inventory or RSI (Carbo, 1984). The RSI is designed to identify students' preferred learning modalities and show their perceptual strengths and weaknesses related to reading. According to her responses on the profile, Donni did not appear to be strongly auditory or visual, but showed a dominant preference for tactile and kinesthetic modalities for reading. She also preferred quiet, no talking, dim lighting and a warm room temperature. Her best times to read were shown as before noon and early evening.

Donni and I discussed these results and explored ways to structure her reading/study environment to accommodate these preferences. The results confirmed why Donni disliked reading in the library because "it was always cold and they have those bright lights." Although it contradicted her RSI profile, Donni related that listening to soft music had helped a lot. "I listen to it all the time when I'm studying."

Several times during the second month, as I probed to pinpoint specific difficulties in literacy, Donni recollected her earlier experiences in reading: "I was exposed to reading, but it was in a kind of negative way . . ." She recalled her parents' harsh approach to homework, especially her reading assignments, saying that her parents did read to her:

> But in such a boring kind of way. They'd make me sit there, you know, when they were trying to teach me. I don't remember them reading to me for the fun of it . . . It was never presented just for the fun of it.

In fact, Donni noted that reading didn't become fun until she went to live with her great aunt after her parents' divorce and her near-fatal car accident. She was eighteen at the time. Donni's aunt had "stacks of books and magazines everywhere—she read all the time. She wasn't the greatest housekeeper, there was a lot of dust." Donni credited her aunt with enabling her to attend the university, saying that she is "paying a big portion of the bill."

In describing her great aunt, Donni's tone was completely different than in describing her parents. "We weren't encouraged to be our individual selves at home. My sisters had low self-esteem, too."

### The Final Month of Intervention

During the third month, Donni and I continued to pursue strategies for success through the writing conferences, study skills tutorials, and instructional support from her other instructors. A new pattern emerged during this time as Donni began to realize signs of progress. For the first time, she was clearly passing in all three courses. She admitted that a reluctant confidence was beginning to unfold, especially in comparison to her previous experiences in college courses.

> Everything, I think, is coming together. I'm glad I have you to talk to about it . . . I don't really foresee me failing. I see me making at least all Cs . . . I'm excited 'cause I know where I'm messing up. Where I did mess up at. But it's like so many other things are coming my way. . . . Overall, I'm doing great.

However, at other times, Donni echoed earlier perceptions of her problems in reading:

> I really do like to read . . . I just don't have time to read more than just what I've gotta read right now. But, um, reading is not a problem, it's really not a problem . . . it's studying, studying for the tests . . . what to study is the problem. I mean I may not be the fastest reader, in order for me to comprehend, I have to read slowly. . . . I really do want to be successful, and I'm just scared of it. I'm totally scared of it.

### The Final Interview

During our final session, I asked Donni to reflect upon what she had gained from the interaction and what she had learned about herself. She explained that "the positive influence I've gotten all around campus has helped me a lot," citing specific learning strategies we practiced and also help from her roomate in studying for tests.

Donni jubilantly predicted her grades, "I think I came out with two B's and a C." (I later found out that it was actually a B and two Cs; still her best semester thus far.)

I asked, "What did you learn about yourself this semester?"

Donni replied, "That I need to study [laughter]. Definitely, I need to study."
She also recapped some of the changes, like dim lighting and soft music,
that she had made to improve her study environment.

When asked if she would like to continue the tutorials, she expressed
an interest in resuming our sessions in the fall: "I'd like that because the way
I see it, I started at midterm to get my grades up. I need help with the tests."
Donni also set goals. She wanted to continue learning how to digest information from the textbook chapters and become more proficient at taking
notes during lectures.

Donni also was beginning to come to terms with the role of her parents
in relation to her perception of her problems in reading. She reflected on her
grades and her personal goals versus her father's goals for her: "Right now
the problem is home. You see I don't really have a home anymore. I live
with my great aunt. It's a big mess. My dad doesn't want me to come here
[the university]."

Looking to the summer, Donni speculated on taking an algebra or history course. She brought up the idea of getting help (tutorials) over the summer. She also added, "I have plans to read to my niece, get library books and
make it fun. . . ."

## Discussion
### *What specific reading difficulties did Donni have?*
The data from Donni's test scores in high school revealed that Donni's
reading comprehension, vocabulary, language, and study skills had been
several years behind her grade level and fell below expected norms for successful entrance into college. Although she did read some material fluently,
her college textbooks were difficult for her to interpret and understand. Donni
described the material as boring and she stated that she was easily distracted
when reading.

Donni's study skills also were weak. She seemed to have difficulty with
self-monitoring, summarizing, identifying key points, visualizing relationships
within the information in the text, listening to and taking notes during lectures, and recalling what she had studied.

Donni also demonstrated difficulties in oral and written communication.
She described being afraid to read orally in front of a group. Feedback from
her speech teacher confirmed her nervousness in oral presentations.

With respect to written expression, interview questions she wrote for
sociology were too general and were unfocused. The English teacher described her journal entries as "too brief" and said her essays also lacked focus and organization. In our sessions Donni was confused about differences
in types of paragraphs and the various modes of expository writing.

In addition, Donni expressed a great deal of grade anxiety and fear of failing. This seemed to restrict her motivation to read and ability to study. She often said that she could read, but had difficulty in finding the time and making herself do it.

### *What were Donni's perceptions of the causes of her reading problems?*

At the beginning of the intervention, Donni described herself as a poor reader. She stated that she felt it took her a long time to read and that she read slowly. She did not believe she read well orally, and she said that she "messed things up" the first time she read them.

Donni negatively described her early experiences in reading. She recounted her parent's approach to helping her with reading as harsh. She expressed feelings of inferiority from being placed in a remedial program in elementary school and tracked in the below-level reading classes throughout junior high.

### *How did Donni's perceptions of her reading ability change during the semester?*

Early in the semester, Donni distinguished between reading and studying when she stated that reading was *not* the problem, studying was the problem. She later qualified this statement by explaining that she did not know how to study or she studied things in the wrong way. After three months of tutorials in study skills, Donni concluded that she needed to study more and wished to continue cultivating better study skills and habits in the fall semester.

During the first half of the semester, Donni expressed a great deal of fear and anxiety of failing. She did drop one course, but set goals in the remaining three. At midterm, her negative attitude shifted to a more confident stance as she felt that she was getting her assignments under control. She became more enthusiastic in our sessions and described things as coming together. She was confident that she would pass all three courses. She finished the semester with a "B" in English and two "Cs."

Donni also changed the way she described her reading ability during the intervention process. At first she referred to herself as a "slow reader." In the final interview, she stated, "I need to read slowly in order for me to comprehend." She attributed some of her low self-esteem to not being encouraged to be an individual at home, and she expressed a desire to be different: "It's like I'm in a shell, and I want to come out."

## Conclusions

One overarching theme or pattern emerged through the analysis of the data: namely, many of Donni's difficulties in reading seemed linked to the affective domain. First, Donni expressed a lack of motivation to read in terms of time constraints, purpose, and interest. Second, she confided not knowing how to study and concluded her lack of success in school stemmed from this difficulty. Third, she demonstrated a low sense of self-esteem and negative self-perception as a learner. Finally, having previously experienced failure in school, Donni revealed a high level of anxiety and fear toward grades and failing in general.

Following the three month period of intervention described earlier, Donni completed nine credit hours successfully with a 2.3 G.P.A. She earned a "B" in English, a subject based upon literacy and one she had failed previously. Also, during the semester, Donni's perceptions of herself as a learner and the causes of her reading problems changed as she explored strategies to improve her study and communication skills, self-assessed her learning, and experienced academic success.

While the role of affect has been left unexplored in most adult literacy intervention programs, this study confirms several major premises of attitude development. As hypothesized by Ajzen and Fishbein (1980) and others, attitudes are learned behaviors which exist within systems. Attitudes within a system also are interrelated, varying in intensity, quality, and degree, and they give rise to motivated behavior (Fishbein & Ajzen, 1975; Liska, 1984; Shaw & Wright, 1967).

Recent research suggests that perceived failure dramatically impacts human performance, particularly in relation to tests (Maimon, 1995). This impact can be positive or negative depending upon how the individual responds to perceived failure. In Donni's case, it seemed that efforts declined, strategies were impaired, and performance was seriously diminished by perceived failure. This type of response to failure is defined as internal helplessness due to exposure to uncontrollable events, including course assignments and tests. According to this theory, although individuals believe there are responses that would produce successful outcomes, they believe they do not posess these responses. Failure to attain goals is attributed to internal factors.

The relationship of the affective domain to learning is further corroborated by research into the nature of self-concept and its bearing on attitude development and achievement. An empirical body of research strongly suggests a positive correlation between self-concept, positive attitude, and achievement (Alexander & Filler, 1976; Bandura, 1989; Cothern & Collins, 1992). Numerous studies attest that literacy behaviors in the home influence literacy behaviors at school. Likewise teachers must be supportive in order to facilitate positive attitudes toward learning (Brophy, 1988; Cothern & Collins, 1992; Durkin, 1966; Morrow, 1986). These studies reveal the inestimable role that affective factors play not only in learning to read but in sustaining reading habits.

## Strength and Limitations

One of the strengths of case study design is that it tends to have a high degree of internal validity (Merriam, 1988). The internal validity of this study is strengthened through the triangulation of data, member checks, and peer examination from the other professors who provided feedback. However, the short time period of observation, one semester, may limit its validity. The study also is limited to a single case and therefore the findings are isolated to that subject. While the findings are not generalizable to other students, the design and process are described in detail so that additional studies may be replicated with other students in similar circumstances.

## Implications

While the process of holistic intervention described here is more time-consuming than more traditional forms of learning assistance such as college study skills courses and peer tutorials, the success achieved by this student warrants attention to the process. Dialogue between the instructor and student was an essential ingredient in promoting and monitoring this student's success. Further studies could be designed which examine the effects of this dialogue on student motivation and performance. Additional research that identifies and examines adult literacy programs that are prescriptive and individualized is needed. This information could be helpful to colleges and universities who seek to implement holistic learning assistance with adults.

Many questions remain unanswered. Other studies that specifically explore the relationship of failure to self-perception and achievement among adult learners are needed. Also, despite apparent relationships between affect and learning to read, the influence of affective factors and ways to teach strategies that stimulate affect are largely missing from the texts designed to prepare future reading teachers. Research concerning how affective factors are related to literacy acquisition and are taught in reading methods courses is necessary. This case study ended with greater inquiry than insight and a heightened curiosity into the complexity of factors intertwined in working with adult learners.

---

## References

Ajzen, I., & Fishbein, M. (1980). *Understanding attitudes and predicting social behavior.* Englewood Cliffs, NJ: Prentice Hall.

Alexander, E., & Filler, R. (1976). *Attitudes and reading.* Newark, DE: International Reading Association.

Athey, I. (1971). Language models and reading. *Reading Research Quarterly, 7,* 16-110.

Bandura, A. (1989). Regulation of cognitive processes through perceived self-efficacy. *Educational Psychology, 23* (5), 729-735.

Belenky, M., Clinchy, B., Goldberger, N. & Tarule, J. (1986). *Women's ways of knowing: The development of self, voice, and mind.* New York: Basic Books.

Brophy, J. (1988). *Research on teacher effects: Uses and abuses. Occasional paper no. 16.* Instititute for Research on Teaching, College of Education, Michigan State University. Washington, D.C.: The Office of Educational Research and Improvement.

Carbo, M. (1984). The reading styles inventory. Roslyn Heights, NY: National Reading Styles Institute.

Cothern, N. & Collins, M. (1992). An exploration: Attitude acquisition and reading instruction. *Reading Research and Instruction, 31*(2), 84-97.

Durkin, D. (1966). Children who read early. New York: Teachers College Press.

Estes, T. (1987). Illusions (and realities) of schema theory. In D. Lumpkin, M. Harshbarger, & P. Ransom (Eds.), *Seventh Yearbook of the American Reading Forum* (pp. 106). Muncie, IN: Ball State University.

Fishbein, M., & Ajzen, I. (1975). *Belief, attitude, intention, and behavior: An introduction to theory and research.* Reading, MA: Addison-Wesley.

Frager, A. (1993). Affective dimensions of content area reading. *Journal of Reading, 36* (8), 616 - 622.

Glaser, B., & Strauss, A. (1967). *The discovery of grounded theory.* Chicago: Aldine.

Goetz, J. P., & LeCompte, M.D. (1984). *Ethnography and qualitative design in eduational research.* Orlando, FL: Academic Press.

Hochschild, A. (1979). Emotion work, feeling rules, and social structure. *American Journal of Sociology, 85,* 551-575.

Liska, A. (1984). A critical examination of the casual structure of Fishbein-Ajzen attitude-behavior model. *Social Psychology Quarterly, 47,* 61-74.

Maimon, L. (1995). The effects of perceptions of failure and test instructions on test performance of community college students. In W. M. Linek & E. G. Sturtevant (Eds.), *Generations of literacy: The seventeenth yearbook of the college reading association* (pp. 145-160). Harrisonburg, VA: The College Reading Association.

Marshall, C., & Rossman, G. (1995). *Designing qualitative research.* Thousand Oaks, CA: Sage.

Mathewson, G. (1992). Model of attitude influence upon reading and learning to read. In *Theoretical models of reading: Update and new directions.* 1992 Annual Convention of the International Reading Association Publication Session.

Merriam, S. (1988). *Case study research in education: A qualitative approach.* San Francisco: Josey-Bass.

Morrow, L. (1986, April). *Promoting responses to literature: A children's sense of story structure.* Paper presented at the National Reading Conference, Austin, Texas.

Oldfather, P. (1993). What students say about motivating experiences in a whole language classroom. *The Reading Teacher, 46* (8), 672-681.

Rosenblatt, L. (1938). *Literature as exploration.* New York: Noble and Noble.

Rosenblatt, L. (1978). *The reader, the text, the poem.* Carbondale, IL: Southern Illinois University.

Ruddell,R., & Speaker, R. (1985). The interactive reading process. In H. Singer and R. Ruddell (Eds.), *Theoretical models and processes of reading* (3rd ed., pp. 751-793). Newark, DE: International Reading Association.

Shaw, M., & Wright, J. (1967). *Scales for the measurement of attitude.* New York: McGraw-Hill.

Schumacher, S., & McMillan, J. (1993). *Research in education: A conceptual introduction (3rd ed.).* New York: Harper Collins.

Smith, F. (1986). *Insult to intelligence.* New York: Arbor House.

# EMERGING
# ISSUES

# ANALYZING QUALITATIVE DATA USING THE TRIFOLD

**Donna E. Alvermann**

University of Georgia

**Stephen F. Phelps**

Buffalo State College

**Rick Umpleby**

Brunson County High School

## Abstract

*The purpose of this paper is to present a step-by-step description of how to use the trifold, an analytic tool for systematically recording and interpreting qualitative data. A brief history is provided to give a context for this tool. The trifold is described using data from an actual study, and information is provided on how to adapt the trifold for other means of data representation.*

One of the most time consuming but important tasks of qualitative data analysis involves making sense of the data as they are collected rather than waiting until the end of a study to write up the findings. The notion of *writing* as a method for shaping how we represent our data, rather than concentrating solely on the *write-up* (Alvermann, O'Brien, & Dillon, 1996) at the end is in keeping with Harry Wolcott's (1990) advice to write early and often. It is this notion which gave impetus to the trifold's development.

The phrase "shaping how we represent our data" is reflective of the research approach that informed the development of the trifold. It was a constructivist approach following Guba and Lincoln's (1989) constructivist paradigm. Basically, this approach to qualitative inquiry assumes that because "observer[s] cannot (should not) be neatly disentangled from the observed, . . . findings or outcomes of an inquiry are themselves a literal creation or construction of the inquiry process" (Schwandt, 1994, p. 128). Hence, the trifold, which allows observers to construct meaning from the data as they are collected, is a useful analytic tool in the sense that it helps them keep track of events as they unfold, rather than waiting until the end of data collection—something Wolcott (1990) warns against.

The trifold is particularly useful in classroom observation studies where university-based researchers and teacher researchers co-construct meanings surrounding the classroom teacher's practice. The act of co-constructing, or shaping and representing the data, is a necessary component of the constructivist paradigm. It is, as Schwandt (1994) has observed, the "'dialectic' of iteration, analysis, critique, reiteration, reanalysis, and so on that leads eventually to a joint (among inquirer and respondents) construction of a case (i.e., findings or outcomes)" (p. 129).

## Background

The trifold was originally developed by Donna (Alvermann, Umpleby, & Olson, in press) to solve a problem that surfaced as a result of Rick Umpleby's move to a site 150 miles distant from the university where Donna taught. Donna and Rick, a ninth-grade English teacher, had received a grant from the National Council of Teachers of English to conduct a collaborative school/university-based study during the year the move occurred. The purpose of the study was to explore what five ninth-grade students (who were labeled at risk of dropping out of school) and their teacher, Rick, would do to bring meaning and life to the literacy activities that were part of the school's basic-track English/language arts curriculum.

Although Donna made weekly (and sometimes daily) observations in Rick's classroom, the geographical distance separating the two of them made it impossible to meet between observations to construct meaning from the data. What was needed was a way to analyze the data independently that would be in a format that could be shared in person after the next weekly observation. This was essential because the on-going data analysis informed subsequent data gathering procedures, interview questions, and instructional activities.

As is so often the case, necessity proved to be the mother of invention. The trifold is a procedure for continuously analyzing field notes, transcriptions of interviews and videotaped lessons (as well as any number of other data sources) when two or more individuals are involved in a research project and separated by time and space. In fact, it was a slightly modified trifold from the one described here that allowed members of a multicase study (Alvermann, et al., 1996) to analyze qualitative data across five sites spread over three states nation wide. In that study, whose purpose was to discover adolescent readers' perceptions of their classroom experiences in discussing regularly assigned content area texts, Steve Phelps joined Donna and three other university/school-based researchers in using trifolds to check the trustworthiness of the assertions generated across sites.

A step-by-step procedure is outlined next to provide an example of the trifold that was used in the two studies described above. Four figures accompany the outlined procedure in an attempt to illustrate how the trifold worked with actual data. Figures 1 and 2 are the front and back of an actual trifold; Figures 1A and 2A are typed copies of the same trifold. The data came from the first study (Alvermann, Umpleby, & Olson, in press) rather than the second (Alvermann, et al., 1996) because only one site was involved in the former study. Providing examples from all five sites in the second study would have lengthened this article beyond the recommended length for CRA Yearbook submissions.

## Step 1

One begins by simply folding a piece of paper, 8 1/2" x 11" in size, accordion-style so that there are three equal parts (hence, the name *trifold*). As an analytical tool, the front side of the paper (see Figure 1/1A) contains one panel for the person initiating the trifold to describe an event from an observed lesson. Events will vary from one observation to the next and also from one type of data source to the next. For purposes of this article, we are focusing on an event that occurred as part of a discussion in Rick's ninth-

**Figure 1. Front Side of Trifold Used in First Study.**

| Description of an observed literacy event.<br><br>_Jim_<br>Initiator's name    Date<br><br>*[handwritten:]* Students were asked to think/respond to literature with what they thought was about to happen. Sometimes there is no right or wrong answer and we need to base our responses on our interpretations of what we read. | _Donna_ Name<br>Co-researcher's interpretation<br><br>*[handwritten:]* I agree, going Rick is trying to get students to respond in alternative ways -- no right/wrong answers. His success seems contingent upon students' ability to think divergently. That should not be a problem, but what may become a problem is motivating students to care enough about their own views to commit them to writing. I sense a real "oral culture" at work in Rick's classroom. These students are willing to express themselves -- though briefly -- and they don't seem concerned with backing up their statements -- Rick has to pull to get them to give reasons why. The spacing of the lesson may work against reflective thinking. It's a bit too fast and too oral." | _Rick_ Name<br>Co-researcher's interpretation<br><br>*[handwritten:]* The kids are more willing to commit to oral answers than they are to written responses. It takes a feeling of comfort & acceptance before they can begin to write willingly. The pace which is necessary to keep their attention often prohibits real written or oral reflection & meaning. It's almost a catch-22. If you provide a slower pace & more time for responses, you often lose the attention necessary to get the response. |

## Figure 1A. Typed Copy of Trifold in Figure 1

| Description of an episode in an observed literacy event. | [Donna]___Name Co-researcher's interpretation | [Rick]___Name Co-researcher's interpretation |
|---|---|---|
| [Jim]_____ _____<br>Initiator's        Date<br>name<br><br>Students were asked to think/respond to literature with what they thought was about to happen. Sometimes there is no right or wrong answer and we need to base our responses on our interpretations of what we read. | I agree, Jim, Rick is trying . . . get students to respond in alternative ways—no right/wrong answers. His success seems contingent upon students' ability to think divergently. That should not be a problem, but what may become a problem is motivating students to care enough about their own views to commit them to writing. I sense a a real "oral culture" at work in Rick's classroom. These students are willing to express themselves—though briefly—and they don't seem concerned with backing up their statements—Rick has to pull to get them to give reasons why. The pacing of the lesson may work against reflective thinking. It's a bit too fast and too oral? | The kids are more willing to commit to oral answers than they are to written responses.<br>It takes a feeling of comfort & acceptance before they can begin to write willingly.<br>The pace which is necessary to keep their attention often prohibits real written or oral reflection & musing. It's almost a Catch-22. If you provide a slower pace and more time for responses, you often lose the attention necessary to get the responses. |

grade classroom where reader response was the preferred mode of inquiry into the state-adopted literature anthology. The data source was Jim Olson's field notes; Jim was a graduate research assistant on the project. In describing the event, Jim wrote:

> Students were asked to think/respond to literature with what they thought was about to happen. Rick had told them that sometimes there is no right or wrong answer and we need to base our responses on our interpretations of what we read.

## Step 2

In our example, Jim passed his description of the event (see Figure 1/1A, the first panel), which he selected because of its relevance to one of the study's guiding questions, to Donna, who in turn recorded her interpretation of the event (see Figure 1/1A, the second panel). This interpretation was gleaned from her field notes on the same lesson, which she, like Jim, had observed in Rick's classroom. Donna's interpretation was also informed by the videotapes of earlier lessons and by data gathered in previous interviews with the students in Rick's class. After writing her interpretation in the second panel of the trifold, Donna mailed the trifold to Rick.

## Step 3

Rick, like Donna, recorded his interpretation of the event that Jim had selected as a focus. Rick did this independently of what Donna had written. In fact, we had agreed earlier as a research team that each of us would strive to react independently as we wrote our interpretations on the front side of the trifold. This was done to ensure that the event under consideration would receive as diverse an interpretation as possible. The data sources used in Rick's interpretation of the event included his own reflections on the lesson and his knowledge of the students and how they changed from day to day. Rick also had access to Jim's and Donna's field notes (typed versions of these field notes were mailed immediately after a classroom observation had taken place). In addition, Rick could refer to any written reflections he had made on the lesson, to the typed transcripts of earlier videotaped lessons, and to student interviews. However, due to time constraints, Rick typically relied only on his own notes and his sense of how the class was going to write his interpretation of an event.

## Step 4

After Rick had recorded his interpretation of the event, he held onto the trifold until the next classroom observation, which in this case was a week later. At that time, he returned the trifold to the person who had originated

**Figure 2. Back Side of Trifold Used in First Study.**

| Initiator's interpretation | Reconciled interpretation of three observers | Emerging key linkages |
|---|---|---|

it (in this instance, Jim). It was Jim's responsibility, then, to complete the back side of the trifold (see Figure 2/2A). In the example, the first panel of Figure 2/2A contains Jim's interpretation of the event he had selected as the focus. It is important to note that this is the first opportunity that Jim, as the initiator of this particular trifold, had to record his interpretation of the event. The recording of the event on the front side of the trifold was simply a description; interpretation of it by Jim occurred only after the other two members of the team had written their interpretations. This withholding of the initiator's interpretation was done deliberately as a way of not unduly influencing what the other two members of the research team might write.

## Step 5

In the second panel of the trifold's back side (see Figure 2/2A), Jim, as the initiator, attempted to reconcile the interpretations written by himself, Donna, and Rick. The purpose of this reconciliation of views was not to reach consensus among the different observers, but rather to render an overall interpretation of what it meant in relation to the study's purpose and to the questions that guided the research. In the example, Jim wrote:

> How does a teacher deal with classroom management techniques when attempting "alternative strategies" with these students, with any students?

**Figure 2A. Typed Copy of Trifold in Figure 2.**

| Initiator's interpretation | Reconciled interpretation of three observers | Emerging key linkages |
|---|---|---|
| Pacing a lesson is very "context-bound" in that it varies from class to class and lesson to lesson. The concern for classroom management techniques is prevalent with many teachers I meet. What works best for the individual teacher is the best suggestion I have. Faster pace works better with these students, eliminating those long, uncomfortable periods of silence. | How does a teacher deal with classroom management techitniques when attempting "alternative strategies" with these students, with any students? | Alternative strategies; pacing |

This reconciled interpretation was pertinent to the study's purpose, which was to discover what five focal students in the bottom quartile of their ninth-grade English class might do over the course of a year to bring meaning and life to the literacy activities that formed the core of the basic-track English/language arts curriculum. Note that the reconciled interpretation drew from Donna's concern for pacing while teaching in alternative ways, Rick's concern for pacing, and Jim's similar concern, especially as it related to classroom management. The reconciled interpretation also drew from Jim's sensitivity to one of the study's guiding questions, namely, "What did Mr. Umpleby and his students do to build a community of readers and writers?"

## Step 6

In the last panel of the trifold's backside (see Figure 2/2A), Jim, as the initiator of this particular trifold, wrote "alternative strategies" and "pacing" as reminders that the event which he had identified and the various interpretations of it were leading him to think about those two concepts (alternative strategies and pacing) as linkages to the larger data pool (see Erickson, 1986 for a full description of *key linkages* as a theoretical construct). The key linkage from this trifold would later be compared with the key linkages derived from trifolds that Donna and Rick initiated on the same lesson by choosing their own events for the rest of the team's consideration. As in the trifold Jim initiated, the events selected by Donna and Rick were ones that seemed relevant to them, based on the study's purpose and guiding questions. Still later, these three trifolds' key linkages would be compared and contrasted with the key linkages recorded on other trifolds initiated and completed by the three-member research team. In this way, we were able to follow Wolcott's (1990) advice to write often about what we were observing. By comparing and contrasting key linkages that we had identified and that were grounded in our data sources, we were able to find common patterns in the data. These common patterns eventually led to the assertions that we made in the larger study (Alvermann, Umpleby, & Olson, in press).

## Conclusion

Although the trifold is certainly no substitute for face-to-face data analysis sessions, it does provide a useful and systematic means for assuring continuous dialogue among multiple members of a research team who are not in close proximity. Two-member teams would need to adapt the trifold so that it consisted of fewer panels, or alternatively, contained different headings for the same number of panels. Research teams composed of more than three members might want to follow the procedure Steve and Donna followed in their multicase/multisite study. To accommodate the larger number of researchers in the Alvermann et al. (1996) study, Donna initiated the first trifold based on her readings of the various data sources from each of the five sites. Then, researchers at each of those sites responded in a manner similar to the procedure outlined above. To accommodate the larger number of researchers, some of the panels were labeled differently. Also, because of the logistics involved in sharing among the five sites, fewer trifolds were initiated. And, to be sure, time was a factor. As we learned from the first study (Alvermann, Umpleby, & Olson, in press), it was difficult enough to pass a trifold from the initiator to the next person, who in turn mailed it to the school-based researcher 150 miles away—all within a week's time.

The trifold also would seem to have implications for researchers involved in computer-assisted qualitative data analysis. For example, Roponen (1995) has urged researchers using computer packages for analyzing qualitative data to adopt various features from anthropological and ethnographic writing. It is our belief that the trifold would qualify as one type of ethnographic writing tool researchers could use in preparing their data for entry into one of those packages. The conciseness of information called for by limiting interpretations to single panels of an ordinary 8 1/2" x 11" piece of paper would be one way of assuring that qualitative data retained some of their contextual richness while still being workable in terms of data entry into computer packages.

---

# References

Alvermann, D. E., O'Brien, D. G., & Dillon, D. R. (1996). Conversations: On writing qualitative research. *Reading Research Quarterly, 31,* 114-120.

Alvermann, D. E., Young, J. P., Weaver, D., Hinchman, K. A., Moore, D. W., Phelps, S. F., Thrash, E., & Zalewski, P. (1996). Middle- and high-school students' perceptions of how they experience text-based discussions: A multicase study. *Reading Research Quarterly, 31,* 244-267.

Alvermann, D. E., Umpleby, R., & Olson, J. R. (in press). Getting involved and having fun: Dilemmas in building a literate community in one lower-track English class. *Qualitative Studies in Education.*

Erickson, F. (1986). Qualitative methods in research on teaching. In M. C. Wittrock (Ed.), *Handbook of research on teaching* (3rd ed., pp. 119-161). New York: Macmillan.

Guba, E. G., & Lincoln, Y. S. (1989). *Fourth generation evaluation.* Newbury Park, CA: Sage.

Roponen, S. (1995, September). *Writing in computer-assisted qualitative data analysis.* Paper presented at the Conference on Text Analysis and Computers, Mannheim, Germany.

Schwandt, T. A. (1994). Constructivist, interpretivist approaches to human inquiry. In N. K. Denzin & Y. S. Lincoln (Eds.), *Handbook of qualitative research* (pp. 118-137). Thousand Oaks, CA: Sage.

Wolcott, H. F. (1990). *Writing up qualitative research.* Newbury Park, CA: Sage.

# Is Fluency Yet a Goal
# of the Reading Curriculum?

**Timothy V. Rasinski**

Kent State University

**Jerome B. Zutell**

The Ohio State University

## Abstract

*Over the past decade reading fluency has been increasingly recognized as an important and appropriate goal of the elementary reading curriculum. Recent studies, however, have suggested that many students have not achieved appropriate levels of fluency in their reading. This study examined four primary readers of two commercial basal reading programs for the extent to which they promote fluency in students' reading. The study examined fluency instruction indicators such as repeated readings of text, assisted or supported reading, and direct instructional cues to fluency in the teachers' manual. In general, fluency does not appear to be an integral or emphasized part of the reading programs examined. Students' lack of proficiency in fluency, then, may be due to lack of instructional emphasis in popular commercially produced reading programs. The authors suggest that makers of comprehensive reading programs reexamine their products for the extent to which fluency is taught and, where appropriate, to include a greater emphasis on fluency for students.*

---

Reading fluency refers to the ability to read effortlessly, expressively, and meaningfully with attention to appropriate and meaningful phrasing. Stanovich (1986) adds that an important aspect of fluency is for readers to achieve a level of automaticity in the recognition of written words. Over the past decade the role of fluency has been increasingly recognized as an important goal for the elementary reading curriculum (Allington, 1983; Anderson, 1981). Nevertheless, while Allington (1983) recognized the importance of fluency as a goal for the reading curriculum, little was being done instructionally at that time to nurture fluent reading among students.

During the primary grades two critical reading competencies that students must develop for continued growth in reading are word recognition and reading fluency (Chall, 1979, 1983; Chall, Jacobs, & Baldwin, 1990; Freebody & Byrne, 1988; Perfetti, 1985; Stanovich, 1986). In a study of over 600 elementary students experiencing difficulty in reading, Rasinski and Padak (1993) found that fluency was the major reading problem confronting these students. Similarly, results from the 1994 National Assessment of Education Progress (NAEP) found that only 13% of the fourth graders tested achieved the highest level of fluency, while 49% read at a level considered nonfluent (U.S. Department of Education, 1995). Clearly, theoretical models of reading as well as actual data obtained from children's reading suggest that reading fluency is important for proficient reading and that a significant number of students experience difficulty in achieving fluency by grade four.

Despite the importance of reading fluency in the primary grades, existing evidence suggests that it is not an actively pursued goal. Allington (1983) and Anderson (1981) have argued that fluency is a neglected goal of the reading curriculum. Zutell and Rasinski (1991; Rasinski, 1989) have suggested that fluency is not an important part of most college methods textbooks in reading instruction, nor is it a major strand in most basal reading programs. Moreover, recent evidence from studies of elementary students' reading (NAEP, 1995) suggests that nearly half of all students are not fluent in their reading.

The purpose of the present study, then, was to determine the extent to which reading fluency was an actively pursued (taught) goal of reading in the primary grade readers of two popular basal reading programs. The question asked was, "Do children who are provided instruction via a basal reading program, the dominant form of reading instruction in the United States, receive instruction in fluency and instructional activities to promote fluency as part of their reading curriculum?" The question is significant, because if reading fluency is an important goal of the reading curriculum, comprehensive reading programs in the primary grades should demonstrate clear evidence of promoting reading fluency among students.

## Procedures

Two popular basal reading programs—Houghton Mifflin or HM, (Pikulski, et al., 1993a, 1993b) and Silver Burdett and Ginn or SBG, (Pearson, Johnson, et al., 1989a, 1989b)—were surveyed. These particular series were chosen because of their accessibility and their popularity among schools. Both publishers are dominant makers of basal reading programs; the programs themselves are among the most widely used in the United States. The basals produced by these two publishers are consistently among the top five in sales in the United States. Moreover, basals of differing publication dates were examined to determine if changes in the programs could be detected over time. From these two programs a reader from the first grade (identified as

HM 1 *[Too Big]* and SBG 1.2 *[A New Day]*) and the first reader of the second grade (identified as HM 2.1 *[Silly Things]* and SBG 2.1 *[Garden Gates]*) were surveyed. The rationale behind this choice was that it is during this time period, after children have developed some control over decoding words, that students would be expected to consolidate their decoding knowledge and develop a degree of fluency over the texts they read (Chall, 1983).

In an earlier paper, Rasinski (1989) identified what he considered important principles and instructional activities for nurturing reading fluency among students. Among these principles were repeated readings of connected text, modeling fluent reading for students, discussing fluency with students, and providing support for students while reading connected text. This support could be in the form of choral reading, a tutor reading along with the student, the student reading to a proficient reader who offers support and encouragement, or the student listening to a tape recording of a fluent reading while reading the same text. Because reading fluency involves the actual practicing of connected texts, fluency instruction should also include opportunities for students to perform their practiced reading for others.

This study examined every text that students were expected to read or teachers were given the option of assigning for reading for evidence of the forms of fluency instruction identified by Rasinski (1989). The texts were either part of the student reader or were printed in the teacher's edition for sharing with students on the chalk board, overhead projector, chart paper, or other form of presentation. We examined the texts themselves as well as prescribed and optional activities for teachers to assign to students with the texts. Evidence of fluency-related activities were noted and tallied. Descriptive statistics for the extent to which fluency instruction appeared in the basals were then calculated and are reported in the Results section. Fluency-related instructional activities were counted only if they were explicitly prescribed or suggested in the teachers manual.

Although it is clear that teachers can impose their own activities and instruction, including fluency activities, using the basal only as a text and not as an instructional guide, given the extraordinary number of activities suggested in the basals themselves, most teachers probably confine their instruction to activities described in the teacher's manual. Indeed, some scholars have argued that, in reality, reading textbooks dictate the instruction that teachers actually provide their students (Goodman, Shannon, Freeman, & Murphy, 1988; Shannon, 1987, 1989). Moreover, it should be remembered that a central question to our study focused on the extent to which publishers of materials note the importance and recommend instruction in fluency within their own programs.

# Results

Overall, the Houghton Mifflin program had considerably more texts than the Silver Burdett Ginn series at both the first and second grade levels (see Table 1). The Houghton Mifflin program included many optional texts that appeared only in the teacher's manual and were meant to be duplicated by the teacher or presented by the teacher in an enlarged format.

**Table 1. Mean Rereadings by Basal Text.**

|          | Number of Texts | Mean Rereadings of Texts |
|----------|-----------------|--------------------------|
| HM 1     | 104             | 2.49                     |
| HM 2.1   | 77              | 1.75                     |
| SBG 1.2  | 27              | 2.15                     |
| SBG 2.1  | 34              | 2.56                     |

Based on maximum number of rereadings suggested by the teacher's edition.

*Note: HM 1=Houghton Mifflin, Grade 1*
*HM 2.1=Houghton Mifflin, First Reader, Grade 2*
*SGB 1.2=Silver Burdett and Ginn, Second Reader, Grade 1*
*SGB 2.1=Silver Burdett and Ginn, First Reader, Grade 2*

The first type of instructional activity for promoting fluency that was searched for was repeated readings. Several research studies have documented that having students reread brief sections of connected written discourse leads to significant improvement in students' word recognition and overall reading fluency (Dowhower, 1987; Herman, 1985; Samuels, 1979). Any prescribed or suggested rereadings of text that appeared either in the teacher's manual or the students' text were counted (see Tables 1 and 2).

The highest mean level of rereading for any of the texts analyzed was 2.56 for the SBG 2.1 book. This number of rereadings is considerably lower than the 3-5 rereadings of texts suggested by Dowhower (1989). In the Houghton Mifflin program over 70% of the texts at the first-grade level and over 90% at the 2.1 level are read two times or less. For the older Silver Burdett Ginn program 57.2% of the texts at the 1.2 level and 55.9% of the texts at the 2.1 level are read two times or less. This means that for the Houghton Mifflin program less than 30% of the texts at first grade and less than 10% of the texts at the beginning of second grade are prescribed or suggested to be read three times or more to develop fluency. For the Silver Burdett Ginn program, less than half the texts at both levels are read for fluency through practice. It is interesting to note that in the HM first grade book 8 passages are suggested or required to be read over 5 times, with one text suggested to be read 11 times

**Table 2. Repeated Readings per Text.**

| | Number of Readings Per Text | | | | | | | | | | |
|---|---|---|---|---|---|---|---|---|---|---|---|
| | 1 | 2 | 3 | 4 | 5 | 6 | 7 | 8 | 9 | 10 | 11 |
| HM 1 | 30 | 45 | 13 | 5 | 3 | 3 | 1 | 0 | 1 | 2 | 1 |
| % | 28.8 | 43.3 | 12.5 | 4.8 | 2.9 | 2.9 | 1.0 | 0 | 1.0 | 1.9 | 1.0 |
| HM 2.1 | 33 | 38 | 3 | 1 | 0 | 1 | 1 | 0 | 0 | 0 | 0 |
| % | 42.9 | 49.4 | 3.9 | 1.3 | 0 | 1.3 | 1.3 | 0 | 0 | 0 | 0 |
| SBG 1.2 | 9 | 8 | 8 | 1 | 1 | 0 | 0 | 0 | 0 | 0 | 0 |
| % | 33.0 | 24.2 | 24.2 | 3.7 | 3.7 | 0 | 0 | 0 | 0 | 0 | 0 |
| SBG 2.1 | 10 | 9 | 7 | 4 | 2 | 2 | 0 | 0 | 0 | 0 | 0 |
| % | 29.4 | 26.5 | 20.6 | 11.8 | 5.9 | 5.9 | 0 | 0 | 0 | 0 | 0 |

*Note: HM 1=Houghton Mifflin, Grade 1*
*HM 2.1=Houghton Mifflin, First Reader, Grade 2*
*SGB 1.2=Silver Burdett and Ginn, Second Reader, Grade 1*
*SGB 2.1=Silver Burdett and Ginn, First Reader, Grade 2*

by students. This seems to be an excessive number of readings and may lead to student disinterest in reading.

Next, the nature of the readings students were asked to do in each of the books was examined. As noted earlier, Rasinski (1989) identified several types of reading that promote reading fluency, from modeling reading by a fluent reader to providing some sort of support while the student is reading. Perhaps the type of reading that least promotes fluency development is students reading by themselves. Results of the analyses of the types of reading recommended by the two programs are summarized in Table 3. Interestingly, the two programs seem rather consistent at the two levels surveyed. The Houghton Mifflin program is marked by considerable choral reading, particularly at the first grade level (44.8% of all readings at level 1; 15.4% at 2.1). Student performance reading of text is also a strong part of the Houghton Mifflin program. However, a significant portion of the performance reading was suggested without prior practice by students. The Silver Burdett Ginn program, on the other hand, seems to be characterized more by students reading on their own without support (50.0% of all readings for the 1.2 book and 53.1% for the 2.1 book). Indeed, student independent reading is also a major feature of the Houghton Mifflin program.

It is interesting to note that several types of fluency building reading activities such as students listening to a recorded version of a text while reading, students reading to an adult (teacher aide or parent volunteer) in school, or students reading text to family members at home are largely absent from

**Table 3. Types of Readings Per Basal Text.**

| | Teach. reads to students (read aloud) | Students (& tchr.) Choral group read | Students listen to tape while reading | Students read to adult at school | Students read to another child at school | Students read to parent or family at home | Students perform for a group | Students read by self (alone) |
|---|---|---|---|---|---|---|---|---|
| | Modeling | Support | Perform Support | Perform Support | Perform Support | Perform Support | Perform | Unsuprtd. |
| · HM 1 | 25 | 116 | 4 | 0 | 11 | 0 | 39 | 64 |
| % | 9.7 | 44.8 | 1.5 | 0 | 4.2 | 0 | 15.1 | 24.7 |
| HM 2.1 | 8 | 22 | 0 | 0 | 17 | 0 | 47 | 49 |
| % | 5.6 | 15.4 | 0 | 0 | 11.9 | 0 | 32.9 | 34.3 |
| SGB 1.2 | 7 | 7 | 0 | 1 | 9 | 5 | 0 | 29 |
| % | 12.1 | 12.1 | 0 | 1.7 | 15.5 | 8.6 | 0 | 50.0 |
| SBG 2.1 | 22 | 8 | 0 | 0 | 3 | 2 | 10 | 51 |
| % | 22.9 | 8.3 | 0 | 0 | 3.1 | 2.1 | 10.4 | 53.1 |

any of the readers examined. Students performing for a group was largely missing from the 1.2 book of the Silver Burdett Ginn program.

Another aspect of fluency instruction involves teachers directing children's attention to various aspects of fluent reading. Instances of such direct cues were searched for in the programs examined. The results are summarized in Table 4. Very few direct cues to fluency in the teacher's manual of any of the four reading books were found. The second grade reader of the Silver Burdett Ginn series contained the most fluency references (n = 31). Nevertheless, if one considers that such a text is intended to be read for approximately 4 months of the school year, children in the 2.1 Silver Burdett Ginn reader are given about 2 direct instructional references to fluency per week by the teacher. Fewer references are apparent for the other readers.

**Table 4. Direct Instructional References/Cues to Fluency Characteristic**

| Text | Repeated reading of phrases/ sentences | Emphasis on voice expression (loud/soft pitch) | Emphasize/ adjust rate | Phrasing, attention to juncture/ stops | Rhythm pattern | Totals per text |
|---|---|---|---|---|---|---|
| HM 1 | 3 | 5 | 0 | 0 | 6 | 14 |
| HM 2.1 | 0 | 5 | 1 | 0 | 2 | 8 |
| SGB 1.2 | 2 | 6 | 0 | 0 | 0 | 8 |
| SGB 2.1 | 14 | 14 | 0 | 3 | 0 | 31 |

## Discussion

In this study two popular and relatively current commercial reading programs were examined for the extent to which the programs promoted fluency. For each program two readers (one at the end of grade one and one at the beginning of grade two) that represented levels at which reading theory suggests fluency development should be a major instructional concern were chosen. Several limitations constrain the ability to make definitive conclusions on the extent to which fluency is promoted in commercial reading programs. Since the sampled programs represent a fraction of the commercially available programs, and the two levels within each program analyzed represent a small part of the entire reading series, caution needs to exercised in interpreting the results beyond the materials actually examined. Future studies of larger samples of readers may help to confirm these initial findings. The extent to which teachers actually followed the prescribed and suggested instruction that was part of the programs was not examined. Teachers may actually be employing their own instructional techniques without reference to the suggestions in the teacher's manual.

The results reported in this study, however, do give some preliminary indication of the extent to which fluency has become an integral part of commercial reading programs. Reading levels at which reading fluency would most likely be promoted were chosen. All readings and reading activities, whether prescribed, suggested, or made optional in the teacher's manual were counted. Thus, these results suggest the "best case" or most comprehensive opportunities for fluency instruction.

In general, the analyses suggest that fluency continues to remain, at best, a marginal goal of the reading programs examined. Despite the fact that the end of grade one and the beginning of grade two are the times at which fluency should be a considered instructional goal, there were few direct instructional references to aspects of reading fluency in any of the teacher's manuals. In essence, teachers were not encouraged to talk with students about the nature of what makes reading fluent. If teachers decide to bring fluency instruction into the classroom, they have to rely largely on their own expertise and initiative.

Practiced or repeated readings of text in the programs examined, even if students read the maximum number of times suggested by the reading program itself, was not strong. In the four books examined, less than half the texts were wholly or partially read more than twice. The average number of readings per text was less than two for the HM 2.1 book and under three for the remaining books examined.

Also, the type of reading that was most common across all four books was students reading on their own. Relatively few opportunities were available for students to read with the ongoing support of another reader. This is particularly true for students reading to adults, fluent readers in school, or to a parent or family member at home. This finding seems to suggest that commercial reading programs continue to disregard the possibilities for strong support for children's reading development from the home. This is especially remarkable given the ongoing research (Henderson, 1987, 1988) that documents the positive influence parents can have when included in children's education.

While it is encouraging that several of the texts in both programs suggested that teachers read to students, it is distressing that teachers are not more strongly encouraged to capitalize on such an excellent fluency modeling technique. Programs should focus on calling students' attention to the fluent nature of their teachers' reading and encouraging students to emulate their teachers in their own reading.

Finally, the two programs themselves do not seem consistent in the manner and sequence of providing what little specific fluency instruction they do offer, except for not emphasizing it. The Houghton Mifflin program seems to emphasize fluency instruction more at the first grade level than at the 2.1 level. The Silver Burdett Ginn program appears to give greater emphasis to fluency at the 2.1 level. Fluency should be emphasized at both levels with roughly equal intensity. Given that summer vacation normally intervenes between students receiving instruction at the two levels, continuity would demand a strong emphasis on fluency at both levels. Sadly, this does not seem to be the case.

Commercial reading programs have a long way to go to truly make fluency an important part of the reading curriculum, particularly at the instructional levels at which fluency should be actively pursued in instruction. Although other instructional reading programs were not examined, given the fact that the programs often emulate one another in their general instructional focus, it seems reasonable to assume that other programs tend also to minimize their instructional focus on reading fluency. The lack of emphasis on reading fluency in these programs seems highly consistent with the earlier mentioned findings that a large number of elementary students have not achieved fluency and that a major difficulty encountered by students experiencing difficulty in reading lies in fluency.

Commercially developed reading programs will continue to be a mainstay in American reading instruction. With this in mind, it is recommended that publishers of comprehensive reading programs for students in elementary grades work to include fluency as a major goal of their respective programs and that the publishers work to integrate proven fluency instructional techniques within their programs, particularly at grades one and two and in special programs designed for students experiencing difficulty in reading.

It would be relatively easy to include fluency as an integral part of commercial programs. Some specific recommendations are the inclusion and practice reading of brief patterned, rhymed, and rhythmic texts such as verse poetry. Poems for any theme can easily be found or written. Short poems and other texts are meant for performance. The brevity and performance nature of such texts make them naturals for repeated readings. Rasinski, Padak, Linek, and Sturtevant (1994) found that integrating the repeated readings of poems and other short predictable and engaging texts into a second grade reading program led to remarkable gains in reading fluency and overall reading performance by at risk students.

It is also suggested that modeled readings by the teacher or other fluent reader be encouraged. Moreover, such readings occasionally should be accompanied by discussions on the nature of fluent reading—"just what made the teacher's reading fluent and easy to understand?" It would be rather easy to include an occasional minilesson on fluency from time to time in the instructional programs.

Actual reading activities that support the reader while reading, such as paired reading (Topping, 1987) with a parent, other adult, older student, or fluent peer as the tutor; choral reading; student reading to a supportive listener; or tape recorded reading (Carbo, 1978; Chomsky, 1976 ) can easily be incorporated into commercially developed reading materials. These activities have been shown to nurture fluency in student readers. Moreover, the inclusion of parents as an audience for students' repeated readings or as a support for students' own reading, as in paired reading, offers home-based opportunities for increasing students' fluency and overall reading that have been and continue to be ignored in past and current reading programs.

The evidence for the importance of fluency as an appropriate goal for the primary grade reading program is strong. Reading programs that fail to offer students opportunities and instruction to increase their fluency are not optimal programs. This study suggests that the inclusion of fluency instruction in commercial reading programs continues to be a serious concern. We hope that future editions of commercial reading programs will give fluency the serious consideration it deserves.

# References

Allington, R.L. (1983). Fluency: The neglected reading goal. *The Reading Teacher, 36,* 556-561.

Anderson, B. (1981). The missing ingredient: Fluent oral reading. *The Elementary School Journal, 81,* 173-177.

Carbo, M. (1978). Teaching reading with talking books. *The Reading Teacher, 32,* 267-273.

Chall, J. S. (1979). The great debate: Ten years later with a modest proposal for reading stages. In L. Resnick & C. Weaver (eds.), *Theory and practice of early reading.* Hillsdale, NJ: Erlbaum.

Chall, J. S. (1983). *Stages of reading development*. New York: McGraw Hill.

Chall, J. S., Jacobs, V., & Baldwin, L. (1990). *The reading crisis: Why poor children fall behind*. Cambridge, MA: Harvard University Press.

Chomsky, C. (1976). After decoding: What? *Language Arts, 53,* 288-296.

Dowhower, S. L. (1987). Effect of repeated reading on selected second graders' oral reading and comprehension. *Reading Research Quarterly, 22,* 389-406.

Dowhower, S. L. (1989). Repeated reading: Research into practice. *The Reading Teacher, 42,* 502-507.

Freebody, P., & Byrne, B. (1988). Word-reading strategies in elementary school children: Relations to comprehension, reading time, and phonemic awareness. *Reading Research Quarterly, 23,* 441-453.

Goodman, K. S., Shannon, P., Freeman, Y. S., & Murphy, S. (1988). *Report card on basal readers*. Katonah, NY: Richard C. Owen.

Henderson, A. (1987). The evidence continues to grow: Parent involvement improves student achievement. Columbia, MD: National Committee for Citizens in Education.

Henderson, A. T. (1988). Parents are a school's best friend. *Phi Delta Kappan, 70,* 148-153.

Herman, P. A. (1985). The effect of repeated readings on reading rate, speech pauses, and word recognition accuracy. *Reading Research Quarterly, 20,* 553-564.

Pearson, P.D., Johnson, D.D., et al. (1989a) *Garden gates*. Needham, MA: Silver Burdett and Ginn.

Pearson, P D., Johnson, D.D., et al. (1989b). *A new day*. Needham, MA: Silver Burdett and Ginn.

Perfetti, C. A. (1985). *Reading ability*. New York: Oxford University Press.

Pikulski, J. J., et al. (1993a). *Silly things happen*. Boston: Houghton Mifflin.

Pikulski, J. J., et al. (1993b). *Too big*. Boston: Houghton Mifflin.

Rasinski, T. V. (1989). Fluency for everyone: Incorporating fluency instruction in the classroom. *The Reading Teacher, 42,* 690-693.

Rasinski, T. V., & Padak, N. (1993, December). *Chapter I students' reading across multiple performance variables: Profiles of at-risk elementary readers*. Paper presented at the annual meeting of the National Reading Conference, Charleston, SC.

Rasinski, T. V., Padak, N., Linek, W. M., & Sturtevant, E.G. (1994). Effects of fluency development on urban second-grade readers. *Journal of Educational Research, 87,* 158-165.

Samuels, S. J. (1979). The method of repeated reading. *The Reading Teacher, 32,* 403-408.

Shannon, P. (1987). Commercial reading materials, a technological ideology, and the deskilling of teachers. *The Elementary School Journal, 87,* 307-329.

Shannon, P. (1989). *Broken promises: Reading instruction in twentieth-century America*. Granby, MA: Bergin & Garvey.

Stanovich, K. E. (1986). Matthew effects in reading: Some consequences of individual differences in the acquisition of literacy. *Reading Research Quarterly, 21,* 360-407.

Topping, K. (1987). Paired reading: A powerful technique for parent use. *The Reading Teacher, 40,* 608-614.

U. S. Department of Education. (1995). *NAEP Facts*. Washington, DC: U. S. Department of Education, Office of Educational Research and Improvement.

Zutell, J., & Rasinski, T.V. (1991). Training teachers to attend to their students' oral reading fluency. *Theory into Practice, 30,* 211-217.

# CHANGING THEMES FOR PREPARING TEACHERS TO USE COMPUTERS AND MULTIMEDIA FOR LITERACY LEARNING

### Ernest Balajthy

State University of New York
at Geneseo

## Abstract

*Developments in computer and multimedia technologies in the past five years have brought about significant changes in the materials available to teachers of literacy who use computers. Five major changes are described: Increased use of application software, availability of electronic storybooks, improvements in voice synthesis, developments in interactive multimedia, and trends toward "edutainment" software. Implications for use of computers in the teaching of reading and language arts are discussed in the context of a graduate teacher education course.*

Recent developments in computer and multimedia technologies have greatly changed the format and content of materials available to the computer-using teacher of literacy. These changes bring about the need to reconsider the education of today's teachers and future teachers and to update the technology-related content of literacy education coursework. The purpose of this article is to consider a variety of topics related to updating technology components of undergraduate and graduate courses in literacy education.

Attention to these topics is needed as computers become more a part of the everyday life of the classroom. Recent data from New York State, one of the leading states in funding educational technology, suggest that 72% of students and 50% of teachers now use computers regularly (New York State Public Schools, 1994). U.S. Department of Commerce (1994) figures indicate that the ratio of students per microcomputer in public schools has improved from 62.7 in 1984-1985 to 12.2 in 1992-1993.

Market statistics also indicate a rapid increase in the sales of educational software for home use. The 1993 total U.S. sales of such software, was 243 million dollars. A leading operating system, Macintosh, showed a one year growth rate in home education software sales between 1992 and 1993 of 83% (U.S. Department of Commerce, 1994).

In the public schools, use of computers for literacy instruction accounts for some 13% of school computer use, just below the top-ranked categories of mathematics instruction (15%) and keyboarding instruction (14%) (U.S. Department of Commerce, 1994). Attention to the preparation of literacy teachers for use of computer technology in the classroom gained momentum in the early 1980s with the formation of the International Reading Association's Special Interest Group for Microcomputers in Reading. Ad hoc microcomputer committees were also formed in many local, state and national reading associations. For example, in 1985 a symposium was presented at the College Reading Association Conference that brought together a variety of reading educators who were teaching specialized courses that prepared teachers to use computers to teach reading and writing. However, one problem is that most of the material presently available to deal with the specialized topics of computer technology and literacy dates from this same period (Balajthy, 1985, 1986, 1989; Blanchard, Mason & Daniel, 1987; Ewing, 1984; Geoffrion & Geoffrion, 1983; Reinking, 1987; Strickland, Feeley & Wepner, 1987).

Although there has been no such hiatus in publication of general reading and literacy methods textbooks, an examination of these publications shows mixed results in their handling of computers and technology. Some show evidence of careful consideration of the potential applications of technology, while others manage to ignore the issue almost entirely. For example, except for brief and vague suggestions that computers have potential for language experience writing activities, Tierney, Readence, and Dishner's (1995) encyclopedic methods textbook has little or nothing to say about the implications of technology for the various methods they describe. Vacca, Vacca, and Gove (1995) mention the usefulness of word processing for writing process approaches, but other references to computers portray them as drilling and testing devices. Weaver's exhaustive tome (1994) does not mention either the word "computer" or "technology" in its table of contents or index.

On the other hand, some writers devote considerable attention to applications of technology in their textbooks. Putnam's (1996) edited text includes chapters on use of technology for diagnosis and remediation, as well as instruction of disabled readers. McKenna and Robinson (1993) include a chapter in their content area literacy text on using computers. Willis, Stephens, and Matthew (1996) have just published a text entitled *Technology, Reading, and Language Arts.*

The field of computer technology is notorious for its rapid change, and it might be expected that ideas and materials presented and discussed five to ten years ago might be outdated and in need of reconsideration. However, an additional factor has made detailed reconsideration of this issue even more imperative, namely, the move of Apple Computer Corporation and the public schools from the old Apple II platform to the Macintosh platform, with its related multimedia technologies.

Major changes brought about in the mid-1990s that most dramatically affect the relationship of computer technology and literacy education include the following (Balajthy, 1996):

a) Decline of interest in direct instructional software within the field of literacy education, and simultaneous growth of interest in "application" software more amenable to developmental, holistic educational philosophies with their emphasis on authentic learning experiences

b) Development and popular acceptance of electronic books

c) Increased memory capabilities of computers, allowing use of high-quality digitized voice synthesis in place of the older robotic-sounding phonemic voice synthesis

d) Integrated multimedia packages based on CD-ROM and/or video-disc technologies

e) Vastly increased availability of computers in homes. In one year, 1994 to 1995, the number of American homes with both a personal computer and a modem increased from 11 million to 18 million. Some 14% of Americans presently use computer on-line services (Times Mirror Center, 1995).

The remainder of this paper deals with each of these topics in turn, focusing on the practical implications for teacher preparation programs. Each topic is discussed in the context of recent changes in content and structure of a graduate course in Microcomputers in Reading and Language Arts.

## Major Changes Affecting Technology Applications in Literacy Education

In the early 1980s, Taylor (1980) categorized educational technology uses in three ways: computer as tutee, tutor, and tool. In the computer as tutee, children taught the computer by learning to program it. In the computer as tutor, the computer taught the children through tutorials or drill and practice. In the computer as tool, children used the computer to accomplish tasks with word processing, database, and spreadsheet programs. Interest in computer as tutee has declined in recent years as educators have questioned the wisdom of devoting large blocks of classroom time to teaching programming and the importance of programming ability to most vocations. Teachers have also been skeptical about the transfer of problem-solving skills from programming to other domains such as reading and writing.

### Software

Computer-assisted instructional software, use of the computer as a tutor or for drill and practice, is the most widely available type of software. However, tutor software currently receives little attention from researchers and theorists in literacy education. In part, deemphasis on tutor software in literacy education has come about because of increased recognition of the importance of process education, or the belief that students learn by doing. Tool software, on the other hand, can help teachers committed to holistic education engage students in writing and reading their own stories and in other authentic literacy activities (Miller & Olson, 1994).

Teachers may be more amenable to having their children use tool software in class because they themselves are using such software more and more. Doctorow (1994), for example, found that teachers are increasingly using computers to keep track of student progress. Yet despite its potential power as a learning tool, use of tool software such as word processors, databases and spreadsheets accounts for only 6% of school computer use (U.S. Department of Commerce, 1994).

Use of tool software in classrooms can be encouraged in a variety of ways. For example, in a Microcomputers in Reading and Language Arts course, teachers were introduced to telecommunications with a demonstration of the multimedia networking program *Netscape*. They toured several World Wide Web sites such as the Museum of Paleontology and the White House. A visiting speaker addressed the class on the topic of using telecommunications software and e-mail to encourage classroom writing.

Teachers studied and discussed hypermedia creation software. They worked through a demonstration disk of *HyperStudio* and examined several *HyperStudio* projects created by fifth graders. The group was then led through the creation of a *HyperCard* stack, including scanning of pictures for pasting into the stack. They also used *Children's Writing and Publishing Center* to create classroom newspapers, and *Crossword Magic* to create crossword puzzles. In addition, they learned how to use *ClarisWorks* word processor and database with students in their classroom.

### Electronic Books

A new development pertinent to literacy education is the development of the "electronic book" (also called "interactive text"). Electronic books take many forms, depending on their purpose. One type, designed for literacy experiences of beginning and at-risk readers, simulates reading aloud to children. Screen pages and illustrations are presented on the monitor. Children may access voice synthesized pronunciations and definitions (and even translations into Spanish) by pointing the cursor at unrecognized words and pressing a key. Previous research indicates that the latter capability is especially appreciated by students (Ruberg, 1993), and that use of electronic text can enhance comprehension (Miller, Blackstock & Miller, 1994).

The teachers in the Microcomputers in Reading and Language Arts course teachers were introduced to electronic books in a course segment designed to illustrate major changes in classroom technology over the past 10 years. They first examined an Apple IIe series of electronic storybooks, *Houghton Mifflin's Reading Comprehension*. They then examined early Macintosh CD-ROM books by Discis, *Peter Rabbit* and *Benjamin Bunny*. Finally, they examined the recently published Living Books series by Broderbund, including *Just Grandma and Me*, and *Arthur's Teacher Trouble*, as well as Putnam/NewMedia's *Anthony's Big Magic*.

### Voice Synthesis

Increased memory and processing capabilities for hardware has made possible some voice recognition and the widespread use of digitized voice synthesis, which allows computer production of easily understood human-sounding voices. Older technologies usually depended solely upon print or graphics, with occasional use of robotic-sounding phonemic voice synthesis. For example, the *Optimum Resource Reading Program* provides a series of drills based on letter cluster linguistic phonics elements in words. Students wear headphones with attached microphones into which they can speak answers. A letter cluster appears on the screen, such as "li," and the student is asked to say its sound. The computer then analyzes the voice input to determine whether the answer was correct.

Students in the course used both phonemic and digitized voice synthesis software, such as *Houghton Mifflin Reading Comprehension*, and *KidWorks 2*. These programs employ phonemic synthesis to allow unfamiliar words in a story to be pronounced and to read aloud student-written compositions. *KidWorks 2* also has a component that allows children to read segments of their own compositions aloud into a microphone. The readings are digitized, stored on disk, and can be played back at later times.

### Interactive Multimedia

Another fascinating development is the introduction of interactive multimedia materials, which combine the capabilities of computers with such multimedia devices as CD-ROM and videodiscs. In the *Martin Luther King, Jr.* interactive multimedia package, for example, teachers used a workstation equipped with a videodisc player and monitor connected by cable to a computer. The computer provides a large amount of print information, such as the verbatim speeches of King, summaries of news events from his life, a time line of important events, a glossary, and digitized photographs. The videodisc player provided video segments of King's life and the events surrounding it. Teachers used the computer to control the videodisc player, clicking on icons to access still pictures or videos of television news clips and King's speeches.

They also used CD-ROM-based software in class software presentations, including *Coral Kingdom* and *Microsoft Dinosaurs.* This software includes interactive exercises to promote learning and a wide variety of still photographs, diagrams, short video segments, and a large amount of text, some of which is read aloud to students using digitized voice synthesis.

### *The Home Market for Software*

Computers are available in almost 50% of American homes. Many of these computers sit idle, but increasingly parents whose jobs call for frequent use of computer technology are buying and using computers for home tasks. Their interest in using these computers as educational tools for their children has led to unexpected developments. First, since most businesses use hardware developed by or compatible with IBM formats (such as MS-DOS, Windows or Windows 95), parents tend to buy hardware of that variety. This has led software developers to increase their attention to educational software that fits those formats, a change from the 1980s when almost all software for children was designed for Apple computers. Home education software sales for the Windows format, for example, increased 614% between 1992 and 1993 (U.S. Department of Commerce, 1994).

A second development results from parents' lower concern with learning behaviors than teachers in their software purchases. This has led to the development of "edutainment" software, software that combines high entertainment value with few educational objectives. In many cases, the "edu" part of the software plays a decidedly minor role in comparison to the "tainment." Third, parents want a broader payback for their money than schools demand. A school might be willing to spend $50 for a piece of software that will be used with 30 students each year over a several year period to practice one activity. In order to attract home buyers who only have one or two children to spend that same $50, software publishers realize that they have to provide a variety of high interest activities. This has led to multiple-activity software such as the 5-disk *The Backyard,* which offers 6 major games for young children relating to science, mapping skills, animal habitats, and a host of minor activities.

The relationship of entertainment and education in software is a controversial one and was frequently discussed in the Microcomputers in Reading and Language Arts class. The issue arose most frequently in conjunction with the Broderbund series for preschoolers that includes *The Playroom* and *The Backyard,* as well as the Broderbund "Living Books" series of electronic storybooks. Teachers were consistently impressed with the entertainment value of such software, but extremely dubious about their classroom usefulness. They sympathized with Hirschkron (1995), a reviewer who formulated three cardinal rules for successful edutainment software: "Include animals, make funny noises, and squash as many objects as possible" (p. 83):

I asked if the kids thought [edutainment software] taught them anything. One of my [child] reviewers assured me that it did. 'What?' I asked. He thought for a minute and answered, 'How to have fun.' As if they need help.

Overall the field of literacy education is in need of a renewed examination of the potential of computer-related technology in the classroom. This reexamination should focus on serving the needs of a generation of children for whom computers are an integral part of everyday life. New theoretical orientations within the field, advocating authentic literacy experiences and creating communities of learners, can be combined with recent developments in technology to provide teachers and students with a new level of sophistication in the use of computers in the language arts classroom.

## References

Balajthy, E. (Ed.) (1985). *Preparation of Teachers for Microcomputer Instruction in Reading and Language Arts: Proceedings of a College Reading Association Symposium*, October, 1985. Newark, DE: International Reading Association Special Interest Group on Microcomputers in Reading.

Balajthy, E. (1986). *Microcomputers in reading and language arts*. Englewood Cliffs, NJ: Prentice Hall.

Balajthy, E. (1989). *Computers and reading: Lessons from the past and the technologies of the future*. Englewood Cliffs, NJ: Prentice Hall.

Balajthy, E. (1996). Using computer technology to aid the disabled reader. In L. R. Putnam (Ed.), *How to become a better reading teacher: Strategies for assessment and intervention* (pp. 331-343).Englewood Cliffs, NJ: Merrill.

Blanchard, J. S., Mason, G. E., & Daniel, D. (1987). *Computer applications in reading* (3rd ed.). Newark, DE: International Reading Association.

Doctorow, R. (1994). *The development of standards in reading and writing for kindergarten through grade 8*. Educational Resources and Information Clearinghouse. [ERIC ED 377441]

Ewing, J. (1984). *Reading and the new technologies*. London, England: United Kingdom Reading Association.

Geoffrion, L. D., & Geoffrion, O. P. (1983). *Computers and reading instruction*. Reading, MA: Addison Wesley.

Hirschkron, A. (1995). The kids behind the stereotype. *New Media, 5*, 83.

McKenna, Michael C., & Robinson, Richard D. (1993). *Teaching through text*. New York: Longman.

Miller, L., Blackstock, J., & Miller, R. (1994). An exploratory study into the use of CD-ROM storybooks. *Computer Education, 22*, 187-204.

Miller, L., & Olson, J. (1994). Putting the computer in its place: a study of teaching with technology. *Journal of Curriculum Studies, 26,* 121-141.

New York State Public Schools. (1994). Technology update—1994. *Technology Applications Quarterly,* Spring.

Putnam, L. (Ed.) (1996). *How to be a Better Reading Teacher.* Englewood Cliffs, NJ: Merrill.

Reinking, D. (1987). *Computers and reading: Issues for theory and practice.* New York: Teachers College Press.

Ruberg, L. (1993). *The impact of digital technologies on the elementary school classroom.* Paper presented at the International Visual Literacy Association, Rochester, NY, October. Educational Resources and Information Clearinghouse. [ERIC ED 370 566]

Strickland, D. S., Feeley, J. T., & Wepner, S. B. (1987). *Using computers in the teaching of reading.* New York: Teachers College Press.

Taylor, R. (Ed.) (1980). *The computer in the school: Tutor, tool, tutee.* New York: Teachers College Press.

Tierney, R. J., Readence, J. E., & Dishner, E. K. (1995). *Reading strategies and practices: A compendium* (4th ed.). Boston: Allyn & Bacon.

Times Mirror Center. (1995). *Report on Americans and Technology.* New York: Times Mirror Center for the People and the Press. U. S. Department of Commerce, (1994). *Statistical abstracts of the United States* (114th ed.). Washington, DC: U. S. Department of Commerce.

U. S. Department of Commerce. (1994). *Statistical abstracts of the United States* (114th ed.). Washington, D. C.: U. S. Department of Commerce.

Vacca, J. A. L., Vacca, R. T., & Gove, M. K. (1995). *Reading and learning to read* (3rd ed.). New York: HarperCollins.

Weaver, C. (1994). *Reading process and practice: From socio-psycholinguistics to whole language.* Portsmouth, NH: Heinemann.

Willis, J. W., Stephens, E. C., & Matthew, K. I. (1996). *Technology, reading, and language arts.* Boston: Allyn and Bacon.

## Software References

Arthur's Teacher Trouble [Computer software]. (1993). Novato, CA: Broderbund Software.

Big Anthony's Magic [Computer software]. (1993). NewYork, NY: Putnam New Media.

The Backyard [Computer software]. (1993). Novato, CA: Broderbund software.

Benjamin Bunny [Computer software]. (1991). Toronto, Canada: Discis Knowledge Research.

Children's Writing and Publishing Center [Computer software]. (1988). Fremont, CA: The Learning Company.

ClarisWorks [Computer software]. (1995). Santa Clara CA: Claris Corporation.

Coral Kingdom [Computer software]. (1992). Pleasantville, NY: Sunburst/Wings for Learning.

Crossword Magic [Computer software]. (1990). Chicago, IL: Mindscape.

Dinosaurs [Computer software]. (1992). Redmond, WA: Microsoft.

Houghton Mifflin Reading Comprehension [Computer software]. (1989). Hanover, NH: Houghton Mifflin Educational Software Division.

Hypercard [Computer software]. (1995). Sante Clara, CA: Claris Corporation.

HyperStudio [Computer software]. (1994). El Cajon, CA: Roger Wagner Publishing.

Just Grandma and Me [Computer software]. (1992). Novato, CA: Broderbund Software.

KidPix [Computer software]. (1990). Novato, CA: Broderbund Software.

Kid Works [Computer software]. (1992). Torrance, CA: Davidson & Associates.

Martin Luther King, Jr. [Computer software]. (1990). Warren, NJ: Optical Data Corporation.

Netscape [Computer software]. (1995). Mt. View, CA: Netscape Communications Corporation.

Optimum Resource Reading [Computer software]. (1990). Norfolk, CT: Optimum Resource.

Oregon Trail [Computer software]. (1990). Minneapolis, MN: MECC.

Peter Rabbit [Computer software]. (1991). Toronto, Canada: Discis Books.

The Playroom [Computer software]. (1991). Novato, CA: Broderbund Software.

Scholastic's Electronic Portfolio [Computer software]. (1993). Jefferson City, MO: Scholastic New Media.

Spell It [Computer software]. (1992). Torrance, CA: Davidson & Associates.

Voyage of the Mimi and Voyage of the Mimi II [Computer software]. (1990, 1993). Pleasantville, NY: Sunburst/Wings for Learning.

Word Munchers [Computer software]. (1985). Minneapolis, MN: MECC.

# A Qualitative Study of the Literacy Environment in One Home School Setting

## Valerie G. Hall

Ball State University

## Abstract

*The purpose of the study is to present a personalized qualitative description of the literacy environment in one home where parents taught their own children. Through the theoretical perspective of hermeneutic phenomenology, the interactions of each family member during literacy instruction are interpreted. Data are analyzed using the constant comparative method. Overall, findings indicate that literacy lessons are structured, planned, and organized in this home schooling situation. The parents initially appear to provide individualized instruction through creating an appropriate learning environment. The physical arrangement of the home setting, parental attitudes and their influence on literacy education, and freedom of the students to explore their interests are discussed. The influence of the public school classroom environment on literacy instruction is considered as the home environment is examined.*

## Introduction

Lee (1960) provided an example of a child learning to read naturally in her book *To Kill a Mockingbird.* In this story the fictional character, Scout, expresses her experiences learning to read at home with her father. She does not know how or when she first began to understand that the symbols on a page have meaning. She often sat on her father's lap as he read newspapers and other materials to her. As her eyes followed the page, she learned to read in a relaxed natural way in a home setting. Scout provides an example of ways children can learn about books: by watching adults read, listening to stories, and finding answers in books.

The value of family literacy interactions in relation to literacy development and a literate life has been well documented in the research literature (Heath, 1982; Taylor, 1981; Taylor & Dorsey-Gaines, 1988). As the ultimate application of the parental role in education, some parents embrace the complete involvement of teaching their own children. They are typically well-educated, religious people interested in providing their children with a positive and supportive educational environment at home (Knowles, 1988; Knowles, Muchmore, & Spaulding, 1994; Mayberry, 1989; Van Galen, 1988). These parents believe they are capable of teaching their children because they know their children better than anyone else does. Painter concurs with this notion in her reference to parents' oral discourse with preschoolers, "It is being a member of the child's inner circle that enables the parent to ask the most appropriate questions" (1985, p. 39).

Because some parents have taken the responsibility to educate their own children, it has become important for literacy educators to consider cooperative efforts with these families (Knowles & Muchmore, 1994; Rakestraw, 1987; Ray & Wartes, 1991; Webb, 1989). Beyond the examination of the needs of parents who home-educate their children, public school teachers could consider how to involve their students' parents in their classrooms (Bauch, 1994; Berger, 1991; Chavkin & Williams, 1993; Holt, 1983; McCaleb, 1994; Morrow, Paratore, Gaber, Harrison, & Tracey, 1993). As Potter reminds, "It must be the family who helps to maintain the continuity of the child's education" (1989, p. 28). Only through observations of literacy interactions between parents and children can educators gain an understanding of how to work with parents in the education of children. Although many issues of home education are discussed in research, the area most overlooked is that of pedagogy. Learning about how parents teach their children can assist teachers in collaboration with parents.

In the research related to home-education, the apparent lack of data concerning the teaching methods of parents indicates the great need for long term, ethnographic observation in a variety of homes where children are home-educated by their parents. An examination of the literature reveals a lack of qualitative, in-depth data describing instruction and social interactions in these homes. In some research "gaining access to private homes for observation has been a major impediment" (Hafer, 1990). For example, Hafer studied published materials used by those who home-educate their children because he could not gain access to a family who would allow him to observe in the home. However, as a teaching parent with active involvement in a home school support group and regular attendance at the annual Indiana Association of Home Educators conventions, I know many parents who home-educate their children and who are open to observation. I have established rapport with these individuals and this gives me access to a group of people often unavailable to other researchers.

This paper is one component of a larger study intended for the purpose of documenting what occurs during literacy lessons in one home where children are home-educated by their parents and understanding the events from the parents' and children's perspectives. The purpose of this paper is to describe the literacy environment in one home school setting. The literacy environment is an important factor in the development of instruction in this home school setting. As in this home, the atmosphere in public and private schools is critical to education. The research question that guided and focused this portion of the study was, "What is the relationship between the home environment and literacy instruction?"

## Methodology

This study is an in-depth qualitative description (Patton, 1990) of what happens in a home-educating family during literacy instruction and an interpretation of the perspectives of the participants. In order to gain an understanding of the phenomenon of literacy instruction and the setting in a home where children were home-educated by their parents, I chose to focus on one case. In this intrinsic case study, I examined one family because of the importance of understanding their particular motivations, beliefs, literacy events, and practices (Stake, 1994). I was interested in this particular case for what could be learned about this one family, not because they represent all other families where children are home-educated by their parents. Although my primary focus and interest was in this one family, I hoped to gain insight into the issue of home education as it relates to other parents who home-educate their children, public school teachers, and parents whose children are in the public schools.

## Design

My theoretical perspective is hermeneutic phenomenology in the sense that I attempt to describe the "structure and essence of experience of this phenomenon for these people" (Patton, 1990, p. 69). In the phenomenological tradition I sought a deep understanding of the meaning of the daily experiences of this family. Through observations via fieldnotes, audiotaped lessons, interviews with the parents, written reflections of the parents, and content analysis of textbooks, manuals, and student work, I was able to understand what education means to each family member. With hermeneutics I applied interpretation of these lived experiences to determine the meaning to the family members. As a result of observation of instruction in this home, I provide a description of the environment in addition to an interpretation of what the setting means to the participants. I provide this information because hermeneutic phenomenology is both descriptive and interpretive in nature. Thus, in following the hermeneutic phenomenological framework, I attempt to "construct a full interpretive description of some aspect of the lifework, and yet remain aware that lived life is always more complex than any explication of meaning can reveal" (Van Manen, 1990, p. 18).

In describing this phenomenon, I was reminded that I can never completely help readers understand the educational experiences of this family. To the family, education was a part of life and occurred all day in many situations. If the family went on a week long camping trip, the children learned about a variety of life skills even when they were not using their textbooks or following traditional plans. Although I could not be with the family every hour of every school day, I did interpret what I observed and verified my interpretations by consulting the parents about their teaching.

## Participants

I selected one family from the same home education support group that I had attended for five years. This support group of twenty families met every other week for group activities with different mothers sharing the leadership and teaching roles during these sessions. I knew Mrs. Anderson from watching her assist with group field trips and organize and teach projects at the support group. I chose a family with four school-aged children to allow observation of interactions between children and variations in the teaching of children who differ in age. Because I was interested in examining literacy interactions, I wanted to see several children as they interacted among themselves and with their parents. I also selected the Andersons because they are representative of the largest group of parents who home-educate their children—those who do so out of religious motivation (Mayberry, 1989). According to criteria outlined by several researchers (Gladin, 1987; Mayberry, 1989; Van Galen, 1988; Wartes, 1988), the family I selected is representative of typical families who home-educate their children. The family is Caucasian, Protestant, upper middle class, and both parents completed degrees at major universities.

In order to understand the children, I gathered data on their interests and abilities through interviews and observations. Nathan, the only boy in the family, is thirteen years old and working at approximately fifth grade. His mother describes him as being uninterested in reading and less capable in reading and writing than the average child. He loves sports and enjoys mechanics and working with arts and crafts. Nathan demonstrates his dependability in caring for his sisters and helping in the home when his parents leave the house for an hour or two.

The next oldest child, Victoria, is ten and doing third grade work. She appears very happy, displaying a smile constantly. Like her brother, she did not begin to show skill in reading until recently. Because Mr. and Mrs. Anderson read to the children when they were young and provided them experiences useful for building background knowledge, Mrs. Anderson attributes their reading below grade level to a lack of interest and motivation. She is hopeful that providing a stimulating environment without undue pressure will encourage the children in their academic development. Victoria loves to help clean house and assist with her two younger sisters. She likes to teach the two younger girls lessons and tell them what academic work will be required when they are older like she is. She spends time feeding and watching animals in the yard, organizing her coin collection, and cooking.

The third child, Ann, is eight years old and in approximately first grade. She enjoys doing school work, and like her older brother and sister, is happy to show her work. She loves doing creative projects and often becomes distracted from her assignments when she becomes absorbed in a craft project. She likes sewing and other needlework, playing with dolls, and making paper crafts.

The youngest child, Elizabeth, is six years old and doing preschool work. She loves doing all kinds of academic work, cleaning house, roller skating, and working dot-to-dot pages. She easily accepts the guidance of her brother and two sisters and observes them as they study. She seems to desire to please her parents and works diligently and enthusiastically.

## Environment

I observed the Anderson family in their home as they engaged in educational lessons. Although their instructional activities occasionally included field trips and athletic practices, most of the events occured in and around the home. Because this is a unique instructional setting, a description of the home is essential to a clear understanding of teaching and learning in this environment.

The front door of the Anderson home opens into the living room. Four stuffed chairs are in front of a large picture window with end tables and lamps spaced between the chairs. A piano is positioned on the wall next to the chairs. A couch faces the chairs for a comfortable arrangement for group lessons. A hallway goes from the living room to three bedrooms and a bathroom. Large bookshelves, filled with a variety of reading materials, line the wall by the hallway and around the corner into the dining room. The dining room and kitchen are attached to the living room. The living room is open to the dining room, so the four student desks and the dining room table are visible from the front door. A large chalkboard in the middle of a bookcase is further evidence of learning activities. Games and a globe are on a small bookshelf next to the row of desks.

The children do written work at their desks, sit on the floor or in a chair to read or play games, or sit on the couch with Mrs. Anderson when reading to her. When a child wants to work alone in a quiet place, the child goes to his or her bedroom or the guest room at the side of the dining room. During a group parent-directed lesson, Mrs. Anderson stands by the piano or sits at the end of the couch while the children sit in the large comfortable chairs. I observed from locations near the children, moving around the home to watch all of them. Because I am the instrument of observation, it is necessary to illustrate my experiences in both home and public school settings.

## The Researcher

To place this study in a proper qualitative context, it is important to know the researcher and the role I assumed. Like the Andersons, I taught my son for seven years, and I chose to teach him in order to instill Christian values while spending time with him. My experiences with home education were both a limitation and an asset. Because I had supported the philosophy of home education for several years, I could not be completely objective. On the other hand, during the years I taught my son, I met many families who also home-educated their children. I attended several conferences for home educators and examined a variety of secular and Christian instructional materials. Because of my contacts with home educators and my understanding of their motivations, these parents readily allowed me to spend time with their family. The family trusted me as a parent and a teacher. As a teaching parent, I was profoundly aware of the benefits and rewards as well as the difficulties and demands involved in teaching my own child. This background assisted me in understanding this family and the experiences of each participant. The Anderson family members may also have been more genuine in expressing themselves because of our close relationship through our home teaching experiences.

In addition to my experiences as a parent teaching my son, I taught in elementary classrooms for five years. I worked with parents in my classrooms and valued the support they could give their children. I read professional journals and studied theories of literacy learning. As I continued to teach my son for two years while I studied, I applied some of the pedagogies I gathered through my course work and discussions with other teachers. My experiences in public school teaching and home education permitted me to observe the Andersons through the lenses of both a literacy educator and an involved parent. As Van Manen wrote about his research on parenting, I can also say, "I am not *just* a researcher who observes life, I am also a parent and a teacher who stands pedagogically in life" (Van Manen, 1990, p. 90). As the role of the researcher is critical in qualitative research, so the process of data collection and the verification through triangulation are important factors in the rigor of the study.

## The Process

In my role as a researcher, I carefully selected the data sources and the method for collecting the data. On my first visit in the Anderson home, April 1993, I noted the physical surroundings and observed Mrs. Anderson as she provided reading instruction for the children. This visit with the Andersons, along with observations in three other homes, provided me with background information to begin my research of literacy instruction in a home where children were home-educated by their parents. At this visit I established the procedure of tape recording reading and writing lessons as they occurred with parent and child. I also began gathering samples of children's work and instructional materials while writing fieldnotes based on my observations of literacy instruction. On this visit, I conducted my first interview with the parents. Following this initial visit, I visited the Andersons twice in August 1993 for an overview of instruction as the school year began. In January 1994, I began more regular visits. For four visits, I focused on one child at a time, following that child's activities from room to room. This allowed me to see the structure of one child's schedule throughout the day.

After gaining a perception of each child, I spent four days a week with the family from February 7 to March 3, 1994. During this concentrated time, I was able to observe the continuity of a unit of study. Although I observed activities in all subject areas, I focused on reading and writing and the interactions during those lessons.

After observing literacy instruction for consecutive days through one unit of study, I returned to visit the Andersons in the evening when Mr. Anderson was involved in the teaching. During this evening visit, I sat in a chair in the living room to observe the group lesson Mr. Anderson conducted with the entire family. He stood at the dry erase board while Mrs. Anderson and the children sat in chairs around the room.

Data were analyzed using the constant comparative analysis method (Glaser & Strauss, 1967). I generated themes or categories of behaviors and actions from the data, beginning with the process of open coding and proceeding to the development of core categories (Strauss, 1987). Specifically, I worked "back and forth between the data and the classification system to verify the meaningfulness and accuracy of the categories and the placement of data in categories" (Patton, 1990, p. 403). In the analysis of the phenomenon of literacy instruction in the home, I looked for patterns and themes that emerged from the data, constantly considering new data to collapse categories or generate new ones.

Following my generation of assertions and supportive categories, I shared my charts with the family and asked for their input. They supported my interpretations, surprised by all that they were doing as they taught. Through this process of data analysis, I generated assertions that supported the finding that in this home, teaching was structured, planned, and organized. The assertion that is the focus of this paper is that the parents provided individualized instruction through the learning environment. In this study I was able to observe approximately twenty-five lessons over time as they naturally occurred in a home-education setting.

## Discussion

In this study it was evident that the parents initially established the learning environment, then continued to adjust the setting, materials, and methods as they taught and evaluated their instruction. Within the discussion of the learning environment, I examine the physical arrangement of the home setting, parental attitudes and their influence on literacy education, and freedom of the students to explore their interests.

### Home Setting

As stated in their philosophy of education, the Andersons realize the importance of the home setting to the type of instruction they want to provide. "The home environment and day-to-day life situations provide the ideal setting and opportunity to apply knowledge" (Note from Anderson family, 9-27-85). Additionally, in interviews with the parents and observations in their home, it was apparent that Mr. and Mrs. Anderson provided the children with constant reminders of love and acceptance. Even decorations in the home depict the importance of the children and positive character qualities.

In addition to the reminders on the wall, each child has a photo album full of pictures of him or her along with other family members. The children enjoy looking at the pictures and retelling events surrounding these pictorial reminders. Nathan has his own room with an aquarium, test tubes, and model airplanes. Although the three girls share a room, each has her own space and knows where she keeps her possessions. The collection of photographs and the individual living space illustrates the way Mr. and Mrs. Anderson value each child.

In the instructional setting, all the children have desks in the dining room so they can work together if they desire. Nathan also has a desk in his room where he often prefers to work. A guest bedroom attached to the dining room has two desks where children work when they want to be away from the others. The morning group lesson is held in the living room with each child sitting in a large stuffed chair or on the floor. Mrs. Anderson usually sits on the couch near a dry erase board that she occasionally uses in the lessons. In sum, Mr. and Mrs. Anderson seek to provide a comfortable setting conducive to learning, allowing for individual differences and preferences. The children appear to feel that they are considered as individuals and have personal space for learning in the type of setting they each desire.

## Parental Attitudes

Along with the physical setting of the home, the attitudes of the parents are vital to establishing an environment they deem appropriate for their children's learning. Interviews with the parents and fieldnotes of observations provide evidence that Mr. and Mrs. Anderson respect each child as an individual. When Mrs. Anderson works with one child, they sit on the couch together, sometimes with arms around each other. Occasionally when Mrs. Anderson kneels beside a child's desk when giving assistance, the child leans over and gives Mom a kiss.

When a child needs discipline, Mrs. Anderson discusses the matter privately in a bedroom, helping the child keep his or her dignity while settling the situation. During the day, Mr. Anderson occasionally talks with Nathan by phone to discuss his attitude toward his mother. Data also indicated that Mr. and Mrs. Anderson are positive and encouraging in response to the efforts of the children.

For example, even when a child wanted to do a lesson in a way other than what the parents had prepared, Mr. and Mrs. Anderson were considerate of the child's wishes. For example, when Ann was ready to start her reading lesson, she wanted to do something different: "Ann asked Mrs. Anderson if they could start the book over so I could hear all the stories. Mrs. Anderson said that would be good practice. After Ann read a story especially well, Mrs. Anderson praised her" (fieldnotes, 2-25-94).

The parents enjoyed working with their children and express this in their interactions. This positive, encouraging attitude is essential in the education of the Anderson children because this atmosphere seems to motivate the students to do their best. The children appeared to feel good about themselves and exuded confidence that they could succeed. The way the parents worked with the children allowed these young people freedom in selection of materials and activities.

## Student Freedom

Because of the atmosphere established through the home setting and the Andersons' attitudes, the children in this home have the freedom to pursue their individual areas of interest. As indicated through content analysis and observation fieldnotes, the children could proceed independently with much of their own work through reading their assignment notebooks. Each child does some of the scheduled assignments, works on projects, and returns to other work. The flexibility of the schedule allows the children to pursue their interests during the day while they have energy. They do not need to wait until late afternoon when they might be too tired to be interested in creative activities.

Nathan provides an example of this freedom. He loves science and cooking, so he often does projects in the kitchen. One day he made a cranberry drink based on a video they had seen the day before. When he interrupted his mother to offer her a drink, Mrs. Anderson stopped her interactions with Ann long enough to thank Nathan for the float and to discuss what he had learned about cranberries from the video. She encouraged the children to work on projects of interest to them and expressed her interest in each child's work.

In addition to cooking, Nathan pursued other activities. He designed and built a bird cage to help his sister with her interest in animals. Nathan also took a "safe sitters" class and could be trusted to care for his three sisters for a short time while his parents were away from home. Once, when Nathan was left with the responsibility of caring for his sisters, he surprised his parents with an apple pie in the oven on their return.

Victoria also has time to pursue her interests. She loves animals and spends hours preparing and placing food for the birds and squirrels that come to the Andersons' patio. She loves exploring in the woods behind the house and observing the Canadian geese that visit the pond.

Ann is artistically creative and is provided time to make interesting projects. On one occasion when she called her mother to the kitchen sink, I went to observe what she had made. "Ann showed her mother her 'new invention,' a pipe cleaner shaped into a large circle with a handle. She dipped it into dish soap and water and blew huge bubbles" (fieldnotes, 2-15-94). Ann also enjoys cutting and pasting, making crafts she uses in her play.

When Elizabeth finished her school work, she played with Ann. Elizabeth was highly motivated. She usually continued her school assignments until they were finished, rather than participate in other activities during the day. The freedom of the Anderson home education setting provides many opportunities for individual creative expression for each child. The children seemed relaxed without pressure to complete specific assignments at a given time. They were interested in a variety of areas and excited about developing their own abilities.

## Implications

In the examination of research, some aspects of literacy instruction related to home education are also of concern to public school educators. Classroom teachers and home-educating parents confront the issue of establishing a literacy environment and cooperation between homes and schools. Creating an appropriate learning atmosphere in both home and public school settings is important because children need a rich literacy environment and a safe place for taking risks that will stimulate and encourage their learning. The other issue confronting parents and teachers is that of cooperation between homes and schools. Concerns surrounding this issue are twofold: (a) whether public school professionals should assist home-educating parents, and (b) whether public school teachers should encourage the involvement of parents in curriculum and classroom matters.

Children are the greatest beneficiaries when parents are involved in schooling. Children thrive in an atmosphere where caring adults cooperate to meet children's needs. Public school teachers and home-educating parents might both benefit if given opportunities for open communication. With shared knowledge, parents and teachers can develop instruction that addresses the needs of the whole child. As teachers model literacy strategies (Routman, 1991), they can also model collaborative efforts. Optimally, children would sense the cooperative attitude and learn to develop this trait in their relationships with others in the school setting. When parents and teachers work as partners in the education of children, they create an environment conducive to learning and beneficial to all. As noted by Taylor and Dorsey-Gaines:

> Every attempt should be made to create an atmosphere that places value on the children's growing sense of competence and independence so that their lives are not separated from the outside world. Such policies, if promoted by our schools, would depend upon close contact between teachers and parents. Family and community involvement in school programs would be essential, and our children would surely benefit from the connections that were being made in their everyday lives. (1988, p. 210)

Although this study of literacy instruction focused on parents who chose to take the major role of educating their children, this research has implications for parents accepting a different role. Teachers have often been encouraged to involve parents in the classroom because of the potential benefits to parents and their children. As the Andersons learned about child development through working with their children, so parents working in the classroom could learn more about their children and the lessons they are learning at school. Although the Andersons developed their own instruction, parents of children in public schools could observe techniques they might use at home to support classroom instruction. Since parents are privy to useful background knowledge about their children, teachers could benefit from this parental wealth of information. For example, the teacher could quickly become acquainted with a child by acquiring background knowledge about the child from the parents. This facilitates providing instruction that is meaningful to each student.

This case study has provided in-depth information about the literacy environment in one home school setting. Continued research related to a variety of models that attempt to increase parental involvement is essential because some models have been more successful than others. We need to examine why and how successful programs work. Areas for future study should include: the characteristics of successful programs, parental responses, student reactions, and how parents collaborate with teachers.

In summary, many parents, like the Andersons, take their obligations to their children extremely seriously: "We are responsible to see that our children become mature and balanced by giving them protection, provision, and direction" (Note from Anderson family, 9-27-85). Because these are also the basic desires of most school systems, parents and teachers must explore ways to work together to provide the best environment for children's learning and emotional support.

---

# References

Bauch, J. P. (1994). Categories of parent involvement. *The School Community Journal, 4*(1), 53-60.

Berger, E. H. (1991). *Parents as partners in education.* New York: MacMillan Publishing.

Chavkin, N. F., & Willams, D. (1993). Minority parents and elementary school: Attitudes and practices. *Families and Schools in a Pluralistic Society.* Albany: State University of New York Press 77.

Gladin, W. E. (1987). *Home education: Characteristics of its families and schools.* Doctoral thesis, Bob Jones University. Greensborough, SC.

Glaser, B. G., & Strauss, A. L. (1967). *The discovery of grounded theory: Strategies for qualitative research.* New York: Adline Press.

Hafer, G. R. (1990). *An analysis of writing instruction in the home school.* Unpublished doctoral dissertation, Purdue University.

Heath, S. B. (1982). What no bedtime story means: Narrative skills at home and school. *Language in Society, 11,* 49-76.

Holt, J. (1983). *How schools can cooperate with home schoolers. Education Digest, 49,* 2-5.

Knowles, J. G. (1988). Parents' rationales and teaching methods for home schooling. *Education and Urban Society, 21,* 69-83.

Knowles, J. G., & Muchmore, J. A. (1994, April). *Yep! We're grown-up home schooled kids— and we're doing just fine, thank you very much.* Paper presented at the annual meeting of the American Educational Research Association, New Orleans, LA.

Knowles, J. G., Muchmore, J. A., & Spaulding, H. W. (1994). Home education as an alternative to institutionalized education. *The Educational Forum, 58,* 238-243

Lee, H. (1960). *To Kill a Mockingbird.* Philadelphia: Lippincott.

Mayberry, M. (1989). Home-based education in the United States: Demographics, motivations, and educational implications. *Educational Review, 41,* 171-180.

McCaleb, S. P. (1994). *Building communities of learners: A collaboration among teachers, students, families, and community.* New York: St. Martin's Press.

Morrow, L. M., Paratore, J., Gaber, D. Harrison, C., & Tracey, D. (1993). Family literacy: Perspective and practices. *The Reading Teacher, 47*(3), 194-200.

Painter, C. (1985). *Learning the mother tongue.* Oxford: Oxford University Press.

Patton, M. Q. (1990). *Qualitative evaluation and research methods.* Newbury Park: Sage.

Potter, G. (1989). Parent participation in the language arts program. *Language Arts, 66*(1), 21-28.

Rakestraw, J. G. (1987). *An analysis of home schooling for elementary school-age children in Alabama.* Doctoral dissertation, University of Alabama, Tuscaloosa, AL.

Ray, B. D., & Wartes, J. (1991). The academic achievement and affective development of home-schooled children. In J. A. Van Galen & M. A. Pitman (Eds.), *Home schooling: Political, historical, and pedagogical perspectives* (pp. 43-62). Norwood, NJ: Ablex Publishing.

Routman, R. (1991). *Invitations: Changing as teachers and learners K-12.* Portsmouth, NH: Heinemann.

Stake, R. E. (1994). Case studies. In N. K. Denzin & Y. S. Lincoln (Eds.), *Handbook of qualitative research* (pp. 236-247). Thousand Oaks, CA: Sage Publications.

Strauss, A. L. (1987). *Qualitative analysis for social scientists.* Cambridge: Cambridge University.

Taylor, D. (1981). *Family literacy: The social context of learning to read and write.* Unpublished doctoral dissertation, Teachers College, Columbia University, New York.

Taylor, D. & Dorsey-Gaines, C. (1988). *Growing up literate: Learning from inner-city families.* Portsmouth, NH: Heinemann.

Van Galen, J. A. (1988). Ideology, curriculum, and pedagogy in home education. *Education and Urban Society, 21,* 52-67.

Van Manen, M. (1990). *Researching lived experience: Human science for an action sensitive pedagogy.* New York: The State University of New York Press.

Wartes, J. (1988). The Washington home school project quantitative measures for informing policy decisions. *Education and Urban Society, 21,* 42-51.

Webb, J. (1989). The outcomes of home-based education: Employment and other issues. *Educational Review, 41,* 121-133.

# TEACHERS HELPING TEACHERS: OHIO'S EVEN START PEER ASSISTANCE TEAM PROJECT

**Nancy D. Padak**
**Timothy V. Rasinski**
Kent State University

**Connie S. Ackerman**
Ohio Department of Education

## Abstract

*Since 1993 the authors have been collaborating with local program co-ordinators and selected volunteers to develop and pilot a Peer Assistance Team project for Ohio. In brief the project aims to provide (a) a framework for relatively new (i.e., second year) Even Start programs to engage in systematic self-study and (b) peer support for solving program-identified problems through on-site visitation.*

The Even Start Family Literacy Program (ES) was authorized by the Elementary and Secondary Education Act (1965), as amended by the Hawkins-Stafford Elementary and Secondary School Improvement Amendments of 1988 (Part B, Chapter 1 of Title I; PL 100-297). According to law, ES programs are intended to

> improve educational opportunities of the Nation's children and adults by integrating early childhood education and adult education for parents into a unified program. . . . The program shall be implemented through cooperative projects that build on existing community resources to create a new range of services. (PL 100-297, Sec. 1051)

ES programs are 4-year demonstration projects, awarded through competitive grant programs. Because of the mandate for integrated programming, ES focuses on the family rather than just parents or children. Family literacy practitioners see great potential in the ES model. However, they also see substantial challenges, not the least of which is developing a system of support for fledgling programs. This support is especially critical because so few models of successful and fully integrated family education exist (Dickinson, 1994).

Since 1993 we (two professors and the State ES Coordinator for Ohio) have been collaborating with ES program coordinators and selected volunteers to develop and pilot a Peer Assistance Team (PAT) project for Ohio. In brief, the PAT project aims to provide (a) a framework for relatively new (i.e., second year) Even Start programs to engage in systematic self-study and (b) peer support for solving program-identified problems through on-site visitation. In this article we summarize all aspects of the PAT project to date. We conclude with recommendations for others wishing to use the PAT model to support family literacy programs.

## Background

Aside from the general belief that professional development can and should include peer interaction and support, we developed the PAT project for two major reasons. The first reason was that various sets of "quality indicators" or program criteria were converging upon the field of family literacy. Even Start is based on objectives related to adult education, early childhood education, and parenting education that local programs are to use for implementation and evaluation. In addition, state ES Coordinators met with consultants from RMC (a national consulting group) in May, 1993 and again in October, 1994 to develop a *Program Quality Guide* (1994). This guide was based on ES objectives, that consisted of lists of "quality considerations" and "problem signs/red flags/areas of concern," also to be used for program enhancement. At nearly the same time, the National Center for Family Literacy (NCFL) developed the *Family Literacy Program Quality Self-Study* guide (1994), which addressed many of the same issues in a different format. Also, as part of the National Literacy Act of 1991, federally-funded adult education programs, including ES programs that receive such funds, were directed to develop and then use "Indicators of Program Quality" to improve their programs.

Clearly, interest in ways to enhance adult literacy programs, family literacy programs, and ES programs is high among various audiences. However, the sheer number of competing formats and tools made this potentially important task complex, confusing, and time-consuming for ES programs. One major goal of the PAT project, then, was to streamline and coordinate these various tools into a framework that ES projects could use efficiently and effectively.

A second reason for undertaking the PAT project related to the need to broaden the network of collegial support among ES programs in Ohio. Prior to the PAT project, the only formal mechanisms for problem-solving among ES programs were consultation with the State Coordinator and periodic statewide meetings. As the number of programs throughout the state grew, the amount of time that could be devoted to any one program naturally diminished. Furthermore, since the State Coordinator's responsibilities include compliance reviews and other evaluative tasks, she recognized that programs might hesitate to seek support by sharing their problems and concerns. For both of these reasons, we believed that a framework for peer support would make a valuable addition to state-sponsored ES activity.

## Planning

The planning process for the PAT project centered on three major tasks: (a) developing a common vision for what the PAT process might become, (b) developing consensus about what tools to use, and (c) identifying and training PAT members who would provide on-site assistance. All three tasks were completed with the assistance of the coordinators of all Ohio ES programs (N=18), who were encouraged to share ideas with their staffs and to provide us with staff feedback.

### Creating a Common Vision

Meetings were held with ES coordinators to explore the PAT "vision" and address any concerns. We sought consensus at all stages of the project. In general, inclusive discussions were followed by specific focus on possible problems or concerns, after which the group decided on solutions to problems.

From the outset, coordinators were enthusiastic about project potential but concerned that PAT activities not focus on compliance or evaluation; rather, they desired support and counsel from their peers. All involved recognized the fine line between problem-solving and evaluation. A second concern among coordinators was that the process take as little time as possible. They already were completing paperwork for state reports, their local evaluations, and in some cases the national evaluation. They feared the extra burden on their overworked staffs, and they also wanted a framework that would allow PAT members to explore the variety of ES activities within a single ES program in as efficient and timely a manner as possible. Finally, coordinators hoped that results of PAT visits would be useful, i.e., would help them develop and refine their programs.

### Developing Tools

The local ES coordinators also assisted in the process of developing tools. These tools were used both by the programs that were visited and by the visitation teams. The former used the tools to guide the self-study that preceded the site visit, and the latter used the tools to frame their on-site interactions. Initially, we used a modified Delphi technique (e.g., Huse &

Cummings, 1985) to develop a set of tools based on standards provided by the National Center for Family Literacy (NCFL, 1994). First, a mailing to all local programs asked for ratings of importance and exemplars for particular standards. Local coordinators' perceptions were tallied, and lists of comments were compiled. These standards then were shared at a statewide meeting. At this time coordinators expressed concern about the extent to which standards spoke directly and explicitly to the ES objectives, as opposed to more generic types of family literacy programs. Consequently, the standards were revised to capture and reflect both the ES objectives and the NCFL standards.

The final list of program standards (see Appendix) includes five areas of focus: program planning, family selection and orientation, adult academic programs, parenting programs, and early childhood programs. Within each area of focus, several indicators are identified. For example, in the "Family Selection and Orientation" area of focus (which corresponds to ES objectives 2, 3, and 4 and NCFL standards 1.10, 1.11, 1.12, 1.13, and 1.14), the indicators are (a) recruitment is comprehensive, ongoing, and shows evidence of collaboration with other agencies, (b) selection is systematic, and (c) intake procedures are comprehensive and "friendly." The final set of focus areas/standards and indicators within them was approved by local ES coordinators at a meeting in October 1994.

Next, both the areas and the indicators were enhanced and synthesized to develop several other documents for use throughout the process. We developed lists of possible sources of information about each indicator (see Appendix). We also developed several guiding questions to help both local programs and PAT members think about the key issues related to the indicators (see Appendix). Finally, we developed some charts (see Figure for an example) that were intended to assist (a) local programs in a self-study that summarized and synthesized information for PAT members to use and (b) PAT members in summarizing and synthesizing the results of their study of the programs. We hoped that these instruments would guide program staffs and PAT visitors in a thorough yet efficient exploration of each area and indicator.

### Identifying and Training PAT Members

All ES programs received written requests to nominate potential PAT members. A description of the PAT process accompanied this request, as did a brief nomination form, which sought demographic information about the nominee and asked for a brief description of "why you feel this person would be a good member of the Peer Assistance Teams." Comments also were solicited about nominees' knowledge and experience in ES, their ability to work with others, and their experience in providing formative evaluation and feedback for others. Seven ES staff personnel were nominated, and all agreed to

**Figure 1. Self-Study Summary.**

Program: _____      Date: _____

Area: Program Planning

| Indicators | Strengths | Evidence | Questions/ Concerns |
|---|---|---|---|
| 1.1 Planning Team | | | |
| 1.2 Project Goals | | | |
| 1.3 Physical Plans | | | |
| 1.4 Staff Development | | | |
| 1.5 Program Evaluation | | | |
| 1.6 Product Development/ Dissemination | | | |

serve. One subsequently withdrew from the project, as she had resigned from her position within ES. The 6 remaining PAT members formed 2 teams.

We held two meetings with the PAT teams to help team members understand the entire process and to facilitate their planning. The first meeting focused on the overall PAT process and other general issues, while the second provided PAT teams with time and support for planning their site visits. At the conclusion of this second meeting, both teams believed that they were ready to pilot the process.

## Field Test

Year 2 ES programs were selected to participate in the pilot project. This selection was based on (a) timing, since projects in their second years have worked out start-up problems but still have time to undertake major refinements, should they be necessary, and (b) the strength of the two Year 2 projects in 1994-95. We believed that initial focus on strong projects would enable a more thorough field test of the PAT *process*, because it would be unlikely that major programmatic issues would occupy PAT members' attention. PAT members would be able to focus on positive aspects of programs as well as areas of concern. Both Year 2 ES programs agreed to participate as visitation sites in the pilot process.

Each pilot program completed a self-study prior to PAT visitation. Programs used the focus areas, indicators, and guiding questions to (a) identify their strengths, (b) list evidence that could document these strengths, and (c) generate questions and concerns. To provide further focus for the PAT visits, we suggested that programs summarize their self-studies by articulating four major strengths and four areas of concern. Self-study documents were sent to the PAT teams.

Program visitations occurred in March and April, 1995. Schedules for activities during the visitations were developed by PAT teams, in collaboration with personnel from local ES projects. At the conclusion of the visits, PAT teams prepared reports, which included both commendations and recommendations.

## Evaluation of the PAT Process

We developed a mail survey to supplement evaluation information gained through conversation with both PAT members and ES program personnel. The survey sought perceptions about the most significant outcomes of the process, both positive and negative, whether the PAT program should continue, and if so, what modifications should be considered. All participants, both PAT members and representatives of ES programs, returned the surveys. Survey responses were read and analyzed inductively.

In the evaluation, local ES program personnel identified several positive outcomes of the PAT process. They viewed the self-study as helpful because it required a broad look at their programs and the development of clear explanations of problem areas. They appreciated the face-to-face positive reinforcement received during the PAT visitations, and they found written suggestions in the PAT reports helpful.

Likewise, PAT members identified benefits. They saw value in the brainstorming process used to help local programs solve problems, especially when persons involved in problem-solving represented diverse roles within Even Start. They also saw the PAT process as a professional development opportunity for themselves. Finally, they appreciated learning that problems that plagued their own programs were shared by others. For example, one PAT member valued the "realization that there are shared concerns (recruitment, attendance, integration of curriculum, etc.) among ES programs." This feeling was particularly strong among PAT members who were instructors, since they, unlike program coordinators, generally have few opportunities to discuss issues across programs.

Both ES program personnel and PAT members recommended that the program continue with refinements. One suggestion was to expand the number of ES professionals available as PAT members. These persons should be knowledgeable about "best practice" and representative of the diversity of expertise (e.g., adult education, early childhood education, parenting education) among those involved in family literacy programs. Several people also recommended additional time for on-site visits, especially for larger ES programs.

A final recommendation was to continue clarifying the purpose of PAT visits, including the role of PAT members. Despite extensive discussions with both ES coordinators and PAT members, the survey revealed some concern about a perceived fine line between program assistance and program review or evaluation. For example, one ES coordinator wrote, "I am not especially comfortable with peers evaluating a program that they will be competing with for funding in 2 years. . . ." Moreover, at least one PAT member indicated that she felt some "defensiveness" among local ES staff at the beginning of the visit. All involved believed this "assist vs. evaluate" issue was critical to continued success of the PAT project. All also believed the problem could be solved through additional conversations.

## Conclusion

Peer Assistance Team activities will continue in Ohio because all involved believe that the concept and actual program have great potential for providing support for Ohio's ES programs. Local programs had help solving local problems, and the PAT members profited from professional development opportunities.

Other educational programs could benefit from the mentoring or teachers-helping-teachers approach we employed. For such efforts to be successful, however, several ingredients seem to be critical. First, sufficient planning time for all aspects of the project must be allocated, and the planning group should represent all stakeholders in the process. The documents that ultimately supported the PAT project in Ohio went through at least four iterations before final versions were developed. This process was time-consuming but necessary, as the final documents represented consensus among ES programs, in our case the key stakeholders.

Second, pilot testing on a small scale, along with careful evaluation of the pilot tests, is another critical element. Evaluation results can be used to refine the overall program, after which the program can "go to scale."

Third, the documents we developed may provide support for other family literacy efforts. Since the areas and indicators (see Appendix) reflect priorities of both Even Start and the National Center for Family Literacy, they provide a comprehensive framework for viewing components of family literacy programs. As such, they can provide a foundation for family literacy program development or support.

Finally, projects like the PAT belong to the local personnel who develop them. In our case university personnel served to coordinate and facilitate document development. The state coordinator's involvement was limited to the provision of funds to support the project. Other available instruments, such as those developed by RMC and the NCFL, paint vivid pictures of high quality family literacy programs, but ownership on the part of the local staff that is critical to program improvement may be lacking.

All stakeholders must understand that the purpose of the PAT process is assistance and not evaluation. All PAT efforts must be aimed solely at helping program staffs understand and improve their own programs.

---

## References

Dickinson, D. (1994). *Bridges to literacy: Children, families, and schools.* Cambridge, MA: Basil Blackwell.

Huse, E., & Cummings, T. (1985). *Organization development and change.* St. Paul, MN: West.

National Center for Family Literacy. (1994). *Family literacy program quality self-study.* Louisville, KY: Author.

RMC. (1994). *Even Start program quality guide.* Washington, DC: Author.

# Appendix: Even Start Peer Assistance Teams Sources of Information/Guiding Questions

## *Area 1.0: Program Planning (ES 1,5,11,12,13; NCFL 5)*

### 1.1 Planning Team

*Sources of Information:*
List of committee members and organizations or agencies; minutes; evaluations; interviews.

*Guiding Questions:*
Are members of the advisory council representatives of appropriate agencies? Is membership balanced between educators and others? Do program participants have a voice?

Does the advisory council meet regularly? Is problem-solving a primary purpose of the meetings? How are decisions made, communicated, and implemented?

Do the major collaborative agencies work actively to develop and strengthen links among their organizations? To what extent do ES and other cooperating agencies report satisfaction with collaborative efforts? What benefits and what barriers do they report?

Do non-ES collaborators understand and value ES?

Do instructors receive support from the ES coordinator? Does the coordinator receive support from agency administration? Do staff receive support from the governing agency? Does the staff meet regularly?

Are there written job descriptions? Do staff members know their responsibilities?

### 1.2 Project Plans Related to Project Goals

*Sources of Information:*
Proposal; minutes; surveys; interviews; evaluation reports.

*Guiding Questions:*
Is the cycle of planning, evaluating, and modifying the program ongoing? Who participates in this process? How does it occur?

Are ES staff familiar with all the goals and objectives guiding their project? Do staff with different responsibilities (e.g., adult educators, ECE educators) meet regularly to plan coordinated instruction?

Does the program offer an appropriate balance of activities for the entire family?

### 1.3 Physical Plans

*Sources of Information:*
Documentation of transportation schedules, stipends, fiscal accounting, etc.; child care attendance sheets or rosters; observation; interviews with students and staff.

*Guiding Questions:*
Are program sites in convenient locations (e.g., near public transportation, adequate parking, handicapped accessible)? Is the site clearly identified on the outside of the building? Is it easy for learners to find classrooms?

Is the program schedule flexible and convenient? Is it easy for parents who need to drop out temporarily to reenter the program?

Is the physical environment comfortable, safe, and appropriate for all learners? Is security available? Are emergency exit routes indicated? Is a telephone available? Are access areas, restrooms, and classrooms clean? Are heat, light, and ventilation adequate? Are non-smoking policies observed?

Are classrooms large enough to accommodate varied activities? Are furnishings appropriate?

Are support services (e.g., transportation, child care, counseling) readily available?

Do families exit the program for reasons other than participation barriers?

### 1.4 Ongoing Staff Development
*Sources of Information:*
Calendar of events; evaluations of staff development sessions; agendas from training activities; documentation of each staff member's staff development opportunities; interviews.

*Guiding Questions:*
How are new staff prepared for their ES responsibilities? Do they report satisfaction with preservice staff development activities?

How is the staff development plan developed? Who participates in its development?

Does the staff development plan focus on a limited number of topics over an extended period of time? Are topics directly related to the improvement of instruction? Do staff help choose topics? Are topics related to identified staff needs?

To what extent do staff attend staff development opportunities? To what extent does staff development promote collaboration among people with different ES responsibilities?

Does staff provide feedback on staff development opportunities? Is feedback used to plan further efforts?

Have all adult basic instructors been trained to teach beginning readers? to address learning disabilities? to teach writing? to teach math?

Have early childhood educators and parent educators received training appropriate to their roles?

Are annual performance reviews conducted for all staff members? Does the coordinator work with each staff member to help him or her plan for individual improvement?

### 1.5 Program Evaluation
*Sources of Information:*
Local evaluation reports; student interviews; attendance records.

*Guiding Questions:*
Do local evaluation results indicate whether ES is affecting participants positively?

Do local evaluation results indicate the relative effectiveness of program components?

Are evaluation results used to modify the program design and the written plan?

Are evaluation results available to and understandable for all ES staff?

## 1.6 Product Development/ Dissemination
*Sources of Information:*
Documentation.

*Guiding Questions:*
Is product development proceeding as originally planned?

What is the quality of products developed by the project?

How have products been disseminated?

What other dissemination efforts are evident in the project?

## *Area 2.0: Family Selection/Orientation*
## *(ES 2,3,4; NCFL 1.10,1.11,1.12,1.13,1.14)*
### 2.1 Recruitment
*Sources of Information:*
Evidence of flyers, brochures, other printed recruitment documents; evidence of collaboration with and referrals from other agencies; surveys; interviews.

*Guiding Questions:*
Is there a proactive recruitment plan that includes multiple methods? What media are used to promote the program?

Does the coordinator contact social service agencies to make them aware of the program? Does the program appear to be well connected to other community agencies?

Is recruitment considered part of everybody's job? Is recruitment ongoing? Is the recruitment budget appropriate to the size and scope of the project?

What special efforts are made to recruit those most in need of literacy services? to recruit special populations?

Do students (current and past) report that they are encouraged to recruit others?

### 2.2 Selection
*Sources of Information:*
Written selection criteria; numbers of low level adults, of ADC/JOBS recipients, of SSI, of teen moms, and of men.

*Guiding Questions:*
Does the program have written selection criteria?

Are families most in need selected for participation in the program?

### 2.3 Intake and Orientation
*Sources of Information:*
Evidence of orientation attendance and content; self-evaluation instruments; interviews with parents.

*Guiding Questions:*
Does the intake and orientation process make ES expectations clear to parents? Do families receive printed materials about the program?

Is the intake process easy and "friendly"? Do students report satisfaction with program orientation?

Are staff knowledgeable about other community resources? Do parents learn of other community agencies that can help them?

Are current students involved in orienting new ones?

## *Area 3.0: Adult Academic Programs (ES 6,10; NCFL 1)*

### 3.1 Relevant Content
*Sources of Information:*
Classroom observation; review materials and lessons plans; interviews.

*Guiding Questions:*
Does content demonstrate respect for adult learners by building on their interests and respecting their backgrounds and traditions?

Are staff aware of adults' interests and needs? Does the adult education program relate directly to parents' goals? Do students report conversations with adult educators about their goals?

Do students report using authentic materials (i.e., not only workbooks) and having discussions of "life skills" issues?

### 3.2 Integrated Curriculum
*Sources of Information:*
Interview teachers and learners; review curriculum documents; consider directives from school system or state.

*Guiding Questions:*
Do learners engage in meaningful writing and reading daily?

How are themes chosen? Are they relevant? Do learners participate in curriculum decision-making?

Can instructors show (or explain) the curriculum? Do materials and activities support the planned curriculum? To what extent are basic skills integrated with learning about content related to parenting or other issues of interest to learners?

Do parents report satisfaction with the adult education component?

### 3.3 Instructional Formats
*Sources of Information:*
Observation; review materials; interviews with teachers and learners.

*Guiding Questions:*
Is sufficient time provided for instruction?

Do participants demonstrate respect for one another?

Is there appropriate variety in the methods and materials used in the adult education program?

What special provisions are made for instruction for beginning readers? for speakers of other languages? for learners with special needs?

Does instruction vary to meet students' needs? Do learners report participation in small group activities? large group instruction? Are computers available for student use?

### 3.4 Teacher as Resource and Facilitator
*Sources of Information:*
Observation; interviews with teachers, learners, coordinator/ teachers' supervisor.

*Guiding Questions:*
Does the adult education staff value ES?

Have adult educators and parents developed positive relationships?

Do adult educators consciously work to support parents' personal and academic self-esteem?

Do teachers have knowledge of appropriate resources and instructional methods?

Do learners report adequate individual attention?

### 3.5 Adult Learner Assessment
*Sources of Information:*
Review assessment plan, tests given, and feedback forms shared with parents; review attendance and retention data.

*Guiding Questions:*
How are learners assessed? How are assessment results shared with learners? How are assessment results used to guide further instruction?

Are parents encouraged to set attainable, meaningful goals? Do parents periodically assess their own progress toward goal attainment? Can parents explain their progress toward meeting their goals? Do families stay in the program until their goals have been met?

Do families persist in the program? Do all families participate equally in all core components?

Do staff contact families whose attendance is poor?

## *Area 4.0: Parenting Programs (ES 7,8; NCFL 2)*

### 4.1 Relevant and Appropriate Content
*Sources of Information:*
Review curriculum; observation; survey and interview parents.

*Guiding Questions:*
Do parents report satisfaction with the parenting education component?

Is parenting education integrated into other areas of the curriculum?

Does the parenting program build on parents' interests and needs?

Are parent development and child development issues and questions appropriate and addressed frequently and directly? Does content help parents form reasonable expectations for their children and learn how to support their growth? Is attention paid to beliefs and attitudes about raising children?

Do parent-child activities have literacy connections?

## 4.2 Appropriate Activities
*Sources of Information:*
Review amount of time devoted to parenting programs; review lesson plans for variety of activities; observation.

*Guiding Questions:*
Is enough time regularly spent in parent education? Are instructional sessions varied? Are parents actively involved? Are activities based on sound instructional and learning theory and research?

Do parents actively participate with their children? Do ES staff provide assistance?

Do parenting education activities support peer interaction, among both parents and children?

Do activities a) encourage active manipulation of a variety of objects, and b) engage children in problem solving? Are story reading or telling and writing routine parts of sessions?

## 4.3 Transfer, Application To Home
*Sources of Information:*
Observation at home visits; review parents' portfolios; interview parents.

*Guiding Questions:*
Are classroom activities such that they can be easily replicated using materials commonly found in the home?

Are home visits sufficient in amount and duration and aimed at increased literacy and school readiness?

How do ES staff assess the extent to which transfer takes place (observation, survey, interviews) ?

## *Area 5.0: Early Childhood Programs ( ES 9; NCFL 3 )*

## 5.1 Goals
*Sources of Information:*
Review curriculum to match goals to project application; review records of parent/child time; interview parents and teachers.

*Guiding Questions:*
Does the early childhood component have articulated goals that are consistent with ES and "best practice" ?

Are goals comprehensive? Do goals address all areas of children's development?

## 5.2 Developmentally Appropriate Curriculum
*Sources of Information:*
Observation; review lesson plans; interview teachers and parents; review staff inservice records.

*Guiding Questions:*
Is a licensed or nationally recognized early childhood curriculum used? If not, how is it validated?

Is the adult-child ratio small enough that children can receive individual attention and develop positive relationships with ECE educators?

Are there multiple opportunities for child-initiated learning?

## 5.3 Varied and Appropriate Materials and Activities

*Sources of Information:*
Review materials; interview parents; observe.

*Guiding Questions:*
Do parents report satisfaction with the early childhood education component?

Are materials sufficient, varied, interesting, and appropriate for children's use?

How do teachers implement the program? Is there a high degree of interaction? manipulation of objects? problem solving? story reading and writing?

Are activities varied? Do children have peer interaction time and independent activity time, as well as time for teacher-led instruction?

Does learning focus on direct, firsthand, and interactive experiences?

Is the classroom a literacy-rich environment?

## 5.4: Child Learner Assessment

*Sources of Information:*
Review assessment plan, assessments used, and feedback forms shared with parents; interview parents.

*Guiding Questions:*
Do children seem happy to be in the classroom? Are they active learners?

Are assessment plans written? Are they appropriate? Do they relate to ES goals and the curriculum?

How often (and how) are children assessed? Are assessment tools and methods appropriate for children? How are assessment results shared with parents? How do assessment results guide further instruction?